In this important book, Professors Cohen and Lewis, leading China scholars of different generations, have drawn on the r  *Act in 2009, as well as Taiwan's broader . upon China, under its new leadership, to le lenge to China is not only a scholarly tour-that is essential if the citizens of the People's rights they deserve and their government is great power.* —**Judge John M. Walker, Jr.,** (Second Circuit

Taiwan has successfully made the transition from authoritarianism to democratic governance and correspondingly from a police-centric to a court-centric legal system. Through a meticulous case study of the abolition of the offense of liumang *[hooliganism], the book provides a fresh and insightful perspective on the rise and fall of that notorious penal institution in Taiwan and the interaction between political liberalization and police accountability. Taiwan's experience says to China that robust legal reform not only strengthens democracy, but may also cata-lyze it.* —**Professor Fu Hualing,** Director of the Centre for Comparative and Public Law, University of Hong Kong Faculty of Law

Elections alone do not make a democracy. To be fully democratic, states must give up the convenience of arbitrary power and place themselves under the law. In this gem of a book, Jerome Cohen and Margaret Lewis show how the Taiwanese state did just that. Whether ransoming racing pigeons or "eating the same fish twice," the authors weave together legal detail with juicy interview data and charming case studies to create a narrative that is persuasive, informative, and engaging. This short, readable book explains Taiwan's legal system, details its legal reforms, and offers guidance (and hope) to reformers everywhere—including those in the People's Republic of China—who are working to rein in police power and secure the rule of law. —**Shelley Rigger,** Senior Fellow at the Foreign Policy Research Institute's Asia Program and Brown Professor of East Asian Politics at Davidson College

CHALLENGE TO CHINA

HOW TAIWAN ABOLISHED ITS VERSION OF RE-EDUCATION THROUGH LABOR

For Sir Joseph,
With thanks for your support!

US-Asia Law Institute
NYU School of Law

Jerry & Maggie

Oct 7, 2013

CHALLENGE TO CHINA

HOW TAIWAN ABOLISHED ITS VERSION OF RE-EDUCATION THROUGH LABOR

Jerome A. Cohen & Margaret K. Lewis

© 2013 by US-Asia Law Institute, NYU School of Law
US-Asia Law Institute Books is an imprint of Berkshire Publishing Group

 **US-Asia Law Institute
NYU School of Law**

Berkshire Publishing Group
122 Castle Street
Great Barrington, Massachusetts 01230-1506 USA
Email: info@berkshirepublishing.com
Tel: +1 413 528 0206
Fax: +1 413 541 0076

Challenge to China: How Taiwan Abolished Its Version of Re-Education Through Labor is available through many ebook and database distributors. Special print/digital bundle pricing is also available. Contact Berkshire Publishing (info@berkshirepublishing.com) for details.

Page and cover design by Anna Myers.
Index by Amanda Prigge.

Library of Congress Cataloging-in-Publication Data

Cohen, Jerome Alan, author.
    Challenge to China : how Taiwan abolished its version of re-education through labor/Jerome A. Cohen & Margaret K. Lewis; US-Asia Law Institute.
      pages cm
    Includes bibliographical references and index.
    ISBN 978-1-61472-932-7 (hardcover : alk. paper) — ISBN 978-1-61472-933-4 (ebook) — ISBN 978-1-61472-934-1 (pbk. : alk. paper)
    1. Disorderly conduct—Taiwan.   2. Hoodlums—Rehabilitation—Taiwan.
    3. Human rights—Taiwan.
I. Lewis, Margaret K., author. II. New York University. US-Asia Law Institute, sponsoring body. III. Title.
    KNP430.5.C64   2013
    345.51249′0243—dc23   2013032128

CONTENTS

PREFACE AND ACKNOWLEDGEMENTS

We started this project at a time when proposals for reforming "re-education through labor" (RETL) were bubbling in Mainland China, yet calls to abolish the analogous punishment in Taiwan for "hooligans" (*liumang* 流氓) were nearly silent. Eight years later, the reform paths have played out quite differently than the initial situation suggested: RETL remains firmly in the hands of the police on the Mainland, whereas Taiwan completely abolished *liumang* offenses in 2009. Now that the new leadership in Beijing has publicly put RETL reform back on the agenda, it is an opportune time to reflect on Taiwan's experience and consider what lessons Mainland reformers might draw. Surely Taiwan did not repeal *liumang* offenses solely in order to encourage the Mainland to do the same, but Taiwan's success in curbing arbitrary police power stands as a challenge to the Mainland to follow through on years of false starts when it comes to reining in the most egregious exercises of unfettered police power.

Our goal in writing this book was not only to draw attention to an underappreciated aspect of legal reforms in Taiwan, but also to consider how its experience might be relevant to its neighbor across the Taiwan Strait. In order to best capture both written laws and real-world practice, this book relies on Taiwan's conventional laws, rules, and regulations; judicial decisions and other government publications; scholarly writings; newspaper and magazine articles; conversations with judges, prosecutors, lawyers, police, and scholars; as well as visits to government agencies, police stations, and even the institutions for punishing *liumang*. The patience and earnestness with which our informants explained Taiwan's legal system and their aspirations to us, as well as their willingness to explore creative solutions, are commendable. Names have been redacted from all conversations, as was promised to the people with whom we spoke.

This project was generously funded by a grant from the Smith Richardson Foundation. We are deeply grateful for their commitment to a project that was aimed not merely at short-term legal reform but also at long-term reflections on changes to criminal justice systems in Taiwan and the People's Republic of China. We may never know to what extent our work on this project—including a conference we stimulated in Taipei in 2006 that brought together police, judges, prosecutors, lawyers, and academics to discuss the topic and that publicized our concerns—influenced the ultimate decisions that led to the repeal of *liumang* offenses. Nonetheless, we feel confident that this project generated additional momentum for repeal of what had been an often overlooked and increasingly antiquated punishment. We likewise hope that this book helps stimulate momentum to reform, and perhaps even repeal, RETL. To reach a broad audience in Taiwan and the Mainland, this book is also being published in Chinese by Yuan Zhao Publishing in Taiwan.

We are especially indebted to Professor Jaw-perng Wang of National Taiwan University School of Law for the countless hours that he and his hardworking research assistants contributed to this project. This book truly would not have been possible without their cooperation. We benefited greatly from the help of Professor Chin-shou Wang of National Cheng Kung University, who conducted many relevant interviews with judges in Taiwan. We are also greatly indebted to Yu-jie Chen, a Taiwan lawyer who is a Research Scholar at NYU School of Law's US-Asia Law Institute and a J.S.D. candidate at NYU School of Law, for her careful confirmation of our research into Taiwan's legal publications and her invaluable insights into Taiwan's legal system. We are further grateful for the translation assistance of Yen-chia Chen, who has an LL.B. from National Chengchi University College of Law in Taiwan and recently received his J.D. at Indiana University Robert H. McKinney School of Law. And we thank Yanmei Lin, Associate Director of the US-China Partnership for Environmental Law at Vermont Law School, for her assistance translating several of the initial draft chapters. Jeremy Daum, Clint Bergstrom, and David Willard all provided helpful comments on the draft English manuscript. We also thank the staff of Berkshire Publishing Group, especially Karen Christensen and Bill Siever, for their extraordinary cooperation in bringing this book to press in a timely and attractive manner. Finally, we thank our colleagues, the staff members of NYU School of Law's US-Asia Law Institute, who have provided help throughout the life of the project, both with respect to commenting on our research and administering the grant.

Jerome A. Cohen & Margaret K. Lewis
August 2013

 US-Asia Law Institute
NYU School of Law

CHAPTER 1:
INTRODUCTION

I. THE BOUNDS OF POLICE POWER

Every civilized society needs police. Yet, unless police power is subjected to limits and to certain external checks and balances, civilized society will be threatened, if not destroyed. Every modern country has a long history of seeking to find *le juste milieu*: the right formula for attaining the benefits that police protection can confer without suffering the burdens that an out-of-control police system can impose.

Although police generally have many powers at their disposal to help them ensure public order and safety, the harshest—short of killing—is the ability to detain people, to remove them from home, work, and social life and to incarcerate them for significant periods. The challenge comes in determining in what circumstances police should be permitted to exercise that power. This entails difficult decisions concerning the appropriate institutions, persons, and procedures for best protecting the public while also guarding against abuses of individual liberty.

In all countries, this is principally the business of the criminal justice system—to define what conduct is sufficiently harmful to warrant detention, and to designate the institutions, persons, and procedures required for fairly processing the cases of those singled out for punishment. Criminal justice thus often employs not only legislators and police, but also prosecutors, lawyers, judges, justice department personnel, lay assessors, and others who are allocated roles in an effort to approach a case from multiple perspectives and through procedures designed to satisfy the needs of both efficiency and fairness. It is the participation of these non-police actors, serving together with the police in accordance with legislated standards and procedures, that legitimates the police power to initiate the criminal process by detaining suspects and keeping them in custody for prescribed periods.

Some countries, however, in addition to providing for the conventional criminal process to remove anti-social elements from society, authorize the police alone to inflict detention for periods of varying duration after complying with few or none of the safeguards that rightly apply to most criminal cases. Police are sometimes also empowered to unilaterally issue warnings, require that people report regularly to authorities, place people under surveillance, or otherwise impose restrictions on their ability to go about their lives that fall short of actual detention. Even if not expressly labeled "criminal sanctions," the impact of supposedly "non-criminal" police detentions and other restrictions can be as damaging as formal punishment, both in terms of deprivation of liberty and the ramifications on a person's physical, emotional, and economic well-being. These alternative processes generally exclude the participation of prosecutors, lawyers, judges, and others. Although countries using such methods are usually neither democratic, liberal, nor "Western" in their governmental systems, their use of unchecked police power—especially to impose long-term detention—is a continuing source of controversy, both to their domestic and international audiences.

This is the situation in the People's Republic of China today, as it has been for the entire era of Communist rule since its start in 1949. Police in the PRC have always had a panoply of choices for keeping someone locked up at the exclusive discretion of the police. Most notoriously, since the mid-1950s, they have had the power to dispatch a very broad range of people to what gradually became known as "re-education through labor" (RETL), without the need to gain approval from the procuracy (prosecuting authorities) or courts, or to allow the intervention of lawyers. The term of such detention, currently (as of 2013) limited to three years, can be extended to a fourth year by the Committee for the Administration of Re-Education-Through-Labor, which administers RETL sentences. The detention may be reviewed by a court in accordance with China's Administrative Litigation

Law, but only after the person has been sent off for "re-education." That review process is not invoked in most cases and, even if it succeeds (as it does on rare occasions), offers only modest comfort to a person who has continued to be detained during the lengthy litigation process.

Police across the Taiwan Strait previously employed a similar supposedly "non-criminal" sanction to put so-called and vaguely-described hooligans (*liumang*[1] 流氓) behind bars for up to three years. This counterpart system of the Republic of China on Taiwan (ROC or Taiwan),[2] however, was gradually reformed in order to restrict police power and to offer greater procedural protections before its ultimate abolition in January 2009. Taiwan's experience is therefore highly relevant and enlightening for countries seeking to set bounds upon police power. It should be of particular interest to legal officials, lawyers, scholars, and law reformers in China, as well as abroad, who hope to eliminate RETL. This is why we have undertaken this study.

---

[1] We use the pinyin Romanization of the Chinese characters for the term instead of translating "*liumang*" into English. Considering the lengthy development of the unique concept of *liumang* in Taiwan, it is not surprising that the term does not lend itself to easy translation. Varyingly translated as "hooligan," "hoodlum," and "gangster," *liumang* does not fit squarely into the definition of any of these words. "Hooligan" evokes images of youth—especially young sports fans—who have crossed the line from exuberant to destructive behavior. Although "hoodlum" does not carry the same youthful connotation, it still implies a certain thuggish quality that does not necessarily embrace the full panoply of *liumang* behavior. The nuances among the various terms related to "hooliganitis" were humorously explored in a 1981 *New York Times* piece (William Safire, *On language, New York Times*, § 6 (Magazine) at 9 (16 August 1981)). Finally, "gangster," by definition, indicates that the person is involved in some sort of shady, if not blatantly criminal, organization. Although the concept of *liumang* includes people involved in gangs, a person can act entirely independently when engaging in *liumang* behavior. "*Liumang*" further has a non-legal aspect and has played into popular culture both in Taiwan and Mainland China. For example, in his article titled "Wang Shuo and *Liumang* ('Hooligan') Culture," Geremie Barmé (1992, 28) explains, "*Liumang* is a word with some of the most negative connotations in the Chinese language. Here the expression is used in an attempt to describe both a social phenomenon and its cultural refraction." As with the term "*liumang*," the *Liumang* Act has a variety of translations, most notably "Act for the Prevention of Gangsters," "Anti-Hoodlum Law," and "Anti-Hooligan Act."

[2] In this study, we use "Taiwan" to refer to the territory under the effective control of the ROC government (including the island of Taiwan itself as well as Matsu, Penghu, and Kinmen [a.k.a. Jinmen or Quemoy]), unless otherwise specified.

II. RE-EDUCATION THROUGH LABOR

RETL was first formally promulgated in October 1957, at the height of the Communist Party's "anti-rightist" campaign, to legitimize long-term police confinement of hundreds of thousands of the Party's critics who had surfaced during the ill-fated campaign to "let a hundred flowers bloom, let a hundred schools contend." What originally emerged as an expedient mechanism for removing "rightists" from society soon became a reliable tool that the police could wield when confronting other unwanted elements, including prostitutes, homosexuals, drug addicts, petty thieves, and those who refused to work. RETL, of course, did not suddenly spring full-blown from the head of Chairman Mao Zedong, but was based on a broad range of police practices that even antedated the Communist government; some of these other police detention practices have continued to co-exist with RETL.

"Re-education through labor" (*laodong jiaoyang* 勞動教養, or simply *laojiao* 勞教) has often been confused with "reform through labor" (*laodong gaizao* 勞動改造, or simply *laogai* 勞改), which was the name of the punishment meted out to many of those convicted by the formal criminal process. Confusion arose, even among people in China, from more than the similarity in names. For many years, detainees sentenced to the former, even though they were not deemed "criminals," were often confined together with those sentenced to the latter at notorious "labor camps" where they were forced to work and live in harsh conditions. The term "reform through labor" has formally ceased to exist, although labor camps are still maintained as alternatives to conventional prisons.

The social stigma accompanying RETL is supposed to be less than that attached to criminal punishment, and RETL prisoners are compensated for their labor to a greater extent than "criminals." Yet other treatment received by the two classes of prisoners has often been identical. Only in recent years, as concern grew over the abuses to which RETL has lent itself, has there been an effort to separate the places of confinement of the two varieties of inmate and to distinguish RETL's regimen from that of those receiving criminal punishment.

Nevertheless, in certain respects, the RETL sanction has been even more severe than criminal punishment. For example, originally RETL sentences were indefinite, while most criminals were sentenced to a fixed term of years. In 1979, when the 1957 regulation that had first formally authorized RETL was revived after the chaos of the Cultural Revolution (1966–1976), the sentence became limited to a maximum term of three years, in response to a nascent wave of criticism over its abuses. The custodial authorities were empowered to impose an additional fourth year upon those who continued to need "re-education" at the end of their term. Even now, many criminals whose offenses are arguably more harmful to society than those of RETL offenders find themselves sentenced to far shorter terms than the maximum three or four years that can be dispensed to RETL offenders.

As mentioned above, RETL has not been the only supposedly "non-criminal" detention measure in the police arsenal for confronting anti-social conduct, although it has proved the most significant and enduring. In the crackdown that followed the 4 June 1989 Tiananmen massacre, another kindred sanction called "shelter and investigation" 收容审查 proved far more important to the police, who used it to detain large numbers of people thought to be protesters or their sympathizers. But "shelter and investigation," which allowed the police to detain and investigate people without any involvement by the procuracy or the court, was eliminated as part of the comprehensive 1996 reform of the nation's Criminal Procedure Law.

That still left the police with another weapon for long-term administrative detention—"shelter and repatriation" 收容遣送. This measure helped to fill the gap created by the demise of "shelter and investigation" and was especially useful in restraining and returning to their home districts hordes of petitioners who had descended on urban centers to lodge their protests against alleged government abuses. A dramatic change occurred, however, when in 2003 a young university graduate named

Sun Zhigang died in police custody shortly after having been detained for "shelter and repatriation." Thanks to pressure from the media, the Internet, and some courageous legal challenges to the constitutionality of "shelter and repatriation," that sanction, too, fell victim to the reform spirit that was gradually gaining strength. The State Council mooted the legal challenges by rescinding the authorizing regulation. As criticism of RETL also mounted, many observers wondered whether RETL would also fall victim to the reform era.

III. EFFORTS TO ELIMINATE RETL

The period 2003–2005 represented a high point of the rising tide against RETL. Some optimistic, influential, and energetic law reformers believed that the time had finally come to eliminate RETL and put an end to the ability of the police to impose long-term administrative detention. In 2004, more than 420 delegates to China's National People's Congress (NPC) signed a petition calling for the repeal of the RETL system.

Few reformers voiced opposition to police-imposed programs targeting prostitution and drug addiction because those programs often called for detention of not more than six months. Nor did many reformers appear to be unduly concerned about the continuing power of the police to impose short-term detention—no more than fifteen days for a single offense—for a broad range of minor offenses under the then-prevailing Security Administration Punishment Regulations. In fact, when those regulations were replaced by China's first Security Administration Punishment Law in 2005, that new law contained several procedural reforms of police practice that presaged comparable reforms that would be enacted during the 2012 revision of the Criminal Procedure Law, which took effect on 1 January 2013.

This reformist trend, in turn, spurred greater recognition that continuing RETL's four-year maximum term would be too inconsistent with the rational punishment program that was emerging. How, they asked, could one justify reforms that were bringing due process of law to formal criminal justice while leaving untouched the power of the police to evade those reforms by choosing to apply RETL? Although calls for reform of RETL quieted after 2005, they returned with renewed vigor in 2012.

China's Ministry of Public Security (MPS), however, still represents a formidable opponent. Having lost two of its three major instruments for swiftly curbing social disorder and deterring dissidents—"shelter and investigation" and "shelter and repatriation"—it remained determined not to lose the third—RETL.

Since 2005, the MPS has fought to stall efforts in the NPC to abolish RETL.[3] Following the reform push in the early 2000s, the MPS even reiterated its commitment to RETL in 2005 by issuing the "Implementation Opinion Regarding Further Strengthening and Improvement of Re-Education Through Labor Review and Approval Work." Yet, in order to comply with the demands of current legislation governing deprivations of liberty, even the MPS acknowledged that, if RETL is to continue, it must finally be authorized by a law enacted by the NPC or its Standing Committee. At present, the only authorization for RETL is a smattering of national and local decisions and regulations.

The problem is, what should be the content of such a proposed law? While there have been numerous proposals to reform RETL, there is no consensus among them. Nor were RETL reforms included in the 2012 comprehensive revision of the Criminal Procedure Law. To date, RETL remains distinctly separate from the formal criminal justice process.

At the time of completing this book in the summer of 2013, renewed discussions were underway regarding possible reforms to RETL. In the lead-up to the 18th Party Congress in the fall of 2012, rumors began to circulate that the new leadership might take up RETL reform

---

[3] The following section draws in part on the work of Sarah Biddulph, who offers a detailed discussion of proposed legal reforms (Biddulph 2007, ch. 9).

early in their tenure. In January 2013, reports briefly surfaced that Meng Jianzhu,[4] newly-installed chair of the powerful Political-Legal Committee of the Communist Party and recent Minister of Public Security, directed that the use of RETL be terminated by the end of the year. In March 2013, after the NPC's annual meeting, new Premier Li Keqiang told a press conference that, with respect to RETL reform, "the relevant departments are working intensively to formulate a plan, and it may be laid out before the end of this year." Despite great fanfare in the media regarding the leadership's call for reform, the actual substance of the proposed legislative reforms remains murky.

Many reform-minded academics and people working in the criminal justice system want to make RETL more acceptable by changing its name. As previously noted, "re-education through labor" sounds too similar to "reform through labor" (in both English and Chinese) and is often similar in reality. Moreover, those who have suffered this ostensibly "non-criminal" sanction have been seriously stigmatized by the name. Under RETL as well as criminal punishment, offenders are removed from their families and jobs to undergo labor at a state-controlled facility. The major drafts of a law that would authorize RETL under a new name, which have long been before the NPC but not made available to the public, have therefore reportedly been entitled "The Law for the Correction of Unlawful Conduct."

More substantively, there appears to be much support for reducing the maximum term of RETL from three years to eighteen months or even a year in order to diminish its harshness. This would make it appear a somewhat better, albeit imperfect, fit in the panoply of state-prescribed punishments, ranging from the leniency of the Security Administration Punishment Law's brief detention to the severity of the Criminal Law's potential lengthy prison or labor camp terms (and even the death penalty).

---

[4] All Chinese names in this book are listed with family names first, following the general convention.

The extra year that custodial authorities can tack onto the end of the current three-year RETL term would apparently be eliminated.

Some propose to alter the nature of the sanction in various ways to eliminate its similarity to labor camps. Many RETL centers have long been called "schools" instead of labor camps, and some reformers want to actually make them resemble boarding schools, even giving the "students" weekend furloughs to return home or converting some facilities into "day camps." The facilities themselves may establish so-called "free zones" where the detainees can function relatively freely in a "semi-open" environment. Much greater emphasis will supposedly be placed on "education" instead of labor. This proposal is already reflected in the use of compulsory "legal education classes," which localities have reportedly enacted in response to various policy directives, such as concerns that people are repeatedly petitioning government authorities. Yet another suggested reform is that probation and community service, already available, may be more liberally granted.

Perhaps the most complex area of reform concerns the criteria for determining what kind of conduct and what type of person should be subject to RETL. As things stand, a confusing welter of vaguely written regulatory documents give the police enormous discretion to detain people under RETL for virtually any behavior thought by the authorities to be "anti-social." While awaiting a formal announcement regarding RETL reform in 2013, reports surfaced that facilities in at least four provinces have already taken steps to transition into compulsory drug treatment centers, indicating that perhaps drug addicts would remain a focus under a revised RETL program, even if the name "RETL" itself should be abandoned. Decades of practice have, ironically, done little to clarify matters. One can well understand why reaching consensus on the variety of proposals put forth in this regard has not been easy.

There is widespread agreement that, if RETL is to continue, its examination and approval procedures must be improved. In order to preserve its valuable weapon, the MPS has sought to placate critics by conceding the need for procedural reform in principle and has permitted some limited experiments in practice. For example, lawyers in some cases have been allowed restricted opportunities to represent targets of the process. Many critics insist that a formal, indeed public, hearing must precede any determination, that witnesses be summoned and subject to cross-examination, and that rules of evidence be instituted—reforms that the courts themselves have far from completed in handling criminal cases. One imaginative and optimistic scholar—not a legal expert—went so far as to suggest that a jury system be established to make the decision rather than leave it to the police bureaucracy. This was several years before the recent limited experiments with informal, consultative "juries" for criminal trials in some Chinese provinces.

The Ministry of Public Security, which in 1983 had agreed to relegate custodial but not decision-making responsibilities for RETL to the Ministry of Justice, appears willing to tolerate a number of modest procedural embellishments so long as the MPS retains the ultimate power to decide. Yet that is precisely what opponents of RETL want to prevent. Reverting to an idea embodied in the original RETL regulations, they propose at least requiring the police to share decision-making power with certain other local government agencies. Some recent pilot experiments in designated cities have sought to establish such an arrangement, but thus far these efforts appear still to be dominated by the police.

Some reformers take the position that, if RETL's abolition is not now politically possible, half a loaf will be better than none, and that an attempt should be made to at least partially judicialize the process by requiring that in every case some type of court review take place before a person is consigned to RETL's administrative punishment. Since the Administrative Litigation Law (ALL) became effective in 1990, every person (theoretically) has been allowed to seek court review of an adverse RETL decision, but only after the person's RETL term has commenced. Relatively few people have taken advantage of the opportunity to seek court review, and some have even found the courts closed to them for no valid reason. In any event, the vast majority of such suits have been unsuccessful. This relative lack of success, the fear of police retaliation against those who challenge RETL decisions, and the difficulties of either finding a lawyer or litigating on one's own behalf have combined to make court review of RETL decisions available more in theory than in practice. Nevertheless, in the recent case of Tang Hui, her outrageous sentence to RETL in 2012 for protesting against the punishments given her young daughter's rapists aroused such popular indignation that the authorities had to release her shortly after detaining her. A provincial high court even reversed a lower court decision regarding her request for compensation and awarded her a modest sum under the State Compensation Law.[5] An automatic court review in every case, taken with the help of a lawyer and before the person is sent off, would immediately inject at least a measure of greater fairness into the situation and might become more meaningful over time.

How much of an improvement such judicial review would actually make would depend, of course, on the scope of review, the procedures associated with that review, the degree of autonomy permitted to the court in carrying out its duties, and the extent to which judges are willing to disagree with decisions of the police. Improvement would also depend on the extent of other related reforms, such as access to counsel and clarification of the criteria for determining who should be subject to RETL. Every PRC court continues to be controlled by the Party political-legal committee at the corresponding level, and the most influential voice on that committee has, at least until recently, usually been that of the public security representative.

Nevertheless, even the currently available judicial review has sometimes invalidated RETL decisions. It is possible that, if there were a newly established arrangement requiring court review of every such decision (on the merits, as well as on the regularity of procedures), the arbitrariness

---

[5] Keith Zhai, *Rape victim's mother Tang Hui wins damages over labour camp sentence*, South China Morning Post (16 July 2013).

of RETL determinations might be significantly reduced. This might be accomplished not only through court review itself but also through the greater care that the availability of expanded court review might stimulate in the initial decision-makers.

Yet some reformers want to go further. An increasing number of bold critics have argued—correctly in our view—that, even if the NPC finally adopts a law authorizing RETL, this administrative punishment will still violate the PRC Constitution as well as China's obligations under the signed but-not-yet-ratified International Covenant on Civil and Political Rights (ICCPR). Unless the final power to impose this long-run confinement rests with the courts—and *not* with the police—RETL will remain illegitimate as a matter of law under both PRC constitutional law and applicable international law.

Some reformers therefore hope to transform future RETL decisions by the police into mere recommendations and to give the decision-making power to a special division of the courts. Until January 2009, when Taiwan's counterpart system was abolished, this represented the most recent version of the practice in Taiwan with respect to police efforts to subject so-called hooligans (*liumang*[6] 流氓) to up to three years

---

[6] As further explained in note 1, above, although the word "*liumang*" is commonly translated as "hooligan," the English word fails to capture the broad swath of behavior that the term covered in Taiwan. Accordingly, we have opted to use the Chinese term throughout.

As early as the birth of the RETL system, there has been a deep connection between *liumang* and RETL sanctions. The term *liumang* was employed by the 1957 PRC State Council Decision on RETL in one category that punishes, alongside *liumang*, those who are not engaged in honest work, who commit thefts or frauds that are not prosecuted, and who repeatedly violate public security administration. The 1982 MPS Regulations for Implementing RETL continues to apply RETL to recalcitrant *liumang* whose acts are not serious enough to be considered criminal. What constitutes *liumang*, however, remains undefined in these regulations. At one point, *liumang* was also punishable as a criminal offense. Prior to 1997, the PRC Criminal Law criminalized *liumang* acts, though the definition was not coextensive with that used across the strait. What was formerly *liumang* behavior is now covered by other articles in the PRC Criminal Law, such as those for engaging in brawls and creating disturbances. Despite having largely faded into history, in 2010, *liumang* crimes briefly regained public attention when the media reported on a man who was convicted of "hooliganism" in 1983 but became tangled in an administrative maze and ended up on parole that was later invalidated. He began serving his term again in 1994 and was reportedly China's last remaining *liumang* (Dui Hua Foundation, 8 December 2010).

of "non-criminal" punishment. This is a critical reason why it is important for Mainland reformers to understand Taiwan's relevant experience
and accomplishments. If the PRC is not prepared to *abolish* RETL and
instead only contemplates *reforming* RETL, the PRC should at least
learn the role that Taiwan's courts played in the punishment of "*liumang*"
in accordance with Taiwan's former counterpart to RETL.

IV. TAIWAN'S ANALOG TO RETL

In 1945, at the end of World War II, Taiwan again fell under Chinese
rule, after five decades as a Japanese colony. The government of the
Republic of China (ROC), controlled by President Chiang Kai-shek's
Nationalist Party (Kuomintang or KMT), reintegrated the island into the
ROC's territory. After losing the Chinese civil war to Mao Zedong's
Communist Party on the Mainland in 1949, the KMT regime took
refuge on Taiwan, which was already under its martial law, and made the
island its exclusive base for maintaining the ROC government.

For the subsequent four decades, the KMT suspended parts of the
ROC Constitution[7] and consolidated power in the executive branch and
the military under the Temporary Provisions Effective During the Period of
Communist Rebellion (shortened here to simply "Temporary Provisions";
please refer to the appendix starting on page 209 for a full list of abbrevia-
tions used in this book). The KMT and "a complex structure of external
and internal security organizations" wielded ultimate power over the island
(Winckler 1984, 491). The KMT's ordinarily discreet, albeit tremendous,
day-to-day police power was on full display during high-profile outbreaks

---

The goal of this study is not to undertake a comprehensive comparison of how the concept of
liumang has been varyingly interpreted in China and Taiwan. It nonetheless bears noting at the
outset that *liumang* is a complex term with deep historical roots and nuanced meanings across
different legal systems.

[7] The full text of the ROC Constitution, which was promulgated in 1947, is available from
http://english.president.gov.tw/

of public unrest, from the widespread killing and repression of protestors and dissidents following the "2–28" uprising of 28 February 1947, to the harsh government response to pro-democracy demonstrations culminating in the notorious crackdown following the 1979 Kaohsiung Incident on International Human Rights Day, at which police violently broke up a peaceful political protest and detained its leaders.

Throughout the martial law period, the police and the military easily found support for their actions in suppression-friendly laws and regulations that authorized both criminal and administrative punishments. Although outwardly aimed at *liumang* behavior, such as gang participation and gambling activities, the relevant legal framework for administrative punishments—the Act for Eliminating *Liumang* During the Period of Communist Rebellion ("1985 *Liumang* Act") and its forerunner, Taiwan Province Measures on Repressing *Liumang*—also provided expedient measures for silencing political opponents who did not fit the conventional description of *liumang*.[8] As with RETL on the Mainland, police unilaterally made the decision to condemn *liumang*. They did not need the approval of any prosecutor or court to impose this administrative, rather than criminal, punishment. The punishment imposed on *liumang* at the time was the dreaded *guanxun* 管訓, translated literally as "control and training." "Control and training" was actually an extraordinarily harsh military-administered punishment that could be used to detain any perceived troublemakers indefinitely.[9]

The Law for the Punishment of Police Offenses served as a potent supplementary device for police during the martial law period. Under that law, a counterpart to the PRC's then-prevailing Security Administration

---

[8] The 1955 Taiwan Province Measures on Repressing *Liumang* During the Martial Law Period were replaced in 1985 by the Act for Eliminating *Liumang* During the Period of Communist Rebellion. The more simply named Act for Eliminating *Liumang* followed in 1992 and remained in effect until January 2009.

[9] The 1955 Measures provided a powerful means of locking up people under the guise of "studying life skills" (Art. 6).

Punishment Regulations, police could summarily detain people for up to two weeks at local police stations for a wide range of minor offenses—and with no participation by prosecutorial or court officials.[10]

As explained by one scholar in 1971, "Administrative regulations have defined an extremely broad area within which the police have a free hand to use whatever methods they consider effective and proper" (Tao 1971, 764). Consequently, despite the fact that the KMT had brought with it to Taiwan the ROC's 1935 Criminal Procedure Code 刑事訴訟法, police could easily avoid the judicial process required by the Code. Although the KMT's tight grip on the judiciary during the years of martial law virtually guaranteed desired outcomes if it chose to invoke the formal criminal process, in many cases—especially politically charged ones—it was more convenient to bypass the judicial system by resort to administrative punishments.

The government announced the cancellation of martial law on 15 July 1987, but the actual transition of power from military to civilian authorities took several years. The government only abolished the Temporary Provisions in 1991 and did not dissolve the Taiwan Garrison Command until 31 July 1992, marking the definitive shift to civilian control.

In contrast to the entrenched police repression on the Mainland under Communist rule, the two decades since 1992 witnessed a startling transformation of Taiwan's criminal justice system. Perhaps the most immediately notable shift was the transformation of the draconian, military-administered "*guanxun*" into the Ministry of Justice-administered "*ganxun*" 感訓 or "reformatory training," a more conventional form of imprisonment for which judicial review, albeit truncated, was required in every case.

The waning years of martial law had seen the beginnings of judicial involvement in decisions that had formerly been left exclusively to the police. The 1985 *Liumang* Act had introduced the use of special "public security

---

[10] For a detailed description of policing practices in Taiwan, see generally the work of Jeffrey Martin (2007, 665).

tribunals" 治安法庭 within the district courts to determine whether allegedly serious *liumang* should be incarcerated, but those courts provided little check, both because of daunting procedural barriers to mounting a defense and the courts' general pro-KMT/police propensity.[11] Even Taiwan's 1992 Act for Eliminating *Liumang* ("*Liumang* Act") changed little with regard to procedures. It was not until Taiwan's Constitutional Court 司法院大法官— also known as the Grand Justices of the Judicial Yuan—stepped in that important change began to occur.

In a landmark 1995 judicial interpretation,[12] the Constitutional Court declared five articles of the *Liumang* Act unconstitutional and gave the legislature one year to revise the offending articles. Ensuing legislative reforms curtailed the ability of police to force people to appear before them without any judicial approval and revised the secret-witness system that prevailed in the public security tribunals by authorizing its use only "when necessary." The legislated change regarding the secret-witness system highlighted the importance of the right to confront adverse witnesses, even though it did little if anything to change actual practice. The Court also struck down the policy that allowed the government to require people both to serve time in prison as criminals and, either before or after criminal imprisonment, to undergo reformatory training as *liumang* as a result of the same conduct. Although a second interpretation by the Court in 2001 required only modest revisions to the procedures for confinement of suspected *liumang*, it at least showed a continuing awareness of the controversy over the *Liumang* Act.

Meanwhile, the Law for the Punishment of Police Offenses passed into history. And, once again, the Court played a notable role in the process. In 1990, the Court declared that certain provisions of that law

---

[11] Wang 2002, 554 ("In the context of authoritarian rule, the KMT judicial authorities usually paid limited attention to the dignity or human rights of the accused.").

[12] The three interpretations addressing the *Liumang* Act are No. 384 (1995), No. 523 (2001), and No. 636 (2008).

would cease to be effective on 1 May 1991, because those provisions violated the Constitution's protection of physical freedom. In response, the legislature replaced the offending law with a new Social Order Maintenance Law that addresses mild disruptions of social order and is still in use as of this writing. This law covers a wide array of offenses ranging from illegally using another person's identifying documents, to maltreating animals, to willfully picking another person's flowers or other vegetation (Arts. 66, 79, and 88).

The maximum punishment under Taiwan's Social Order Maintenance Law is detention 拘留 of up to five days. Significantly, the courts—*not* the police—have the power to impose this punishment. The law specifies clear judicial decision-making procedures. If the police, following investigation, believe detention is necessary (although there is a list of minor violations for which detention is never allowed), they must transfer the case to the district court for a ruling by the summary division, in which single judges decide cases based on the files and without requiring a hearing. If the court orders detention and, without a valid reason, the violator does not appear after receiving notice, only then can the police force the person to appear. The law further includes a chapter on "Relief" 救濟 for people who wish to challenge their punishment. In 2009, 6,690 new social order maintenance cases were filed with Taiwan's district courts, representing a noticeable decrease from the 8,754 cases filed in 1998 (Judicial Yuan, 2009a). Of the 6,294 cases closed in 2009, 2,028 people were sentenced to detention. Of those people, 1,569 were sentenced to one day and only one person was sentenced to over three days (Judicial Yuan, 2009b).

This gradual decline in the previously unfettered punishment powers of Taiwan's police must be viewed within the larger context of reforms to the criminal justice system that had gathered strong support. Beginning in the late 1990s, Taiwan's Criminal Procedure Code underwent seismic changes, even while further reforms to the procedures for *liumang* cases appeared to stall and those *liumang* cases remained largely behind closed doors without any prosecutorial involvement and using heavily truncated judicial proceedings.

The National Judicial Reform Conference in 1999 laid out the framework for sweeping criminal procedure reforms that introduced a "reformed adversarial system" 改良式當事人進行主義. This reform sought to elevate the roles of defense counsel and prosecutors in the courtroom, shift judges to a more neutral position, and place the burden of proof squarely on the prosecutors (Lewis 2009, 651). As reforms progressed, the judiciary, legislature, and executive gradually recognized the untenable gap between the new procedures applied to "criminal" cases and those used for "*liumang*" cases. The fact that suspected *liumang* often faced concurrent criminal charges for the same acts underscored the overlap between the *Liumang* Act and the Criminal Code and cast further doubt on the perceived continuing need for the Act.

The stage was thus set for ending the power of Taiwan's police to imprison people without according them the full protections of the criminal process.

V. OPERATION AND TERMINATION OF THE *LIUMANG* SYSTEM

The above summary does not do justice to the sophisticated and detailed workings of Taiwan's *liumang* system and the story of its evolution. Nor does it describe in detail the process leading to its demise in 2009. The following chapters will do this. Indeed, our study brings to light the workings of a system largely unknown even among most legal officials, lawyers, academic specialists, and the general public in Taiwan itself. We therefore hope that our study will be of interest in Taiwan. Our research and analysis should be of special benefit to legal scholars and law reformers in China, and it may also benefit those in China and many other countries who focus on police administration, criminal justice, and comparative law generally.

Chapter 2 analyzes the origins and development of the *Liumang* Act and the long series of efforts by reform-minded individuals in Taiwan's executive, legislative, and judicial branches, as well as legal scholars and practitioners, to adapt the Act to the island's increasing democratization and constitutionalism as well as its changing criminal justice system. In this chapter we seek to answer the following questions: How did the distinctive, supposedly "non-criminal" *liumang* system relate to the formal criminal process? Why was it possible for so long a period for someone to be punished as a *liumang* and a criminal for the same conduct? What kinds of conduct fell within the broad definition of *liumang*? Who made the determination that a person's conduct was sufficiently anti-social to fall within the Act? What procedures and institutional arrangements were followed to make that determination? Was the determination made on the basis of a person's conduct or status or both? To what extent did the *Liumang* Act distinguish between ordinary and serious violators? What were the consequences of this categorization for purposes of applicable procedures, institutions, and punishments? How did procedures, institutions, and punishments of the *liumang* process differ from those associated with the criminal process? What differences existed between the types of personnel who administered the respective processes?

In Chapter 3 we illustrate the concrete application of the *liumang* system. Here, our concern is how Taiwan's system actually worked. To what extent were there gaps between the system prescribed in the legislative and regulatory framework and actual administrative and judicial practice, and why did they exist? To what extent was there anything distinctively "Taiwanese" or "Chinese" about the framework of the system, its implementation, and the environment within which it functioned? What were its goals, and to what extent were they achieved?

Chapter 4 depicts the end of the *liumang* system in Taiwan. What were the political, social, economic, and legal factors that motivated its elimination? How important were the executive branch, the legislature, the regular courts and Taiwan's Constitutional Court in driving this reform? What were the roles of the legal profession, the media, non-governmental organizations, and public opinion in influencing the reform process?

Our concluding chapter seeks to extract the meaning of the life and death of the island's *liumang* system for Taiwan and for China, as well as for other countries where unfettered police power to detain exists. What possible generalizations emerge that might be relevant to law reform beyond Taiwan, especially in China, where the freedom of 1.3 billion people is at stake? This is an exciting story, and we are happy to reflect on it and to make it better known.

CHAPTER 2:
THE LEGAL FRAMEWORK

I. INTRODUCTION: THE *LIUMANG* ACT,
A UNIQUE LEGAL HYBRID

The Act for Eliminating *Liumang* 檢肅流氓條例 ("*Liumang* Act" or LMA)[1] was not only a "special law" technically, in that it constructed a specialized program to be consulted before resort to general laws such as Taiwan's Criminal Code 刑法. It also stood apart in its unique straddling of criminal and administrative law. When asked whether punishments for being a *liumang* were administrative or criminal in nature, one counselor at a facility where *liumang* were held mused that "perhaps they are half and half." That being said, if you asked the average person on the street in Taiwan whether *liumang* are criminals, the answer undoubtedly would be "yes." The common perception of *liumang* goes far beyond people who merely speed, jaywalk, or litter. Instead, they are thought to be thugs, gangsters, or hoodlums. Put simply, a *liumang* is not someone you would want to run into in a dark alley at night.

Throughout the life of the *Liumang* Act, where, exactly, it fell on the technical criminal/administrative divide remained a debated question in Taiwan's legal circles. What is clear is that with its police-dominated determination process, unusual "public security tribunals" 治安法庭, and

---

[1] The full names for relevant laws, rules, and other government documents are contained in the Appendix. The Legislative Yuan (the legislative branch of Taiwan's government) must pass all laws/codes 法 and acts 條例. Taiwan no longer uses "temporary provisions" 臨時條款. Administrative agencies may issue several types of documents without legislative approval, such as implementing rules 施行細則, measures 辦法, provisions 規定, main points 要點, and matters 事項. In the Appendix, we have given each type of document a distinct English translation, except for "*fa*" 法, which we have translated varyingly as "law" or "code" depending on the standard convention.

its distinctive, bifurcated punishment program for minor and serious offenders, the *Liumang* Act was, indeed, special. It was also vague, confusing, and anachronistic when viewed against the protections enshrined in Taiwan's progressive Constitution ("Constitution" or Cst.) and revamped Criminal Procedure Code (CPC). The judiciary, legislature,[2] and executive branch gradually recognized the disparity between the procedures applied to "criminal" cases and those used for "*liumang*" cases.

When we first embarked on this project in 2005, the *Liumang* Act was under scrutiny, but it was still in effect and remained a potent tool for the police. Little did we know at the time that our report would largely become a historical piece. On 23 January 2009, the *Liumang* Act was officially abolished in Taiwan following a vote by the Legislative Yuan, thus bringing to an end more than a half-century of experience with this law and its forebear. We could not be more delighted that the *Liumang* Act has slipped into the past, but we hope it does not also slip from memory. Widely overlooked by scholars during its lifetime, it would be a pity if the *Liumang* Act were now entirely forgotten. The story of its rise and demise is an instructive chapter in the greater narrative of Taiwan's legal transformation.

Here in Chapter 2, we introduce this key piece of legislation and the supporting rules, guidelines, and other legal documents that fleshed it out. Yet these texts only tell part of the story. The *Liumang* Act and supporting documents did not exist in a vacuum. Although people accused of being *liumang* followed a distinct procedural track from those accused of other illegal activities, suspected *liumang* were often simultaneously criminally charged. This overlap was substantial, with one official who oversaw incarcerated *liumang* estimating that ninety percent of the *liumang* in his facility also faced concurrent criminal charges. Likewise, another government employee commented that many inmates were not "pure *liumang*," meaning that they also had criminal cases. While some interviewees thought that

---

[2] In this study, "legislature" refers to the ROC Legislative Yuan, unless otherwise specified. The Legislative Yuan is the highest legislative body of the ROC and consists of popularly elected representatives.

the ninety percent estimate was too high, we were repeatedly told that criminal and *liumang* charges regularly proceeded hand-in-hand. One lawyer who had represented accused *liumang* went so far as to say that ninety percent might be a conservative estimate. Regardless of the exact percentage, it is undisputed that criminal and *liumang* offenses were heavily intertwined.

Beyond the overlap with criminal laws, the text of the *Liumang* Act also incorporated portions of other laws through direct reference.[3] These "gap-filler" provisions rounded out the *Liumang* Act and connected it to the greater administrative and criminal law programs.[4] Moreover, although case law plays only a limited role in Taiwan's European-type civil law system, the Act was significantly revised because of a series of interpretations made by Taiwan's Constitutional Court before the Act's abolition.[5]

Reviewing the formal rules, of course, provides only limited insight into how the system actually operated, but understanding them is a

---

[3] For example, the *Liumang* Act described the contents of a confinement warrant 留置票 by reference to Article 102 of the Criminal Procedure Code. If a public security tribunal later ruled that a person was wrongfully confined as a *liumang*, he was entitled to compensation under the Wrongful Detention Compensation Law (LMA Art. 11).

[4] Despite its hazy status as a criminal and/or administrative law, the *Liumang* Act provided that, when handling *liumang* cases, judges should use the Criminal Procedure Code to fill gaps in the Act (LMA Art. 23). This provision makes sense in light of the fact that judges from the criminal courts, not the administrative courts, heard *liumang* cases and they decided whether or not the accused qualified as a *liumang*. There was no equivalent catch-all provision that the police or other authorities involved in the determination process should look to the Administrative Procedure Code 行政程序法.

[5] Unlike the PRC, where the legislative branch (specifically the Standing Committee of the National People's Congress) holds the power to interpret the constitution, the Constitutional Court interprets the Constitution of the ROC and is charged with unifying the interpretation of laws (Cst. Art. 78). As of the end of August 2013, the court had issued 711 constitutional interpretations. The Organizational Law of the Judicial Yuan 司法院組織法 (Art. 3) provides that there shall be seventeen Justices, though this number was changed to fifteen by the Additional Articles of the Constitution of the ROC 中華民國憲法增修條文 (Additional Articles) (Art. 5), as amended and promulgated on 25 April 2000, and effective from 2003. The court also adjudicates cases concerning the dissolution of political parties that have violated the Constitution (Additional Articles, Art. 5). In 2005, the Additional Articles (Art. 5) were again revised to empower the court to rule on the impeachment of the ROC president or vice president (2005 Taiwan Yearbook). The president and vice president of the Judicial Yuan 司法院, the judicial branch of government, are selected from the Justices. The ROC President selects the two justices who will fill these posts, though the Legislative Yuan 立法院 must consent to the appointments.

23

necessary first step. The next chapter will delve into the former system's nuts and bolts, from the time a person's actions first raised the eyebrows of the police to the eventual, official clearing of the "*liumang*" scarlet letter. The twisting path wandered by accused *liumang* is understandable, however, only when viewed against the backdrop of the underlying legal framework. We first need to know where the *Liumang* Act came from and how it developed over time. This is where we begin.

II. DEVELOPMENT OF THE *LIUMANG* ACT

The *Liumang* Act evolved over more than a half-century. In 1955, six years after moving the Republic of China (ROC) central government to Taiwan, Chiang Kai-shek's Kuomintang (KMT)-dominated government promulgated the Taiwan Province Measures on Repressing *Liumang* During the Martial Law Period 台灣省戒嚴時期取締流氓辦法 ("1955 Measures").[6] The government had earlier declared martial law on the grounds that it was necessary to counter domestic unrest in Taiwan and that the new Communist regime in Mainland China presented an imminent threat of attack (Roy 2003, 78).[7] Though new to Taiwan's legal system, the term "*liumang*" was hardly new to the ROC government: the Mainland had long been rife with *liumang* activity. Indeed, one scholar noted that "[b]y 1920, Shanghai's underworld consisted of an estimated

[6] Prior to ROC rule over Taiwan, which effectively began with the Japanese surrender to Chiang Kai-shek on 25 October 1945, the Japanese colonial government had imposed similar sanctions through the Taiwan Rules for Repressing Vagrants 台灣浮浪者取締規則, which were issued in 1906. The succinct, five-article Rules prescribed punishment (e.g., warnings and forced employment) for people without fixed residences, without regular employment, and who undermined public order and disrupted customs. The term "*liumang*" is not used in the Rules, but the descriptions of the Rules' targets are strikingly similar to those later used by the ROC government.

[7] Although still formally based on the Mainland, the ROC government instituted a military government in Taiwan in accordance with the 1943 Cairo Declaration, which provided for the transfer to China of Taiwan and other specified territories held by Japan (Roy 2003, 56). On 28 February 1947, tensions between the recently arrived Mainlanders (外省人, literally "people from outside the province") and Taiwanese who inhabited the island prior to the KMT's arrival (本省人, literally "people of this province") boiled over and resulted in the violent "2–28 incident," which

100,000 hoodlums (*liumang*)" (Wakeman 1988, 408–440). Taiwan's succinct 1955 Measures served as an efficient, blunt tool for clearing conventional criminal elements off the streets, and the Measures also proved invaluable whenever Generalissimo Chiang's government sought to target political opponents. According to one scholar, the 1955 Measures were "designed to give police administrative control over certain 'undesirable' individuals to whom the criminal law does not extend."[8] Because the ROC offered no mechanisms for raising objections or obtaining judicial relief, the 1955 Measures gave people targeted as *liumang* little hope of challenging their fate.

The 1955 Measures were superseded in 1985 by the Act for Eliminating *Liumang* During the Period of Communist Rebellion 動員戡亂時期檢肅流氓條例 ("1985 Act"). This was the first time that the prohibition against *liumang* was elevated to the status of a law rather than a mere administrative order. The government announced its decision to revise the 1985 Act following the end of martial law in 1987 but allowed the 1985 Act to remain in effect without revision for five years. In 1992, Taiwan

---

is so named for the date (Roy 2003, 67–73). Chen Yi, the ROC-appointed governor-general of Taiwan, declared martial law shortly after the "2–28 incident" erupted (Roy 2003, 70). Martial law was then briefly lifted but reinstated in 1949. Taiwan remained in a state of martial law for the next 38 years. In 1948, the ROC government, while still based on the Mainland of China and involved in a civil war, suspended parts of the constitution and consolidated power in the president's hands under the Temporary Provisions Effective During the Period of Communist Rebellion 動員戡亂時期臨時條款 (Roy 2003, 83).

[8] Tao 1971, 761 (citing *China Year Book*, 1952). Following a long period of political and legal disorder after the collapse of the Qing Dynasty, the KMT-dominated government of Chiang Kai-shek that had gained power formally promulgated a Criminal Procedure Code in 1928 and a Criminal Code in 1935. The Criminal Procedure Code was revised in 1935. Although the 1955 Measures were the KMT-dominated government's first administrative measures aimed exclusively at *liumang*, prior to their issuance, police had other tools to arrest and detain suspects engaged in *liumang*-like behavior. In addition to the Criminal Procedure Code, police could use the 1943 Law for the Punishment of Police Offenses 違警罰法 and 1932 Law for Enforcement of Administrative Measures 行政執行法, though these laws only allowed police to hold people for short periods of time (Tao 1971, 756, 762). Put simply, even before law enforcement authorities had the 1955 Measures at their disposal, they were far from at a total loss for tools to crack down on suspected *liumang*. Nevertheless, the 1955 Measures provided a powerful means of locking up people for extended periods of time under the guise of "studying life skills."

CHALLENGE TO CHINA

replaced the 1985 Act with a supposedly new *Liumang* Act—passed on the last possible day before the old Act lapsed.[9] The newly revised Act, however, looked suspiciously like the old one. While the official mantra leading up to the new Act had been "only revise and do not repeal," many criticized that there was not even much "revision." One popular statement was that the revisions amounted to nothing more than the removal of the six characters "動員戡亂時期" from the title. The deleted phrase literally translates as "period of mobilization and suppressing disorder." In this context, however, it is best (albeit somewhat wordily) translated as "period of mobilization for the suppression of the Communist rebellion," or, as is more commonly used, simply "period of Communist rebellion."

The criticism that the legislature merely took an eraser to part of the title of the 1985 Act is not entirely fair. The new *Liumang* Act included modest revisions, such as modifying the definition of *liumang* and allowing people to object to their designation as *liumang*. For the most part, however, the substance of the old Act remained unchanged. The fact that failure to promulgate any sort of new *Liumang* Act would have resulted in thousands of incarcerated *liumang* being released onto the streets was a potent argument against those who sought the *Liumang* Act's demise.[10]

Arguably, the most significant change in the handling of *liumang* stemming from the end of martial law originated in a provision of the new *Liumang* Act that called for a fundamental shift in its administration from military to civil authorities. The 1992 Act required that henceforth all

---

[9] The transition of power from the military authorities took several years after the government announced the cancellation of the martial law decree on 15 July 1987. The National Assembly abolished the Temporary Provisions Effective During the Period of Communist Rebellion 動員戡亂時期臨時條款 in 1991, and the Taiwan Garrison Command was dissolved on 31 July 1992, marking the shift of police powers to civilian authorities. A number of laws in effect during the period of Communist rebellion, including the 1985 Act, ceased effect on 31 July 1992.

[10] Similar concerns were raised when a constitutional interpretation issued in 2001 set a deadline for revisions to unconstitutional provisions in the *Liumang* Act. As the deadline loomed, one legislator warned, "At least 300 alleged hooligans will be discharged three days later if we fail to properly amend the law. . . . The releases will bring chaos to Taiwan" (*Dropping of hooligan article will bring chaos: Lawmaker, China Post* (20 March 2002) (quoting Su Ying-kuei)).

26

incarcerated *liumang* be overseen by employees of the Ministry of Justice rather than the military (LMA Art. 18). It was at this time that, as noted in Chapter 1, the dreaded "*guanxun*" 管訓[11]—literally "control and training" but actually an extraordinarily harsh military-run punishment[12]—morphed into the Ministry of Justice's "*ganxun*" or "reformatory training" 感訓, a more conventional form of imprisonment. The character "*gan*" 感 alone means to feel or touch in an emotional sense, but it means to help change by persuasion or example when combined with "*hua*" 化, the character meaning to change or transform. It is the reformatory concept of "*ganhua*" 感化 that is captured in "*ganxun*." This change in terminology—seemingly little more than a subtle shift in pronunciation—in fact occurred in 1985. Once the Ministry of Justice took over custodial responsibilities in 1992, however, it began to result in significant improvements in custodial conditions.

One of the authors, who visited a *guanxun* facility in the late 1960s and a *ganxun* facility in 2006, can testify to this dramatic change. The significant improvement in conditions was similarly noted by a counselor at a *ganxun* facility housing *liumang* who made the following comment about "control and training": "There was not a lot of importance attached to human rights [during the martial law period]." Based on the author's personal observations of human rights conditions under martial law, this is a glaring understatement.

---

[11] The term "*ganxun*" was first used in the 1985 Act, which was prior to the assumption of responsibility by the Ministry of Justice (Arts. 8, 12-14, 16). Nonetheless, the term "*guanxun*" is commonly associated with the entire period of military command. Today, the only people subject to *guanxun* are military personnel (e.g., soldiers 士兵 and noncommissioned officers 士官), as provided for in the Punishment Law of the Armed Forces 陸海空軍懲罰法 (Arts. 6-7).

[12] Specifically, the Taiwan Garrison Command 台灣警備總司令部 was in control prior to the Ministry of Justice taking over the job of reforming *liumang* in 1992. The prior military bent was explicit in the Measures for Enforcing the Punishment of Reformatory Training During the Period of Communist Rebellion 動員戡亂時期流氓感訓處分執行辦法, which provided that the military would supervise reformatory training (Art. 12). The Measures, which went into effect on 1 December 1985, were repealed on 30 July 1992. The switch to civilian control did not require a change in all personnel: in 2006, we were told by reformatory officials that a number of instructors still working there dated from the period of military control.

Admittedly, neither the seemingly innocuous phrase "control and training" nor the more recent, similarly benign term "reformatory training" adequately conveys the grim reality of being behind bars under either label. *Liumang* undergoing reformatory training did not trot off to auto shop classes in the morning and return home to their families in the evenings. Nor did the official name of the reformatory training facilities, "vocational training institutes" 技能訓練所, make clear that people were still confined in what was, for all intents and purposes, a prison. Indeed, in Taiwan's training institutes, ordinary convicted criminals were serving criminal sentences in another part of the same building. Euphemistic phrasing is prevalent in criminal justice terminology in every corner of the globe, and Taiwan is no exception, nor is the United States with its "reformatories" and "correctional facilities." In translating terms for this study, we have tried to stay true to their literal meanings but caution readers that terminology can be misleading.

Between its overhaul in 1992 and repeal in 2009, the *Liumang* Act underwent several rounds of revisions—primarily in response to a trio of interpretations by the Constitutional Court.[13] In the first, Interpretation No. 384,[14] issued in 1995, the Court declared that five articles of the *Liumang* Act were unconstitutional and would become null and void on 31 December 1996. The legislature revised the offending articles in 1996 in order to remedy the constitutional deficiencies. First and foremost, the Court determined that Articles 6 and 7, which empowered the police to force people to appear before them without any judicial approval,[15] violated

---

[13] Although the Constitutional Court has been issuing constitutional interpretations since 1949, it took on an increasingly vocal and independent voice as the martial law period ended in the 1980s. As noted by one scholar in Taiwan, "The Constitutional Court was established by the KMT regime and was once a tool of the KMT party. Nonetheless, the Court built itself into a powerful judicial organ that used the law to eradicate KMT ideology" (Chen 2000, 110).

[14] Constitutional interpretations are numbered sequentially—beginning with the first interpretation issued in 1949—and are commonly referred to by these numbers.

[15] Specifically, Article 6, as written at the time of the constitutional challenge, provided that if a person was determined to be a *liumang* and the circumstances were serious, the police had the

28

the guarantee of physical freedom of the person as provided in Article 8 of the Constitution. Article 8 provides that, except in the case where a person is discovered while committing a crime or immediately thereafter (i.e., in *flagrante delicto*), no person shall be arrested or detained other than by judicial or police agencies acting in accordance with "procedures prescribed by law."[16] The Court further emphasized that any law used to deprive people of their physical freedom must be proper in substance and comply with Article 23 of the Constitution, which provides that freedoms and rights enumerated in the Constitution shall not be restricted by law except as may be necessary to prevent infringement upon the freedoms of other persons, to avert an imminent crisis, to maintain social order, or to advance public welfare. On this basis, the Court declared that Articles 6 and 7, as then written, unconstitutionally authorized the police to force people to appear before them without following any necessary judicial procedures.

At first glance, the contents of the *Liumang* Act were "procedures pre-scribed by law," albeit very simple procedures as then written—namely, an internal decision by the police to force the suspect to appear. The Constitutional Court declared that these bare bones "procedures" did not pass constitutional muster. In the reasoning section of Interpretation No. 384,[17] the Court explained that Article 8 of the Constitution requires specific forms and procedures for arrests with and without warrants,

---

power to summon the person without prior warning and, if the summoned person did not comply, to force him to appear at the police station. Article 7 similarly provided that, if a person reengaged in *liumang* behavior within a year after a determination that he was a *liumang*, the police had the power to summon him and, if the summoned person did not comply, to force him to appear at the police station. For people caught while engaging in *liumang* behavior, the police could take them directly into custody without any prior summons.

[16] Article 8 of the Constitution provides, in part, that "physical freedom shall be guaranteed to the people. In no case except that of *flagrante delicto*, which shall be separately prescribed by law, shall any person be arrested or detained other than by a judicial or police organ in accordance with procedures prescribed by law."

[17] For US courts, the holding is often buried in the opinion's text—leading to a favorite pas-time of law school professors of asking new law students, "What is the holding?" In Taiwan, the "holding" is a succinct, clearly marked section at the beginning of the ruling or opinion. The holding is followed by the reasoning, which is so labeled.

whereas the *Liumang* Act authorized police to force people suspected of being *liumang* to appear without any judicially signed and issued documents, whether or not the person was caught in the act. The Court concluded that the *Liumang* Act's failure to differentiate between people caught in the act and people apprehended at a later time violated Article 8 of the Constitution, which clearly distinguishes between the two situations and prescribes different procedures. In accordance with this Interpretation, the articles that addressed the police's authority to summon suspected *liumang* for questioning were therefore revised to require that police first obtain judicial approval or, when exigent circumstances required immediate action, that there be prompt judicial review after the fact.[18]

Second, the Constitutional Court also declared in Interpretation No. 384 that the secret witnesses system set forth in Article 12 of the *Liumang* Act deprived the accused of the right to defend himself and hampered the truth-finding function of public security tribunals established within the Court. As explained in further detail below, the public security tribunals exclusively handled *liumang* cases, though the tribunals were intertwined with the criminal courts because the public security tribunals and criminal courts used the same judges, staff, and facilities. The legislative revisions resulting from Interpretation No. 384 that allowed for secrecy only "when necessary" did little in reality to increase the transparency of the witness system.[19] As discussed below, it was not until 2008 that the Court fundamentally altered the secret witness system.

---

[18] The revised Article 6 provided that when a person was determined to be a *liumang* and the circumstances were serious, the police had the power to summon the person without prior warning and, if the summoned person did not comply after receiving lawful notice and did not have proper grounds for so doing, then the police were required to apply to the court for an arrest warrant. If the facts were sufficient to believe that the person was a flight risk or there were exigent circumstances, however, then the police could arrest him directly, in which case the police were required to obtain judicial approval after the fact. Article 7, as revised, included corresponding language that required a court-issued arrest warrant to force recidivist *liumang* to appear, or judicial approval after the fact when there were exigent circumstances.

[19] As revised in 1996, Article 12 provided that, in order to protect informants, victims, and witnesses, the courts and police shall, when necessary, summon them individually and not publicly to give statements under codenames. Moreover, when the facts were sufficient to believe that

Third, in Interpretation No. 384 the Constitutional Court struck down the practice of requiring people to serve consecutive criminal and *liumang* sentences for the same act. The Court began by noting that, as then written, Article 21 of the *Liumang* Act allowed the imposition of reformatory training after execution of a criminal punishment for the same act, without regard to whether there was a special preventive necessity to do so. This practice, the Court pointed out, resulted in the loss of physical freedom. The legislature revised Article 21 to provide that, when the same acts resulted in both *liumang* and criminal punishment, criminal prison sentences and time spent in reformatory training would be counted against each other on a one-day-for-one-day basis. After the revision, whether the *liumang* or criminal punishment was carried out first depended on the pace of the two proceedings. The Implementing Rules for the Act for Eliminating *Liumang* 檢肅流氓條例施行細則 ("Implementing Rules" or IR) provided that punishments be applied on a "first ruling finalized, first enforced" basis (Art. 46).

Finally, the legislature expanded the relief channels available to *liumang* in response to the Constitutional Court's holding that Article 5 failed to protect the constitutional right to lodge administrative appeals and institute administrative litigation (Cst. Art. 16). As discussed in the next chapter, however, the relief channels remained cumbersome even after this reform.

The *Liumang* Act persevered despite both the blows dealt by the Constitutional Court in Interpretation No. 384 and growing speculation in legal circles that the legislature might do away with the Act in its entirety. An employee in the Ministry of Justice explained to us that, by

---

a witness was under threat of retaliation, the court was instructed to restrict the accused *liumang* and his lawyer from confronting and questioning the witness, as well as from viewing documents in the file with the witness's real name and status. Nonetheless, the *Liumang* Act required that the judge tell the accused *liumang* the essential points of statements or documents used as evidence and give the accused *liumang* an opportunity to state his opinion. Despite allowing secret witnesses, the revised Article 12 required that the testimony of secret witnesses could not be the only evidence supporting a ruling that imposed reformatory training.

1996, he and his colleagues thought the *Liumang* Act was dead, based on statements by the then Minister of Justice after the release of Interpretation No. 384.

This prospect of abolition subsided later that year, however, following a change in personnel at the Ministry of Justice and in response to a perceived increase in crime. In November 1996, Taoyuan County Chief Liu Pang-yu and eight others, including several county officials, were murdered at his official residence. The next month, Peng Wan-ju, the Democratic Progressive Party Women's Affairs Department Chief, was raped and murdered in Kaohsiung. The following spring, Pai Hsiao-yen, the teenage daughter of a famous entertainer, Pai Ping-ping, was murdered: "Demanding $5 million in ransom, the girl's captors sent photos of her, bound with tape, along with her severed finger. They murdered her while her mother was still trying to raise the money, dumping the body in a drainage ditch" (Roy 2003, 207–208). These high-profile murders fueled public concern over deteriorating social order.

After falling out of the spotlight for several years, in 2001, the Constitutional Court again found the *Liumang* Act lacking. Specifically, the Court held that the procedures used for pre-trial confinement of suspected *liumang* violated Articles 8 and 23 of the Constitution. As explained in Interpretation No. 523: "This confinement . . . is a serious restraint on people's physical freedom. Nevertheless, the Act does not explicitly provide the conditions upon which a court may base its imposition of confinement. . . . The Act grants the court discretion to decide the accused's confinement without regard for whether he is still seriously breaching social order, or if he will obstruct the court's hearing of the case by fleeing, destroying evidence, or threatening informants, victims, or witnesses." The Court declared that the offending provisions would become null and void one year from the date of the Interpretation. In comparison to the substantial revisions brought about by Interpretation No. 384, the legislative changes necessitated by Interpretation No. 523 were relatively modest and confined to a single article of the *Liumang*

Act, Article 11. In 2002, the legislature revised Article 11 to include specific criteria for determining whether confinement was required[20] and added two new articles (Arts. 11-1 and 11-2) that detailed procedures for canceling, stopping, and repeating confinement, as well as providing alternatives to confinement (e.g., bail).

After four years of inactivity in the reform process, the legislature again tweaked the *Liumang* Act in May 2006 in order to harmonize its language with that of the Criminal Code. Whereas Article 11 previously allowed for confinement when there was evidence that the person would collude with accomplices if not confined while awaiting a hearing on the merits of his case, the revised *Liumang* Act expanded the language to include collusion with "other principal offenders and accomplices" (LMA Art. 11). The only other revision specified that the amendment would take effect simultaneously with the revised Criminal Code (LMA Art. 25). This was hardly an earthshaking change, and the legislature showed no signs that further revisions were in the pipeline. Nor were politicians or the general public clamoring for reforms. A high-ranking police official in Taipei told us in 2006 that there was not a person in politics who would propose abolition of the *Liumang* Act: "The people need it, the government needs it, and society needs it." While advocating that Taiwan keep the *Liumang* Act, he also recognized that there was room to consider moving the procedures closer to those used in criminal cases, for example, by giving the accused *liumang* a voice during the initial police determination process.

Following the 2006 revisions, there remained only modest momentum for further reform among judges, prosecutors, lawyers and

---

[20] Article 11, following revisions, provided four circumstances under which confinement was warranted: (1) facts indicate that the person is continuing to engage in *liumang* behavior; (2) he has fled or presents a flight risk; (3) facts indicate that he will destroy, fabricate, or tamper with evidence, or collude with other principal offenders and accomplices or witnesses; or (4) facts indicate that he presents a risk of obstructing witnesses' testifying or will endanger or harm the persons or property of informants, victims, or witnesses or other listed categories of people who are connected to the case, including relatives within specified degrees of kinship.

academics.[21] Finally, in the autumn of 2007, the Constitutional Court heard arguments in support of two long-pending petitions for a third constitutional interpretation, both of which were filed by public security tribunal judges.[22] The Court had previously rejected similar petitions, including those supported by a group that had been established under the aegis of the influential Judicial Reform Foundation 民間司法改革基金會 specifically to study the *Liumang* Act. A former member of this group explained that two of the earlier petitions had been rejected for procedural reasons, and the group had subsequently suspended its efforts.

On 1 February 2008, the Constitutional Court issued Interpretation No. 636 in which it held several provisions of the revised *Liumang* Act unconstitutional. Despite hopes that the Court would hold that the *Liumang* Act in its entirety was unconstitutional, it instead continued to chip away at individual provisions. In Interpretation No. 636, the Court parsed the definition of *liumang* and declared two of its clauses unconstitutional because they violated the principle of legal clarity 法律明確性原則. The Court held that the two offending clauses would become null and void one year from the Interpretation's issuance. Although the Court seriously

---

[21] Articles addressing criticism of the *Liumang* Act also occasionally made it into the mainstream press. For example, an article in the English-language Taipei Times published after the issuance of Interpretation No. 523 notes, "The Anti-Hooligan Law (*Liumang* Act), created amidst a large-scale crackdown on gangster rings during the martial law era, has long been in dispute for its departure from international standards of due process." Irene Lin, *Council Rules on Anti-Hooligan Law, Taipei Times* (23 March 2001).

[22] Petitions for constitutional interpretations are not publicly available. The Constitutional Court, however, does publicly issue its decisions not to accept petitions, and these decisions are available through a link on the Judicial Yuan's website (http://www.judicial.gov. tw/constitutionalcourt/). We learned of relevant petitions through various contacts in the courts and academia. Petitions may be filed by government agencies, individuals including judges and other legal officials, juridical persons, and political parties. The details on who may file a petition and relevant procedures are set forth in the Law Governing the Hearing of Cases by the Grand Justices, Judicial Yuan 司法院大法官審理案件法 and its Implementing Rules 司法院大法官審理案件法施行細則. The legal authority for judges, as compared with government agencies and other bodies, to file petitions lies in the Constitutional Court's interpretations, including Interpretations 371, 572, and 590.

questioned the constitutionality of a third clause, it stopped short of declaring the suspect clause unconstitutional and instead called for it to be re-examined and amended. The Court addressed several other aspects of the definition and found no constitutional infirmities, hence leaving the bulk of the definition intact.[23]

In addition, the Constitutional Court revisited the secret witness system set forth in Article 12 of the *Liumang* Act for hearings before the public security tribunal and took the step that it had been unwilling to take in 1995. The Court held that the secret witness system was an excessive restriction on the accused's right to defend himself, and, thus, it violated the proportionality principle 比例原則—the principle that measures must be reasonable, the least restrictive possible and not excessive.[24] The Court also maintained that the secret witness system conflicted with the constitutional guarantees of due process 正當法律程序原則 (Art. 8)[25] and the right to institute legal proceedings 訴訟權 (Art. 16). As with the offending provisions in the *liumang* definition, the secret witness provision was to become null and void one year from the date of the interpretation's issuance—giving the legislature until February 2009 to enact a constitutionally acceptable alternative.[26] In a further move toward strengthening procedural protections for the accused, the Court held that, in accordance with the principle of due process, the accused had a right to make a statement

---

[23] The definition of "*liumang*" and the changes in it brought about by Interpretation No. 636 are detailed in Part III.A of this Chapter.

[24] The Constitutional Court stated in Interpretation No. 471 that this principle is enshrined in Article 23 of the Constitution, which provides that freedoms and rights enumerated in the Constitution shall not be restricted by law except as may be necessary to prevent infringement upon the freedoms of other persons, to avert an imminent crisis, to maintain social order, or to advance public welfare.

[25] The Constitutional Court used the phrase "正當法律程序" in Interpretation No. 636, a phrase that is commonly translated as "due process of law" following the American convention. This phrase is not in Article 8 of the Constitution, but the court has used it to articulate the principle enshrined in the Constitution.

[26] In Interpretation No. 636, the Constitutional Court declared only the first paragraph of Article 12 to be unconstitutional. The second and third paragraphs—regarding the need for evidence in addition to witness testimony and the protection of witnesses, respectively—remained unchanged.

during the initial police process for designating someone as a *liumang*. Moreover, the Court prohibited the police from forcibly transferring a designated *liumang* to the public security tribunal without an arrest warrant.

The Constitutional Court also addressed Article 13(2) of the *Liumang* Act, which provided that it was the function of the public security tribunal to decide whether or not to impose reformatory training, but not to decide the length of the sentence within the statutory one- to three-year period. The actual length of the sentence was left to subsequent determination. Despite expressing concerns that this provision might result in an excessive deprivation of physical freedom, particularly in the case where the person was already incarcerated for less than three years for a criminal conviction before being sent for reformatory training, the Court did not declare Article 13(2) unconstitutional and instead called for it to be re-examined and amended.

In line with its 1995 ruling, the Court upheld the practice that time spent serving a criminal punishment and time spent in reformatory training be mutually set-off on a one-day-for-one-day basis (LMA Art. 21). Finally, the Court refused to hear challenges to several other provisions on technical grounds. In sum, while Interpretation No. 636 marked a positive step in the effort to bring the *Liumang* Act in line with the protections in the Criminal Procedure Code as well as the Constitution, it stopped far short of declaring the Act unconstitutional in its entirety.

The one-year countdown for the Legislative Yuan to revise the *Liumang* Act as required by the Constitutional Court started on 1 February 2008. As the year wore on, it looked increasingly likely that the legislature would once again wait until the final hour to make the required changes. Then, unexpectedly, in December 2008, the legislature held hearings regarding possible abolition of the *Liumang* Act, culminating in the Act's repeal the following month. Chapter 4 discusses in more detail the process by which judges, officials, legislators, and civic groups brought about abolition of the *Liumang* Act. After over a half century of the Act's historical development in Taiwan, it was no longer punishable simply to be a *liumang*.

III. THE CONTENTS OF THE *LIUMANG* ACT AND SUPPORTING RULES

Despite the series of judicially instigated revisions, the basic contents of the *Liumang* Act remained unchanged between its overhaul in 1992 and its repeal in 2009. The Act began with a statement of its legislative purpose: the *Liumang* Act was specially formulated to prevent *liumang* from undermining social order and endangering people's rights and interests (LMA Art. 1). To accomplish this purpose, the *Liumang* Act defined who should be deemed a *liumang*, laid out the procedures for handling *liumang* cases, prescribed permitted sanctions, and provided relief channels through which people could challenge determinations that they were *liumang*.

A. *Liumang* Definition

The *Liumang* Act set forth several categories of people who were deemed *liumang*. A person who fell within one of these categories, however, was properly deemed a *liumang* only if he[27] was at least eighteen years old[28] and his behavior was "sufficient to have undermined social order" 足以破壞社會秩序 (LMA Art. 2). "Undermining social order"

---

[27] Throughout this study we refer to *liumang* as men. This is not to say that there were no female *liumang* because there were, just very few. The officials at training institutes with whom we spoke in 2006 knew of only a couple of female *liumang* undergoing reformatory training in all of Taiwan, and a high police official said that he could count them all on one hand. Female *liumang* were housed in a women's prison, but the prison officials were charged with carrying out their incarceration according to the rules for reformatory training, not for prisons. Prisons are separately regulated by the Law for Carrying Out Punishments in Prisons 監獄行刑法 and its Implementing Rules 監獄行刑法施行細則. For convenience's sake, we will therefore refer to *liumang* as men.

[28] When we asked members of the police whether behavior engaged in before a person was eighteen but discovered after he turned eighteen could be considered *liumang* behavior, we were told that the person had to be eighteen at the time of the act. People under eighteen who engaged in behavior that would otherwise be deemed *liumang* behavior were handled by juvenile courts.

implies more than a mild disruption. Minor infractions like tossing a candy wrapper on the street or jaywalking were thus not considered to undermine social order. Further limiting application of the *Liumang* Act was the requirement that no more than three years elapse between the time of the offending behavior[29] and the time that the suspect was reported, determined to be a *liumang,* or transferred to the court (LMA Art. 3).[30] Prior to Interpretation No. 636, the five categories of *liumang* behavior were as follows:

1) People who organize without authority, are in charge of, control, or participate in, gangs or unions/partnerships that undermine social order or endanger the life, body, freedom, or property of others.

2) People who illegally manufacture, sell, transport, possess, or act as an intermediary for the transaction of firearms, ammunition, or explosives.

3) People who forcibly occupy territory; commit blackmail and extortion; force business transactions; eat and drink without paying; coerce and cause trouble; tyrannize good and honest people; or manipulate matters behind the scenes to accomplish the foregoing.

4) People who manage or control professional gambling establishments, establish brothels without authorization, induce or force decent women to work as prostitutes, work as bodyguards for

---

[29] According to the *Liumang* Act, the three-year period was calculated from the time the offending behavior was established but, if the behavior was continuous or ongoing, then the period was calculated from the time the behavior ceased (Art. 3).

[30] Article 3 of the *Liumang* Act specified that if more than three years had passed since the person engaged in the *liumang* behavior at issue, the police must not report the person, make a determination that he is a *liumang,* or transfer him to the court for a hearing. Consequently, the police needed to allow enough time for the pre-court determination process; otherwise the person might have passed the initial police-dominated determination stage but be rejected by the court because the three-year limit expired in the interim.

gambling establishments or brothels, or rely on superior force to demand debt repayment.

5) People who are morally corrupt or who wander and act like rascals and the facts are sufficient to believe that they have habitually undermined social order or endangered the life, body, freedom, or property of others.

In Interpretation No. 636, the Constitutional Court declared two categories in the definition unconstitutional and announced that they would become null and void in one year. First, the category of people who "tyrannize good and honest people" was to be excised from the list in Article 2(3). Second, Article 2(5) regarding "people who are morally corrupt or who wander and act like rascals" was to be deleted in its entirety. The Court questioned the constitutionality of several other clauses within Article 2(3)—specifically, people who forcibly occupy territory, eat and drink without paying, and coerce and cause trouble—but only called upon authorities to re-examine and amend them. The Court did not clarify what, if any, action it would take if the authorities (presumably the legislature) failed to take action.

The Constitutional Court further stated that the following aspects of the definition *were* constitutional: people who commit blackmail and extortion, force business transactions, or manipulate matters behind the scenes to accomplish the foregoing (Art. 2(3)); and people who manage or control professional gambling establishments, establish brothels without authorization, induce or force decent women to work as prostitutes, work as bodyguards for gambling establishments or brothels, or rely on superior force to demand debt repayment (Art. 2(4)).

Finally, the Constitutional Court did not address the constitutionality of the first or second categories of the definition on technical grounds. In sum, the Court truncated the definition but left substantial portions unchanged. If the legislature had made the minimum required revisions, the definition would thus have read as follows:

1) People who organize without authority, or are in charge of, control, or participate in, gangs or unions/partnerships that undermine social order or endanger the life, body, freedom, or property of others.

2) People who illegally manufacture, sell, transport, possess, or act as an intermediary for the transaction of firearms, ammunition, or explosives.

3) People who forcibly occupy territory; commit blackmail and extortion; force business transactions; eat and drink without paying; coerce and cause trouble; or manipulate matters behind the scenes to accomplish the foregoing.

4) People who manage or control professional gambling establishments, establish brothels without authorization, induce or force decent women to work as prostitutes, work as bodyguards for gambling establishments or brothels, or rely on superior force to demand debt repayment.

As previously noted, some types of *liumang* behavior also qualified as crimes and could be punished alternatively or concurrently under criminal laws, either the general Criminal Code or special laws like the Act for Preventing Organized Crime[31] 組織犯罪防制條例 ("Organized Crime Act" or OCA).[32] Other illegal behavior was unique to *liumang*.

---

[31] A participant in a criminal organization is subject to a fine and a prison term between six months and five years. (Organized Crime Act, Art. 3)

[32] For mild disruptions of social order that are neither criminal nor *liumang* offenses, the police may use the Social Order Maintenance Law 社會秩序維護法. This law covers a wide array of offenses ranging from illegally using another person's identifying documents (Art. 66), to maltreating animals (Art. 79), to willfully picking another person's flowers or other vegetation (Art. 88). Punishments include, among others, detention 拘留 of up to five days, fines, and confiscation (Art. 19). By way of background, the Social Order Maintenance Law was formulated after the Constitutional Court declared in Interpretation No. 251 that certain provisions of the Law for the Punishment of Police Offenses would cease effect on 1 July 1991, because they violated the Constitution's protection of physical freedom.

For example, the phrase "morally corrupt" 品行惡劣 is nowhere to be found in the Criminal Code or any special criminal law. On the other hand, extortion was both a crime and *liumang* behavior.[33] Further, as one lawyer pointed out, "eating and drinking without paying" could also be construed as the criminal offenses of committing fraud or intimidation.

Beyond the difficulty in deciding whether to treat an act as a criminal and/or *liumang* offense, there was also the more fundamental decision whether a suspect actually met the criteria to be properly deemed a *liumang*. First, the person must have engaged in one of the types of enumerated behavior. Some types of behavior were fairly cut-and-dry, such as possession of firearms. There might be some question about constructive possession (e.g., the gun was in the suspect's house or bag but not in his hand), but, for the most part, it was a fairly straightforward factual determination. Other types of behavior were more abstract and thus harder to pin down. For example, what level of conduct qualifies as "coercing and causing trouble"?

Further complicating matters, there was a second fundamental criterion. Even if a person possessed a gun or ran a gambling operation, when did these acts rise to the level of being "sufficient to undermine social order"? Although the "undermine social order" language was expressly stated in only the fifth category of *liumang* behavior, this clause was superfluous because Article 2 already required that all *liumang* behavior be "sufficient to undermine social order." For example, mere gun possession standing alone did not make a person a *liumang*. Instead, the person had to possess a gun and that act of possession must have been sufficient to undermine social order. Thus a person who possessed a gun illegally was not automatically a *liumang*. The 1992 and subsequently updated Implementing Rules attempted to flesh out these and other crucial questions.[34]

---

[33] The Act for Punishing Corruption 貪污治罪條例 prescribes prison terms of at least ten years for people convicted of certain forms of extortion.

[34] Although the "Implementing Rules for the Act for Eliminating *Liumang*" were issued in 1992, the predecessor rules, the "Implementing Rules for the Act for Eliminating *Liumang* During the Period of Communist Rebellion," were issued in 1985.

Article 4 of the Implementing Rules listed three characteristics of behavior that would be "sufficient to undermine social order," but there remained a tremendous amount of discretion vested in the police and judiciary when it came to applying these criteria on a case-by-case basis. First, the Implementing Rules required that the behavior be generalized or "unspecific" in nature 不特定性, meaning that the suspect did not specifically target his alleged victim because of a pre-existing relationship. A true *liumang* was a threat to the population at large. For example, one day he might demand "protection money" from a vendor in the neighborhood, and the next he might steal a moped parked on the street. In other words, the *Liumang* Act was not aimed at punishing feuding friends who ended up in a fistfight. In one case described by a police official, a boss threatened a female employee that her situation at work would suffer unless she slept with him. Because of their work relationship, the police were hesitant to classify this as *liumang* behavior.

Cases of gun possession provide a helpful illustration of the challenges of applying this criterion. A threshold inquiry into whether gun possession was "sufficient to have undermined social order" involved an analysis whether the behavior was unspecific in nature. This murky criterion led to divergent, if not downright contradictory, outcomes. In a 2001 case from Taichung District Court, the public security judge explained that the accused's possession of a gun and ammunition created a clear and immediate threat to unspecific people 不特定人. Yet in a 2004 case from Taipei District Court, another public security judge stated that mere gun possession did not satisfy the "unspecific" element.

Second, the Implementing Rules required that the conduct be an "offensive violation" 積極侵害性. This criterion connoted that the behavior must have the potential to harm others but not be done in self-defense. This fits the stereotypical view of a *liumang* as a thug who relies on illicit force or threats for unjust gain. In one case, the accused *liumang* was sent to reformatory training for robbing three stores. At each store, he carried a knife and said: "I don't want to hurt you, hand over the money." There was no indication in the record that anyone was injured. The judge's ruling explains that the threat to the victims' persons and property was sufficient to satisfy this second criterion.

Our attempts to elicit a concrete description of "offensive violation" from authorities in Taiwan were not particularly successful. A Taipei police officer explained that police would look at the type of "criminal act" 犯行, such as whether the suspect beat people up because they had money. Yet neither he nor other interviewees could articulate a bright line to distinguish when an act satisfied this criterion from when it did not. Our overall sense from these interviews was that a low level of threat was sufficient, and immediacy was not required. Turning back to our example of gun possession, mere possession was generally enough to qualify as an offensive violation—a person need not actually have shot or even brandished the weapon, thus indicating that a latent threat was sufficient.

Third, the acts must have been habitual in nature 慣常性, meaning that the suspect engaged in various or continuing *liumang* behavior. A brief, one-off slip from an otherwise law-abiding lifestyle was generally deemed insufficient. As one police officer explained, *liumang* "do it often." An investigator with the police said that, on the whole, police needed three or more individual acts to report someone as a *liumang*, a requirement that was seconded by another police officer. But this was not a hard-and-fast rule. For example, the same investigator later said that it depended on the type of behavior. In the case of gun possession, mere possession could have satisfied the three characteristics of being "sufficient to undermine social order": (1) the suspect had the potential to endanger unspecific people, (2) that the possession was an offensive violation could be inferred, and (3) the habitual nature could also be inferred. Perhaps being caught once with a single gun was not enough for it to be "serious,"[35] but if the person was caught twice or even once

---

[35] The difference between *liumang* who received only a warning and those who were incarcerated as "serious" *liumang* is discussed below.

but with three or more guns, or if the person had engaged in other *liumang* behavior, then it was a different story.

The "habitual" element referred not only to the frequency of offending conduct but also the duration during which the behavior occurred; for example, how long a person possessed a gun. In a 2004 case from Shilin District Court in Taipei, the judge ruled that the accused be sent to reformatory training for possessing two handguns and ammunition. The judge reasoned that the "habitual" element was satisfied because the accused possessed the gun and ammunition for ten years.

The problem was that there were no objective standards to guide a judge who had to decide what period of time was necessary to make behavior habitual. For example, did the gambling den have to run for one day or one year? In a 1997 case from Taichung District Court, the judge ruled that the habitual element was satisfied even though the accused had run the gambling den for only three days. After recognizing that it was only a three-day period, the judge then proceeded to note that there were a large number of patrons, and the amount of money involved was substantial. On the other hand, in a 2004 case from Taipei District Court, the judge ruled that running a gambling den for only five days was not sufficient to have undermined social order, though this judge noted that the scale of the operation was not large.

At the end of the day, despite the fact that the oft-repeated refrain of "unspecific," "offensive violation," and "habitual" was recited in related rules, court decisions, and interviews, it is debatable whether these criteria derived from the Implementing Rules actually provided meaningful guidance in determining whether a person qualified as a *liumang*. A former public security tribunal judge explained that he and other public security tribunal judges once held a meeting to discuss the definition of "*liumang*" and the meaning of the three defining characteristics of "undermining social order." Working against this attempt at uniformity was Taiwan's newly acquired and hard-won respect for individual judges to decide cases independently. Perhaps not surprisingly, the meeting did not lead to any concrete guidelines.

Even if a person satisfied the general *liumang* definition, the *Liumang* Act added another layer of complexity by separating *liumang* into two categories. Those in the first, milder category received sanctions limited to a warning 告誡 and a one-year "guidance" period—a period of police-administered supervision resembling probation.[36] The term "guidance" 輔導 is a bit of an Orwellian euphemism because during the one-year period the emphasis was more on observing the person's behavior rather than counseling him to reform. These "warned *liumang*" (literally "*liumang* warned and under guidance") 告誡輔導流氓[37] did not see the inside of a courtroom, except in the rare event that one eventually challenged the determination of his status in administrative court. In contrast, a person alleged to be in the second category, a "serious *liumang*" (literally "*liumang* for whom the circumstances are serious") 情節重大流氓, was brought before a public security tribunal, and this tribunal decided whether the person would undergo reformatory training. The average man on the street would likely have no idea that such a distinction existed. The difference in terms of the procedures and sanctions applied to these two separate varieties of *liumang* was, however, substantial.

The next section of this chapter describes the general procedures that applied to warned *liumang* and serious *liumang*, and Chapter 3 explores this two-track system in detail. For now, the key point is that, within the realm of *liumang*, there was an elusive yet crucial legal distinction between low-level *liumang* and those deemed to be of a more dangerous variety. The *Liumang* Act and Implementing Rules attempted to articulate this distinction yet actually provided little in the way of concrete guidance.

---

[36] The criminal law allows for probation 保護管束 for certain offenders (Criminal Code Arts. 92-93).

[37] The phrase "*liumang* warned and under guidance" is used interchangeably with "*liumang* listed in the register and under guidance" 列冊輔導流氓. This register was maintained by the police and contained the names of all *liumang* currently under guidance. Warned *liumang* were also colloquially referred to as "ordinary *liumang*" 一般流氓, a term that was used by several interviewees who took part in this study.

The Implementing Rules explained that the determination whether someone was a serious *liumang* should be made by examining and considering the entire circumstances, but with particular attention paid to the following factors (Art. 5):

1) The degree [severity] of the means and implementation of the act.
2) The number of people harmed and the degree of harm.
3) The degree to which social order was undermined.
4) The person's attitude after engaging in the behavior.
5) Whether the person presented a risk of flight or of seriously undermining social order.

In addition to these five relatively subjective factors, the Implementing Rules set forth four scenarios in which the circumstances were "certainly" serious, provided that the behavior was sufficient to undermine social order or endanger the life, body, freedom, or property of others (Art. 5):

1) People who organize without authority or are in charge of, or control, gangs or unions/partnerships that undermine social order.
2) People who illegally manufacture, sell, transport, possess, or act as an intermediary for the transaction of firearms, ammunition, or explosives.
3) People who use violent, coercive means to forcibly occupy territory; commit blackmail and extortion; force business transactions; tyrannize good and honest people; or manipulate matters behind the scenes to accomplish the foregoing.
4) People who manage or control professional gambling establishments, force decent women to work as prostitutes, or rely on superior force to demand debt repayment.

If these descriptions in the Implementing Rules trigger a sense of *déjà vu*, then you have been reading carefully. They parrot much of the language in the *Liumang* Act's general definition of *liumang* with a few notable additions and deletions. Most obviously, the entire fifth category regarding "morally corrupt" people is absent. As previously noted, in 2008, the Constitutional Court struck down this entire category as unconstitutional, thus increasing the percentage overlap in the definitions of warned and serious *liumang*. Item three above is nearly identical to the parallel provision in the general definition, with the addition of "violent, coercive means" and the deletion of "eating and drinking without paying" and "coerce and cause trouble." Just because "eating and drinking without paying" is not on the list, however, does not mean that someone who engaged in this behavior could never rise to the level of a serious *liumang*. Rather, it simply meant that the behavior was not automatically deemed serious and the decision had to be made with regard to the overall circumstances and general considerations outlined above.

In view of the fact that the descriptions of various *liumang* behavior—and what constituted *serious* behavior—in the *Liumang* Act and Implementing Rules raised more questions than they answered, government entities sought to clarify matters through internal guidelines. Issued in 1992 by the National Police Agency (NPA) and subsequently revised to comply with the evolving *Liumang* Act, the Provisions on Police Handling of Cases under the Act for Eliminating *Liumang* 警察機關辦理檢肅流氓條例案件作業規定 ("Police Provisions" or PP) detailed the procedures for handling *liumang* cases from the initial investigation to the final removal of a *liumang*'s name from the police-maintained *liumang* register. The Police Provisions, which were the culmination of a series of such guidelines,[38] also spelled out criteria for determining whether a

---

[38] The police stopped referring to the following rules because their contents had been incorporated into the Police Provisions: the Supplemental Provisions on Police Handling of Cases under the Act for Eliminating Liumang 警察機關辦理檢肅流氓條例案件補充規定, the Restatement of Police Handling of the Compilation of the *Liumang* Register 重申警察機關辦理流氓業務有關名冊之造冊作業, the Main Enforcement Points for Police Agencies in Handling the Guidance of *Liumang* 警察機關辦理流氓輔導工作執行要點, and the Main Points for Implementing Integrated Reporting for the Work of Eliminating *Liumang* 檢肅流氓工作聯繫會報實施要點. The thirty-four appendices to the Police Provisions included detailed forms for the police to use when carrying out *liumang* work.

person was a *liumang* (Art. 17). Echoing the *Liumang* Act, the Police Provisions specified that a person was a *liumang* if (1) he was at least eighteen years old, (2) he engaged in one type of behavior listed in the *Liumang* Act within the past three years and that behavior was sufficient to have undermined social order, and (3) there were concrete facts and evidence of the *liumang* behavior (Art. 17(1)). A person needed to engage in only one type of *liumang* behavior in order to be deemed a *liumang*. That said, an isolated incident standing alone should, at least in theory, have been insufficient because of the aforementioned requirement that the "sufficient to have undermined social order" criterion included whether the *liumang* behavior was habitual in nature (IR Art. 4). The Police Provisions reiterated this command (Art. 18(5)).

The Police Provisions described a series of additional factors for the police to consider when determining whether a person qualified as a *liumang* (Art. 18). Several factors dealt with technical procedural issues (e.g., whether three years had elapsed since the alleged *liumang* behavior (Art. 18(4)), while others attempted to explain individual acts within the definition. For instance, "coerce and cause trouble" 要挾滋事 was described as using illegal or improper methods to cause a disturbance, including exposing someone's secrets in order to blackmail him, willfully causing a disturbance, or creating a situation where others cannot feel at peace (PP Art. 18(8)(5)). "Eating and drinking without paying" 白吃白喝 was described as relying on force to avoid paying a bill, or refusing to pay a bill after signing it (PP Art. 18(8)(4)). The Police Provisions emphasized that, in order to rise to the level of *liumang* behavior, there must have been some sort of coercion, intimidation, or violent behavior that prompted the victim to refrain from demanding repayment. Without this threatening or violent element, the matter was merely a common civil dispute over a debt and not *liumang* behavior. Perhaps the person was drunk and forgot to pay or was dissatisfied with the food. Or, if a person merely took a few weeks to pay a bill then, as one police officer said to us: "Never mind." Even with this attempt to articulate consistent standards, the bottom line was that the *Liumang* Act invested a tremendous amount of discretion in the police who administered the system.

On the judiciary's side, the Matters that Courts Should Pay Attention to in Handling Cases under the Act for Eliminating *Liumang* 法院辦理檢肅流氓條例案件應行注意事項 ("Court Matters" or CM)[39] provided instructions on how public security tribunals should process and decide *liumang* cases.[40] Originally issued by the Judicial Yuan in 1985, the Court Matters were last revised in 2001. The Court Matters spelled out the nitty-gritty of the procedures for *liumang* cases once they reached the courts. The Court Matters were less helpful, however, in explaining what criteria courts should use when deciding whether a person was a serious *liumang* and, consequently, should be sentenced to reformatory training. In addition to deciding whether the police

---

[39] The courts were previously guided by the Main Points for Courts to Keep in Mind when Handling Cases under the Act for Eliminating *Liumang* 法院辦理檢肅流氓條例案件提示要點. The Judicial Yuan issued this document in 1990, but it was repealed in 1997.

[40] Like all courts in Taiwan, public security tribunals were under the Judicial Yuan and, more specifically, they fell within the criminal divisions of district and high courts. Criminal and civil cases are heard by courts arranged on three levels: district courts 地方法院, high courts 高等法院, and the Supreme Court 最高法院. Taiwan has twenty-one district courts, eighteen of which are on the island of Taiwan, one on Penghu, and the remaining two in Kinmen County and Lienchiang County. Each district court is divided into criminal and civil divisions and further has a summary procedures division 簡易庭. Courts may create additional specialized divisions, e.g., those that handle juvenile, family, or traffic cases. The Taiwan High Court is located in Taipei, with four branches in Taichung, Tainan, Kaohsiung, and Hualien. There is a separate Fuchien High Court with a Kinmen branch that hears appellate cases from Kinmen County and Lienchiang County. In the ROC judicial system, the Supreme Court is the court of final appeal for criminal and civil cases, which are heard by separate divisions within the court. Unlike the district and high courts, which review issues of fact and law, the Supreme Court reviews cases regarding only issues of law, but it does not hear constitutional cases. Administrative cases are handled by separate courts that are organized on three levels: administrative divisions at district courts 地方法院行政訴訟庭, high administrative courts 高等行政法院 and the Supreme Administrative Court 最高行政法院. First-instance cases are heard by administrative divisions at district courts or high administrative courts depending on the type of cases. The decision of the second level court, which reviews only issues of law, is final. This three-level structure went into effect on 6 September 2012. The administrative courts have separate authority from that of the courts that hear civil and criminal cases. Administrative courts hear claims by people who allege that their rights or legal interests were violated by an unlawful administrative action rendered by a government agency.

conducted the investigation and determination in accordance with legal procedures and whether the person engaged in any of the listed types of *liumang* behavior, the judge was instructed to "pay attention to whether the behavior was sufficient to have undermined social order" (CM Art. 25). This advice added little, if any, color to the basic descriptions in the *Liumang* Act and Implementing Rules.

On a more concrete level, the Judicial Yuan published materials discussing specific scenarios, such as whether two people who trapped pigeons on a mountain and then demanded ransom from game keepers should be subject to sanctions as serious *liumang* in addition to facing criminal liability (Judicial Yuan, 2003).[41] If a judge encountered cases that were similar to the bird-napping or other scenarios from the Judicial Yuan materials, the materials were quick to point out that the discussions were for reference and consideration but were not to be used as a legal basis for deciding individual cases. Nor did the Judicial Yuan materials address more philosophical debates such as one judge's question of whether bird-napping is *liumang* behavior directed at pigeons or at people!

The high courts also failed to provide unified guidance. Taiwan's civil law system does not use precedent in the same binding manner as a common law jurisdiction does. Nevertheless, a district court judge prudently noted that, for a lower-court judge, it is not possible, and is indeed improper, to completely disregard the higher court's opinion. Problematically, according to this same judge, the various high courts in Taiwan

---

[41] Surprising as it may be to some foreign readers, holding pigeons captive for ransom is a phenomenon that occurs in Taiwan. Pigeons are used for gambling. Just as people in many countries race horses, people in Taiwan also race pigeons. To quote a Taiwan legal scholar involved in our research project, "A racing pigeon can be as expensive as a luxury car." In New York City, these "flying rats" are generally not held in such high esteem, though pigeon racing does occur around the city. When one member of our research team offered to bring in some pigeons on her next visit to Taiwan, her dinner companions waved their hands in disapproval and retorted that American pigeons were not up to the task. The question whether resourceful New York birds are hearty enough for long-distance competitions in Taiwan will have to be left to future empirical research.

did not necessarily agree on what constituted *liumang* behavior, which led to regional differences. And, because *liumang* cases used a system where the decision of the second level court was final, these cases never reached the Supreme Court, which could have harmonized discordant rulings. As pithily remarked by the same judge: "The high court is boss" in *liumang* cases.

It was further not unheard of for the rulings of individual panels within a single high-court public security tribunal to conflict. Continuing with our pigeon example, in an interview one judge described a controversial case in which he ruled that two people who bird-napped pigeons for ransom were not serious *liumang*. On appeal to the high court, different panels of judges heard the cases of the two accused *liumang*. One panel took the position that the accused was a serious *liumang*, and the other ruled that the behavior did not have the requisite characteristic of being an offensive violation. The exact same factual scenario thus led to two contrasting outcomes. A high-court judge who had reviewed the decisions of public security tribunals also commented on the abstract criteria for determining whether someone was a *liumang* and the resulting lack of uniformity both among the various high courts and among individual judges. When asked what could be done if courts reached different results in the same case, the judge exclaimed that "nothing can be done." After yet another judge commented that courts considered bird-napping to be *liumang* behavior half of the time, we asked the judge who said "nothing can be done" for his own view, to which he replied, "I don't know!"

In the end, the legal definition of *liumang* was inescapably vague. Of course, it is extremely difficult and often undesirable to write laws with excessively bright lines that leave no room for discretion in individual cases. At the same time, there is a difference between calculated room for discretion and extreme flexibility that borders on randomness. The *Liumang* Act leaned far towards the latter pole. Just as US Supreme Court Justice Potter Stewart famously noted about the difficulties of proscribing illicit pornography ("I know it when I see it"),[42] the *Liumang* Act appears to have proceeded along a similar line: Taiwan's police and judges were left to know *liumang* when they saw them.

When the police and judges did see a *liumang*, they usually also saw a criminal, which, as mentioned previously, raised a host of issues. Chief among them was the question of double punishment. Over time, substantive criminal laws increasingly overlapped with the *Liumang* Act, a phenomenon that frequently led to people facing simultaneous criminal and *liumang* charges. Following Interpretation No. 384, and as upheld in Interpretation No. 636, the *Liumang* Act addressed this phenomenon by providing that, if a person was subject to both criminal sanctions and reformatory training for the same act, the time spent in prison 徒刑, in detention 拘役,[43] or undergoing rehabilitation measures,[44] 保安處分 would be deducted from the maximum three-years of reformatory training (Arts. 19 & 21). On the surface, this quick-fix solution appeared to resolve what otherwise would be a constitutional infirmity. Yet, digging deeper, the fact remained that people locked up for both overlapping *liumang* and criminal offenses could serve longer than if the *liumang* or criminal charges stood alone. For example, as discussed further in

---

[42] Jacobellis v. Ohio, 378 US 184, 197 (1964) (Stewart J., concurring).

[43] There are three distinct kinds of detention under Taiwanese law: (1) pre-trial detention 羈押, the criminal counterpart to confinement in *liumang* cases; (2) short-term detention 拘留 that is imposed by administrative agencies; and (3) judge-determined detention as a punishment 拘役, which cannot exceed two months (hence the maximum is usually quoted as fifty-nine days). Time served in this final form of detention could be deducted from reformatory training. The *Liumang* Act used short-term detention 拘留 with respect to the police's ability to ask the public security tribunal to hold a warned *liumang* for up to seven days for failure to appear at meetings during the guidance period (LMA Art. 20; IR Art. 42).

[44] Rehabilitation measures are used, either in addition to other criminal sanctions or on their own, in various situations where people present a special threat to society, such as people who are mentally ill and violent, drug addicts, juvenile offenders, or habitual offenders. Illustrative measures include reformatory education 感化教育 (for juvenile offenders), guardianship 監護 (for insane people or people with limited ability for individual responsibility because of mental infirmities), and forced work 強制工作 (for habitual offenders). Specifics are set forth in the Implementing Law Regarding Rehabilitation Measures 保安處分執行法.

Chapter 3, if a criminal defendant was sentenced to six months in prison and was later committed to reformatory training as a *liumang* for the same act, his six-month imprisonment would have been deducted from the maximum three-years of reformatory training. In reality, because of the prevalence of early release, this deduction would likely mean little. It was rare for *liumang* to spend a full three years at the training institute, and they could be released as early as after having served one year. Moreover, even if ultimately not punished for both, it is unsettling that suspects had to cope with a simultaneous double attack under the *Liumang* Act and criminal laws.

The *Liumang* Act, as expanded by the Implementing Rules, provided the skeleton of procedures used for determining whether a person was a *liumang* as well as what happened once that determination was made. The intricacies of how the system actually operated did not appear in the legislation, but this is hardly surprising, given the inevitable gap between theory and practice in any legal system. The *Liumang* Act established an important framework and introduced a number of key players in the process. The following describes this framework and the various government authorities that were involved in *liumang* cases.

The initial step was for the local police[45] to investigate the target and, after coordinating with "other concerned public security units," conduct an initial examination to decide whether the person qualified as a *liumang* (LMA Art. 2). The Implementing Rules clarified that these other units were the Ministry of Justice's Investigation Bureau 法務部調查局 and the Ministry of National Defense's Military Police Command (originally 國防部憲兵司令部 and later changed to 國防部憲兵指揮部). In general, the Investigation Bureau is charged with investigating violations

---

[45] The *Liumang* Act provided that the police department of a directly governed municipality or the county (city) police department would handle the initial examination (Art. 2). The term "directly governed municipality" 直轄市 refers to cities that are under the direct control of the ROC central government, of which there were two at the time the Act was abolished (i.e., Taipei and Kaohsiung) and five as of 2012.

against national security and certain serious crimes, including drug trafficking, organized crime, major economic crimes, and bribery during elections.[46] In addition to enforcing military law and maintaining military discipline, the Military Police Command implements military police intelligence operations and criminal investigations, secures major government buildings, and can provide backup to civilian police.[47] All three organizations—the police, the Investigation Bureau, and the Military Police Command—held the power to initiate an investigation against a suspected *liumang*. In practice, the dominant player in *liumang* investigations was, almost without exception, the police.

The ROC police force is divided into national and local levels, though both are formally under the jurisdiction of the National Police Agency (NPA), which is part of the Ministry of the Interior. Like the Ministry of National Defense and the Ministry of Justice, the Ministry of the Interior is within the Executive Yuan 行政院, the executive branch of government. The NPA oversees all police work in Taiwan and works on major cases of national concern. Most day-to-day duties, including the investigation of *liumang*, are delegated to the local police departments at the county and city levels.[48] While it was rare for the NPA to be directly involved in the initial evidence collection in *liumang* cases, its Criminal Investigation Bureau 刑事警察局 is charged with investigating high-profile crimes, and evidence collected by this bureau

---

[46] The Investigation Bureau's functions are detailed in the Organizational Law of the Investigation Bureau, Ministry of Justice 法務部調查局組織法.

[47] The powers of the Military Police Command are described further in the Organizational Rules of the Military Police Command, Ministry of National Defense 國防部憲兵司令部組織規程.

[48] The county and city governments also oversee local police, leading to complicated bureaucratic structures as the police answer to both the NPA and local authorities. This dual oversight is graphically depicted on the organization chart of the Taipei Municipal Police Department, which has a line leading directly above to the Taipei City Government but also a diagonal line connected to the NPA. Decentralization does not extend to police training: the Ministry of Interior trains police for all of Taiwan at the Taiwan Police College in Taipei and the Central Police University in Taoyuan.

could be used in *liumang* cases.[49] Nonetheless, the local police usually did the investigation legwork, which generally was intentionally carried out without the suspect's knowledge. This prevented targets from threatening potential witnesses, or paying them off to stay quiet. It also cut down on the probability that targets would flee or try to cover their tracks. That said, people caught while engaging in *liumang* behavior became immediately aware of their problem because they were fast-tracked and taken straight to the station for the police to prepare evidence for the determination process (LMA Art. 10). Other targets might have suspected that they were under investigation because of pending criminal charges that overlapped with *liumang* offenses.

Once the local police decided that they had collected enough evidence to support a determination that the target was a *liumang*, they sent the case up the chain of command. First, a small group from the local police, together with representatives from the Military Police Command and Investigation Bureau, conducted a "preliminary examination" 初審. During this stage, the group decided whether to send the case to the next level. If it was to be elevated, the group then had to decide whether to recommend that the person be treated as a serious or a warned *liumang*.

Following the preliminary examination, the case moved to the "higher-level police agencies" for a "reexamination" 複審, also called a "reexamination and determination" 複審認定 (LMA Art. 2). The *Liumang Act*, however, did not clarify how the "higher-level police agencies" should carry out the reexamination. The details were left to the Implementing Rules, which required that there be a "deliberation committee for *liumang* cases" 流氓案件審議委員會 ("review committee") and that it be

---

[49] The Criminal Investigation Bureau contains a section dedicated to organized crime. Although literally translated as the examining/restraining 檢 and eliminating 肅 section 檢肅科, it is translated as the "Organized Crime Affairs Section" in a brochure from the Criminal Investigation Bureau. We have also seen it translated as the "Anti-Hoodlum Section" on an employee's business card. According to the Criminal Investigation Bureau's introductory brochure, this section is responsible for affairs related to organized crime groups and their affiliates.

composed of police, prosecutors,[50] legal specialists, and impartial people from society (Art. 7). The Implementing Rules failed to specify how many people from each category must be on the review committee. This information was found in the next layer of rules.

The NPA provided the additional rules on the composition of the review committee in the Main Points for the Organization of the Police Committee for the Deliberation of and Objections to *Liumang* Cases 警察機關流氓案件審議及異議委員會編組要點 ("Review Committee Rules").[51] The Review Committee Rules called for six to eight committee members, consisting of at least one prosecutor and no more than one-third legal specialists and impartial people from society (Art. 4). The review committee's evaluation was the final stage for *liumang* who were not considered "serious." Cases involving such plain-vanilla *liumang* were thought to require no court involvement. Rather, the review committee had the power to impose sanctions directly because the sanctions for these low-level offenders were not deemed as harsh as the imprisonment imposed on "serious" offenders.

These low-level offenders had no opportunity to participate in the determination process and usually did not know they were even under suspicion until receiving an official notice of the review committee's decision. In 2008, the Constitutional Court held in Interpretation No. 636

---

[50] By "prosecutors," we mean *public* prosecutors 檢察官. Taiwan's Criminal Procedure Code allows for both public 公訴 and private 自訴 prosecutions. The latter may be initiated by the victim or, in some circumstances, an agent or family member. The person initiating the private suit is called a private prosecutor 自訴人 (CPC Art. 319 *et seq.*). Only public prosecutors were of concern in *liumang* cases, except in the rare case where a *liumang* brought a private prosecution against a witness for perjury or making false accusations (LMA Art. 17). One such case is discussed in Chapter 3. Procedures for public and private prosecutions are set forth in Part II, Chapters 1 and 2, respectively, of the Criminal Procedure Code.

[51] Although called the "deliberation committee for *liumang* cases" 流氓案件審議委員會 in the Implementing Rules, this same entity was called the "committee for the deliberation of and objections to *liumang* cases" 流氓案件審議及異議委員會 in the Review Committee Rules (Art. 2) and the Police Provisions (Art. 16), and it was also colloquially referred to as the "reexamination meeting" 複審會議.

that, in accordance with the principle of due process, accused *liumang* had a right to make a statement during the determination process. Because the legislature repealed the *Liumang* Act, no such change was ever promulgated.

If the review committee determined that the person qualified as a serious *liumang*, the case would then be transferred to the public security tribunal within the local district court. Unlike criminal cases, *liumang* cases bypassed the prosecutors' office and proceeded directly to the court. There was no indictment, just a transfer.[52] Prosecutors played no role in the determination process other than having a single representative on the review committee. The Ministry of Justice, of which prosecutors are a part, was involved in *liumang* cases insofar as its Investigation Bureau contributed to the investigation and preliminary examination stages, though this bureau represents a distinct entity from the prosecutors' offices. After the case left the review committee for the public security tribunal, the Ministry of Justice came into play again, but only with respect to running the training institutes where reformatory training was carried out. It implemented these initiatives through its Department of Corrections, which was in charge of drafting plans and directing work at the facilities.

Public security tribunals were set up within the district and high courts to handle *liumang* cases exclusively (LMA Art. 22). It is misleading, however, to think of public security tribunals as discrete courts that had a visible, independent identity. There was no separate building—or even necessarily a sign or dedicated courtroom—announcing a part of the district court as the public security tribunal. It was simply a name used when a specified judge heard a *liumang* case.[53] For example, in 2006, there were nine public security tribunal judges in the Taipei District Court who were drawn from the court's fifty-nine criminal

---

[52] In a criminal case, the prosecutor must file an indictment with the appropriate court to initiate the prosecution (CPC Art. 264).

[53] The *Liumang* Act provided that the courts may set up "special" tribunals or assign "special" people under the name "public security tribunal" to handle *liumang* cases (Art. 22).

judges.[54] These judges also handled criminal cases, largely out of concern that having only narrow experience with *liumang* cases would stunt their professional development. In smaller courts, such as in Jinmen and Taidong, judges usually heard a variety of cases out of necessity. There can be as few as three to five judges in an entire district court. The public security tribunals' lack of a distinct identity was underscored by their use of the criminal courts' clerks, interpreters, document clerks, court police, and other court personnel.

The public security tribunal's ultimate decision concerned whether the accused was a serious *liumang* and therefore must undergo reformatory training. Technically, the tribunal's holding was either "commit to reformatory training" 交付感訓 or "not commit to reformatory training" 不交付感訓 instead of simply stating that the person was a serious *liumang*. The reason for this wording was that, even if the tribunal concluded that the circumstances were serious, reformatory training would be improper if the accused was under eighteen or insane; the accused was dead; the three-year period in which *liumang* behavior may be considered had passed prior to the transfer of the case to the tribunal; or a public security tribunal had already issued a ruling regarding the same *liumang* behavior, or it was a duplicate transfer (LMA Art. 13). Absent these unusual circumstances, if the tribunal concluded that the accused was a serious *liumang*, reformatory training would follow. Because a decision that the accused was a serious *liumang* was tantamount to a ruling that committed the accused to reformatory training, we use "commit to reformatory training" and "rule that the accused is a serious *liumang*" interchangeably.

In addition to the final ruling whether a person was a serious *liumang*, pending a decision in the case, the public security tribunal

---

[54] Unlike the heavily male-dominated *liumang* population, an increasing number of judges in Taiwan are women, including several of the judges with whom we spoke. Nonetheless, for the sake of simplicity, we also refer to judges using male pronouns.

also had the power to confine the accused under certain circumstances, such as if he was deemed a flight risk. The length of confinement was limited to one month, with a permissible one-month extension (LMA Art. 11). Confinement was rare, with most people given one of several types of supervised release.[55] The *Liumang* Act's use of the term "confinement" underscored the Act's unique nature. "Confine" 留置 is distinct from the term used in criminal cases for pre-trial detention.[56] Yet the difference was in name, not substance. In both *liumang* and criminal cases, the person was held by the police, and almost always in the same facilities.[57]

Unlike at the review committee level, where accused *liumang* did not have the opportunity to voice an opinion, the accused had the right to appoint a lawyer to represent him before the public security tribunal, and the tribunal was required to notify the lawyer and the accused of the hearing (LMA Art. 9, IR Art. 38). Despite these rights, many accused *liumang* appeared without counsel. We asked a training institute employee whether lawyers often visited *liumang* who were undergoing reformatory training, for example, to consult regarding pending appeals or other legal matters. He replied that it had been more common in the past when there were "big brothers" (i.e., high-ranking gang members) who had been caught during large-scale crackdowns on organized crime. By the time of our study, the training institute generally housed low-level

---

[55] As described in greater detail in Chapter 3, the alternatives included bail 具保, custodial release 責付 (i.e., turning over the accused to the custody of another, who becomes answerable for the accused's behavior), or restricted residence 限制住居. In criminal cases, the Criminal Procedure Code provides the same three alternatives when a judge decides that pre-trial detention is unnecessary (CPC Art. 93).

[56] As previously noted in footnote 43, there are three distinct kinds of detention under Taiwanese law.

[57] The Implementing Rules provided that people should be confined in "confinement houses" 留置所 set up by the Ministry of Justice and, if not yet established, then people should be held in "detention houses" 看守所. Confinement was to be carried out with reference to the provisions of the Detention Law 羈押法 (IR Art. 30).

liumang who either did not have the money to hire a lawyer or simply thought a lawyer would be ineffective.

Even when there was a lawyer present, the tribunals did not conduct an adversarial hearing. No prosecutor was involved to serve as an adversary to the accused's lawyer, nor did the police step into the prosecutor's shoes,[58] though police could be called as witnesses or request to appear and state opinions. The hearing was "inquisitorial" in nature, with the judge interrogating the accused and the witnesses like a classic Continental European *juge d'instruction*—a magistrate charged with conducting the crucial pre-trial investigative hearing in a manner that often intimidated the suspect. After Taiwan's adoption of "adversary"-type criminal trials, the gap between the new procedures of criminal trials, featuring a supposedly equal contest between the government and the suspect, and those of its public security trials thus widened substantially, at least in principle.

The hearing was further dissimilar from a standard criminal trial in that the *Liumang* Act provided for a secret witness 秘密證人 system whereby the witnesses' identities were usually withheld from the accused and his counsel (Art. 12). The *Liumang* Act was not unique in protecting witnesses' identities—both the Organized Crime Act[59] and the Witness Protection Law[60] 證人保護法 (WPL) limit access to identifying information—but

---

[58] The police did not assume the prosecutor's role in the courtroom, but one police officer described the police's investigatory role as similar to that of a prosecutor.

[59] The Organized Crime Act provides that, in such criminal cases, witnesses' identifying information be sealed and kept separate and not subject to examination. The judge and prosecutor may also at their discretion bar defense counsel from questioning witnesses or viewing documents with identifying information if facts show that the witness may be subject to retaliatory acts (OCA Art. 12).

[60] The Witness Protection Law was enacted in 2000 to encourage witnesses to testify in "criminal and *liumang* cases" (WPL Art. 1). Despite the explicit mention of *liumang* cases, it was unnecessary for the police and courts to use this law in *liumang* cases because the *Liumang* Act standing alone provided sufficient authority to withhold all identifying information from the accused and his lawyer. The Witness Protection Law only applies to witnesses who are willing to testify and subject themselves to cross-examination, though the witness's identity may be concealed through use of a mask, voice alteration, or other methods (WPL Arts. 3, 11). Protection measures

the *Liumang* Act had traditionally taken secrecy to an extreme that was not seen in criminal trials, except perhaps in some organized crime cases. The Constitutional Court required fundamental revisions to the secret witness system in its February 2008 ruling, but the legislature repealed the *Liumang* Act instead of revising the system.

In addition to the aforementioned use of the term "confine," the public security tribunals used other special terminology that diverged from the standard language of criminal prosecutions. The person before the tribunal was not a "defendant" 被告人 but was instead called the "transferred person" 被移送裁定人 (literally, "the person transferred for a ruling," with the implied meaning that the police were doing the transferring). Prior to transfer, the suspect was the "reported person" 被提報人, i.e., the police had submitted his case for a formal determination whether he was a *liumang*. For convenience's sake, we simply refer to the person as a suspect 嫌疑人 or target 對象 during the investigation phase and as the "accused" or "accused *liumang*" once the police reported him to the review committee for a determination. Lawyers in *liumang* cases came with their own special label. The accused *liumang*'s lawyer was the "chosen lawyer" 選任律師 rather than the "defense lawyer" 辯護律師. And the tribunal's decision was termed a "ruling" 裁定 instead of a "judgment" 判決.[61] These quirks underscore that proceedings before a public security tribunal were markedly different from those of a criminal trial.

---

include issuance of a protective order and temporary relocation, which is limited to an initial period of one year plus a permissible one-year extension (WPL Arts. 4, 13). There is no provision for permanent relocation along the lines of the witness protection program in the United States. The efficacy of relocation is further limited by the realities of Taiwan's geography and population. It is a small place with a close-knit population of approximately twenty-three million people. It is hard to hide. When asked whether secret witnesses were truly secret, one judge responded that people in Taiwan see American movies where people get a new identity, move to another state, and are given a new life. This is not possible in small Taiwan, he said. Additional provisions are set forth in the Implementing Rules for the Witness Protection Law 證人保護法施行細則.

[61] The Criminal Procedure Code specifies that a judgment shall be based on oral arguments 言詞辯論 of the parties unless specially provided otherwise (CPC Art. 221). No oral argument was required in *liumang* cases.

B. Sanctions

As we have seen, *liumang* were subject to one of two types of sanctions, depending on whether they were "warned" or "serious." For a warned *liumang*, following the review committee's determination, the police sent him a written warning and entered his name in a special register that they maintained for *liumang* (LMA Art. 4). The Chinese term used in the *Liumang* Act for "warning," "*gaojie*" 告誡, has a more polite air about it—akin to saying "admonish" or "exhort"—compared to the harsher sounding *jinggao* 警告, described as more "unpleasant sounding" by one police official.

Warned *liumang* underwent one year of "guidance" 輔導—a probation-like sanction that involved periodic interviews and other monitoring. The *Liumang* Act called upon the police to pay attention to the *liumang*'s living conditions at all times during this stage and exhort him to be good (Art. 20). During the guidance period, a warned *liumang* was required to meet with the police at appointed times to report on his living conditions and, if he failed to do so without a valid excuse, the police could apply to the public security tribunal to have him detained for up to seven days (LMA Art. 20). If the warned *liumang* completed a full year of "guidance" without engaging in *liumang* behavior, then the police would remove him from the register (LMA Art. 4).[62] On the other hand, if the police discovered that he engaged in *liumang* behavior during the one-year period, he would

---

[62] The *Liumang* Act specifically provided that, if a warned *liumang* did not engage in *liumang* behavior during the one-year guidance period, after the police reported to the review committee for its examination and approval, the police would cancel the warned *liumang*'s listing on the register, stop guidance, and provide him with written notice thereof. The Police Provisions elaborated that, if the guidance period was complete but the police then discovered that the *liumang* engaged in *liumang* behavior during the guidance period and the police were in the process of investigating the matter, the police could request a deferred cancellation of two months to continue their investigation. If the police were unable to complete their investigation within two months, they were required to report for cancellation in accordance with the procedures in the *Liumang* Act (PP Art. 45(1)).

promptly find himself called into the police station for questioning and perhaps transferred to the public security tribunal for further processing (LMA Art. 7).

For serious *liumang*, it was up to the public security tribunal to decide whether a person was to be so designated and accordingly sentenced to reformatory training, which could last anywhere from one to three years (LMA Art. 19). The judge's role was limited to deciding whether reformatory training was appropriate, but not the actual length thereof, though Interpretation No. 636 called for this provision to be re-examined and amended (LMA Art. 13). The decision regarding the duration of training primarily rested with the authorities at the training institute and their superiors at the Ministry of Justice, who could recommend a person for release at any time after a minimum of one year,[63] provided that the *liumang* met the requirements set forth in the Measures for Enforcing the Punishment of Reformatory Training 感訓處分執行辦法 ("Enforcement Measures").[64] The public security tribunal needed to approve the *liumang*'s release. We heard of no case, however, where a judge sent a person back to do more time against the Ministry of Justice's recommendation.

Having completed his reformatory training, the *liumang* may have been back on the street, but he was not yet out of the woods. So-called "post-reformatory training *liumang*" 結訓輔導流氓—literally, "concluded (reformatory) training, guidance *liumang*" (PP Art. 38)—were subject to a one-year guidance period, just as if they were warned *liumang* (LMA Art. 19). If a post-reformatory training *liumang* backslid during

---

[63] In contrast, subject to certain limitations, parole is available for criminal offenders after they have served half of their term of imprisonment, or twenty-five years of a life sentence (Criminal Code, Art. 77).

[64] The *Liumang* Act provided that the Executive Yuan and Judicial Yuan shall jointly issue measures for the enforcement of reformatory training (Art. 18). The resulting Enforcement Measures replaced the previous Measures for Enforcing the Punishment of Reformatory Training During the Period of Communist Rebellion 動員戡亂時期流氓感訓處分執行辦法.

this period, the police could transfer the *liumang*'s case back to the public security tribunal, and he would likely find himself returning to the training institute (LMA Art. 19).

C. Channels for Reversing a *Liumang* Determination

The determination that a person was a *liumang* was not set in stone. An aggrieved *liumang* could challenge the determination through a multi-layer process. As with sanctions, the *Liumang* Act created a two-track system for relief, depending on the person's status as a warned or serious *liumang*. A warned *liumang*'s first line of attack was to file a written "objection" 異議 with the review committee within ten days of receiving the warning (LMA Art. 5). If this objection was rejected, the warned *liumang* could next file an "administrative appeal" 訴願 with the NPA followed by an "administrative lawsuit" 行政訴訟 with the administrative courts (LMA Art. 5). These last two steps brought into play the Administrative Appeal Law 訴願法 and Administrative Litigation Law 行政訴訟法, respectively.

In contrast, a serious *liumang*'s avenue for relief lay immediately with the courts. He could challenge the public security tribunal's ruling by filing an "appeal of the ruling" 抗告 with the public security tribunal at the high-court level.[65] Unlike the public security tribunal in the district court, where the case was heard by a single judge virtually without exception, the public security tribunal at the high-court level used a three-judge panel (IR Art. 37). In accordance with the special system

---

[65] This process is similar to the Criminal Procedure Code, which states that a party may appeal a ruling to the directly higher court (CPC Art. 403). The term used for this type of appeal, *kanggao* 抗告 (also sometimes translated as "interlocutory appeal"), is different than for appeals of a final judgment, *shangsu* 上訴. Because there was only a "ruling" in a *liumang* case, it was technically impossible for a person to "*shangsu*." A third type of appeal, *suyuan* 訴願, is used for administrative appeals, such as when a warned *liumang* appeals a review committee's determination to the NPA.

for *liumang* cases that provided the decision of the second level court was final,[66] the high court had the final say, subject to a narrow exception (LMA Art. 14): a serious *liumang* could apply for a rehearing 重新審理 of his case when certain major factual errors allegedly occurred, such as that the evidence on which the ruling was based was fabricated or tampered with, or the witnesses' statements were false (LMA Art. 16).[67] If the public security tribunal ruled on rehearing that the accused was wrongly committed to reformatory training, the appellant was entitled to compensation under the Wrongful Detention Compensation Law (LMA Art. 11).

The *Liumang* Act also allowed symmetrical appeal rights for the police.[68] For serious *liumang*, the "transferring agency," i.e., the police, could appeal a public security tribunal's ruling that a person was not a serious *liumang* (LMA Art. 14). While the police's appeal was pending, the alleged *liumang*, if he was confined in the first place, should have been released as a general principle. The court had the power to continue confining the alleged *liumang* pending appeal if the court considered it "necessary" (IR Art. 33), though the legal framework also allowed the person to challenge his continued confinement (CM Art. 24). For warned *liumang*, if the review committee rejected the police's recommendation that a person qualified as a *liumang*, the police were almost always allowed to continue their

---

[66] In contrast, for criminal judgments, the decision of the third-level court, i.e., the Supreme Court, is final, with the exception that cases using summary procedures 簡易程序 are only appealable to the high court (CPC Art. 273). Re-appeals of rulings 再抗告 are allowed in some circumstances in criminal cases (CPC Art. 415).

[67] A *liumang* who sought rehearing was required to apply to the "original ruling court whose ruling becomes finalized" (LMA Art. 16), meaning that if the case went up to the public security tribunal in the high court on appeal, the *liumang* had to apply to the high court. If, on the other hand, the case never reached the high court and was only heard by the public security tribunal in the district court, the application should have been lodged with the district court.

[68] In criminal cases, the prosecution is similarly allowed to appeal (CPC Art. 344).

investigation in order to strengthen the case.[69] This less serious category of *liumang* was not subject to confinement during the period of continuing investigation and, as previously noted, likely did not even know that they were under suspicion. As a result of these procedural mechanisms that allowed for protracted investigations of suspected *liumang*, a suspect's case could stay pending for an extended period of time, especially when tenacious police were involved.

IV. CONCLUSION

The *Liumang* Act charted the general path that an accused *liumang* followed as he proceeded through the system, but it did not convey the intricacies of this process. For that, our research team sought out people involved in various stages of the process: local police, NPA officials, prosecutors who had served on review committees, lawyers in private practice, public security tribunal and criminal court judges, and personnel at training institutes.[70] Based on our discussions with people who had experience with *liumang*-related work and materials provided by them, we were able to get an inside understanding of how the pieces fit together, albeit not necessarily into a neat and tidy picture.

The next chapter explores what happened when people found themselves enmeshed in the system and attempted to untangle themselves—a

---

[69] At some point the review committee could refuse to hear a case or the case would become moot because the three-year period between the behavior and reporting had passed.

[70] Notably absent are *liumang* themselves. In light of the sensitive nature of conducting interviews with incarcerated *liumang*, and the questionable veracity of information we would obtain from inmates during interviews, observed by the authorities, we opted against pursuing this avenue. Sending our teams into the bowels of Taiwan's criminal underworld in search of active *liumang* also did not strike us as a particularly wise move. And our inquiries to various interviewees whether they could put us in touch with reformed *liumang* did not yield any fruitful results.

feat that was doubly difficult because suspected *liumang* were frequently oblivious to the fact that they were under suspicion and, even if alerted, they were hamstrung by their inability to access information comprising the case against them. With the *Liumang* Act now laid out as the backdrop, we turn to the more nuanced story: the journey of two fictitious *liumang* from the streets, through the police and courts, and back onto the streets.

CHAPTER 3:
THE SYSTEM IN PRACTICE

I. INTRODUCTION: THE STORY OF CHEN AND WANG

This is the story of Chen and Wang, two not-so-law-abiding citizens who found themselves entangled in Taiwan's legal system as suspected *liumang*. In order to present Chen's and Wang's complete experiences, we will step back in time to the law as it was in February 2008, after the Constitutional Court had issued its third and final interpretation regarding the Act for Eliminating *Liumang* 檢肅流氓條例 ("*Liumang* Act" or LMA) but before the Legislative Yuan had taken action to repeal the Act. In this twilight period of Taiwan's *liumang* regime, the *Liumang* Act remained a potent tool for the police.

Chen and Wang are not real. Nonetheless, their fictional stories serve as useful heuristic devices to illustrate how the government's efforts to eliminate *liumang* worked in practice. Both underwent investigation and review by the police. At that point, the difference in the severity of their respective *liumang* behavior led them down markedly different paths: Chen's case rested with the police-dominated committee that reviewed *liumang* cases, while Wang's continued past this stage and ultimately landed before a public security tribunal. Likewise, Chen's chance of freeing himself from the *liumang* label was through agency review and thereafter the administrative courts, whereas Wang had to seek relief directly through the general court system by appealing the public security tribunal's ruling.

Chen's and Wang's situations also differed as a result of geography. Wang was located in Taipei and Chen in Tainan. As is reflected in their names, Taipei is in the north (*pei* or *bei* in pinyin[1]) and Tainan is in the south (*nan*). More important than this physical distance was the difference in the cities' relationships to the central government. Although the same rules apply across Taiwan, the agencies handling their cases were different because Taipei is a city organized directly under the central government, while Tainan, until 2010, was a city under Taiwan Province and therefore lacking the autonomy of Taipei. Anecdotally, some interviewees indicated regional differences also resulted in varying perceptions of what constituted a *liumang*. For example, Taipei is a large capital city whereas Tainan is relatively rural, which results in significant differences in public safety. A former member of a police-dominated review committee who later served as a public security tribunal judge explained that, if the police in Taipei thought you were a *liumang*, then you certainly must have done something serious. In contrast, in a less cosmopolitan town in southern Taiwan, lesser misconduct might be able to shock the public.

Of course, two hypothetical cases cannot illustrate all of the many possible subtle variations that occurred once the police identified someone as a suspected *liumang*. Nonetheless, they can help to clarify how two unexceptional suspects meandered through a system that was fraught with ambiguity, secrecy, and uncertainty.

II. INVESTIGATION AND PRELIMINARY EXAMINATION

In Tainan, Chen had taken to racking up bills at several local bars. Chen had been out of work for a while and was rather enjoying his new lifestyle of hanging out in bars with friends, along with making the occasional trip

---

[1] Romanization of the names of places and people in Taiwan is a frustrating endeavor because there is no uniform system, nor is there much rhyme or reason to the multiple methods that are varyingly used. Where a place or person is generally known by a particular name, we have used it (e.g., Taipei) and noted common variants (e.g., Kinmen, which is also known as Quemoy or Jinmen). We have used pinyin as the default system when there is not an already established standard.

to a local gambling den. When repeatedly approached for payment by one bar owner named Li, Chen at first brushed his requests aside. Eventually, when pressed by Li, Chen threatened that he would forcibly adjust Li's facial features if asked again. Chen was, as the Chinese expression literally translates, "using the village people as his fish and meat," i.e., victimizing the locals for his gain. Chen continued to drink without paying.

Meanwhile in Taipei, Wang was running guns for higher-ups in the Bamboo Union 竹聯幫, one of Taiwan's largest and most fearsome gangs.[2] Although not savvy as to greater arms smuggling operations, he frequently carried a few guns in his knapsack for delivery from the storehouse to his "big brothers" (the most important members) in the gang. Wang was only a small fish in the gang, but he had aspirations of working his way up through the ranks.

Although our two shady characters were operating under the police's radar, that changed suddenly. At this point, it helps to understand the structure of policing in Taiwan. Taiwan's police force is structured on four levels: substations 派出所 and stations 分駐所 serve as the

---

[2] Taiwan has a long and colorful history of gangs, including ongoing activities by sophisticated criminal organizations. Bamboo Union, Celestial Alliance 天道盟, and Four Seas 四海幫 rank among Taiwan's most notorious gangs. The 2005 funeral of Hsu Hai-ching, a prominent godfather who, for unknown reasons, bore the sobriquet "Mosquito Brother," brought out a reported 10,000 black-clad gangsters. The media reported that police videotaped the procession in order to review whether any of those in attendance had violated the Organized Crime Act. Rich Chang, *Procession held for 'Mosquito Brother,' Taipei Times* (30 May 2005). Taiwanese gangs are also known for infiltrating politics, for example, Luo Fu-zhu (Lo Fu-chu) and other members of the Legislative Yuan have been notoriously linked to organized crime (Roy 2003, 207). Luo was arrested in 1984 as part of "Operation Cleansweep" and emerged from prison as one of the heads of Celestial Alliance (Chin 2003, 42, 168). In 2001, while serving in the legislature, Luo was indicted for physically assaulting a fellow legislator and, at the same time, determined to be a *liumang*. According to one report, "[Luo]—widely recognized as a thug because of his frequent assaults on his colleagues at the Legislative Yuan—was formally listed as a hooligan on Oct. 24 [2001]." Deborah Kuo, *'Thug' Legislator Returns to Taipei to Face Anti-Hoodlum Law, Central News Agency—Taiwan* (7 January 2002). Beyond these massive criminal enterprises, Taiwan has an array of local, more loosely-knit groups that are engaged in criminal acts, or at least questionably legal behavior. Significant players in local communities are "*jiaotou*" 角頭, which can refer to a local gang or a specific person who is the big man in the neighborhood. *Jiaotou* groups are usually named for the location in which they reside.

neighborhood police units; followed by precincts 分局; the city or county police department 警察局; and, finally, the National Police Agency 警政署 (NPA). The organization of local police across Taiwan is not entirely uniform. Each directly governed municipality 直轄市 (e.g., Taipei, New Taipei City 新北市, Taichung, Tainan, and Kaohsiung), provincial municipality 省轄市 (e.g., Keelung City, Hsinchu City, and Chiayi City), and county has its own police department. In turn, each of these various police departments has subordinate precincts, which then have substations and/or stations. The main difference between substations and stations is that substations are generally found in urban areas, whereas stations are found in less populated, rural areas. Their responsibilities are, for all intents and purposes, the same. Minor differentiations aside, the key point is that most day-to-day patrolling and other neighborhood police work is handled at the station or substation level, which we will collectively refer to as "substations" for convenience's sake.

The police departments in Taipei City and Kaohsiung City, both directly governed municipalities, follow this same structure (e.g., Taipei City has fourteen precincts and ninety-three substations). The wrinkle is that, up until 2010, Taipei City and Kaohsiung City were both enclosed by counties of the same names.[3] Consequently, there was both a Taipei County and a Taipei City police department. The important difference for *liumang* cases was that the cities had their own review committees, whereas cases from the counties of the same names were sent to the NPA review committee. Likewise, when the *Liumang* Act was in effect, there was both a Tainan City and a Tainan County, but *liumang* cases from both of these localities went to the NPA review committee. In short, all *liumang* cases other than those from Taipei City and Kaohsiung City were heard by the NPA

---

[3] In 2010, Kaohsiung County was combined with Kaohsiung City, and Taipei County became New Taipei City.

review committee. Unless specified otherwise, as used in this study, Taipei, Kaohsiung, and Tainan refer to the cities and not the counties of the same names.

Each police department also has hundreds of smaller police beats 警勤區. Each beat has a designated police officer who serves as the contact person for the local residents' administrative affairs. Similar to the police beats are the "responsibility beats for crime monitoring" 刑事責任區, which each consists of an area for which a single police officer is in charge of monitoring crimes.

A. Chen: Drinking for Free in Tainan

Having decided that he did not want to have his face redone by Chen, Li, the aggrieved bar owner, was at a loss about what to do. Li was unwilling to subsidize Chen's drinking habit indefinitely, but, out of concern for retaliation by Chen and his unsavory cohorts, he was also hesitant to file a police report. Unwilling to go to the police, he waited until one day when a police officer from the local police substation was at his bar and then pulled him aside for a quick conversation. The officer had seen Chen about town and heard his name mentioned at the station as someone who had brushed with the police before.[4] After leaving Li's bar, the officer decided to ask his colleagues and other bar owners whether Chen was making a pattern of this behavior. The investigation was underway.

The local police under the Tainan City Police Department set about building a case to prove that Chen was a *liumang* in accordance with the Provisions on Police Handling of Cases under the Act for Eliminating *Liumang* 警察機關辦理檢肅流氓條例案件作業規定 ("Police Provisions" or PP) (Art. 11). The demarcation between the substations' and

---

[4] Called the "public security population" 治安人口 according to a police investigator with whom we spoke, such people are reputed to have criminal habits and, hence, are of particular concern to the police. In short, the police keep a special eye out for these people.

precincts' responsibilities blurred at this stage.[5] Both could be involved in collecting evidence, though the main investigatory work in *liumang* cases fell on the precinct-level police, as is generally done with criminal cases as well. Within precincts, there are "investigative teams" 偵察隊 which, as the name suggests, head up investigations for criminal cases and, previously, *liumang* cases as well. Substation police, by comparison, are generally "administrative police" 行政警察 who conduct routine patrols, answer calls for assistance, and handle management of administrative affairs. At the central level, the Criminal Investigation Bureau under the NPA had the authority to conduct investigations in *liumang* cases throughout Taiwan, though their involvement was generally limited to rare cases of national concern.

A single investigation could have involved police from several substations and even various precincts or departments. One investigator explained that each precinct has approximately eight substations, though he also noted that this number varies. It was unusual for the entire case against a suspected *liumang* to fall within a single substation, and some *liumang* engaged in behavior in areas under the jurisdiction of several

---

[5] The Police Provisions did not clearly differentiate between the responsibilities of precincts and substations. They did, however, separately detail the various responsibilities of (1) the precincts under the police departments of directly governed municipalities 直轄市 and the county (city) 縣(市) police departments (PP Art. 6); (2) the police departments of the two cities that were directly governed municipalities at the time the Police Provisions were in effect (PP Art. 7); and (3) the NPA (PP Art. 8). The first group had a litany of responsibilities with respect to *liumang* cases: investigate thoroughly, collect evidence, conduct the preliminary examination, report the person, carry out warning and guidance, supervise the register, give notices and arrest suspects, order the arrest of a wanted person, transfer the person to court, appeal court rulings, stop guidance, report the cancellation of an entry on the register, send the transferred person under guard for enforcement of reformatory training, enforce detention rulings against people undergoing guidance and deliver related documents, and other related work (PP Art. 6).

Moving up the food chain, the second group (i.e., then only Taipei and Kaohsiung police departments) were responsible for the review (examination and review) determination, deciding objections to cases, examining and approving the cancellation of an entry on the register, and directing and supervising the precincts' work (PP Art. 7). Third and final, the NPA had parallel responsibilities to the second group for all areas outside Taipei and Kaohsiung. In addition, the NPA decided all administrative appeals 訴願 in *liumang* cases, including appeals from cases in Taipei and Kaohsiung (PP Art. 8).

different precincts or departments. This roving behavior befits the description of *liumang* as being unspecific in their choice of victims. For example, a "touring" 周遊 *liumang* might have been away from his home area and demanded money for the safe return of a stranger's car to which he took a liking. It was possible, though less likely, for *liumang* to confine their activities to the jurisdiction of a single substation. Such so-called "local despots" 惡霸 extorted money from area residents without venturing further afield.

Investigations in *liumang* cases were not limited to the regular police. The Ministry of National Defense's Military Police Command and Investigation Bureau were also empowered to investigate *liumang*. Depending on the individual circumstances, evidence collection for a single case—including the taking of witnesses' statements—could thus involve varying combinations of government agencies in diverse locations and at different levels of the official hierarchy. Chen's case was not an exception to the general trend. His behavior reached beyond the jurisdiction of a single substation.

The police began by collecting evidence that Chen had repeatedly failed to pay his bills.[6] Having determined that Li was at risk for reprisals for reporting Chen to the police, they took down Li's statement under the code name "A1," as was the standard police convention.[7] The Police Provisions walked the police through the types of questions that they

---

[6] "Concrete facts and evidence" 具體事證 that a person engaged in *liumang* behavior could include written confessions, transcripts of oral proceedings, photographs, and even a prosecutor's indictment for criminal charges brought in connection with the same alleged misconduct, among other evidence (Implementing Rules for the Act for Eliminating *Liumang* 檢肅流氓條例施行細則 (Implementing Rules or IR) Art. 4).

[7] The Police Provisions instructed police to take a witness's statement in a quiet, peaceful place where they would not be disturbed and to advise witnesses of the protective measures that they take to keep statements confidential (PP Art. 12). Statements taken in the same case by the military police or other public security entities generally used different letters with each witness being given a number, e.g., B1, B2, etc. by a second agency and C1, C2, etc. by a third agency.

should ask, some of which were predictable questions about time, place, and people involved in the incident (PP Art. 12(5)). Other questions probed into the witness's motivations: was there any reason for enmity between the two sides, such as outstanding debts or other disputes? Still others addressed the witness's willingness to appear in court and, if the witness was unwilling, why? After completing the standard line of questioning, the police asked Li the final three questions in the Police Provisions (PP Art. 12(5)): Was everything that you said true? Do you understand that you will be legally responsible for giving false statements? And, do you have anything else you want to add?

The police also spoke with patrons who frequented the bar. One gave a statement, under the code name "A2," that he once saw Chen refuse to pay his bill and raise a fist in a threatening gesture. That patron also offered up a wad of unclear receipts from his own store in the neighborhood that he claimed represented debts that Chen owed him. The police declined to use these as evidence because they were unable to determine whether the receipts were indeed Chen's (PP Art. 12). Without Chen knowing, in order to avoid solely relying on evidence from secret witnesses, the police took a photo of him sitting in Li's bar one night. The *Liumang* Act provided that evidence from secret witnesses could not be the only evidence when a public security tribunal decided whether or not the accused was a serious *liumang* and therefore deserved reformatory training (LMA Art. 12). But if the police took reformatory training off the table as an option in the case, it technically would have been legal for the police to rely solely on secret witnesses in determining that Chen was a *liumang* subject to only a warning and guidance. There were, however, compelling reasons to go beyond secret witnesses in all *liumang* cases even when not explicitly required by law. Not only was exclusive reliance on secret witnesses bad police practice—it was generally not hard to find additional evidence—but it was often the case that the police decided whether a person should be treated as a warned or serious *liumang* only after reviewing the accumulated evidence.

Regardless of whether the police eventually decided to go after Chen as a serious or a warned *liumang*, the overwhelming response from interviewees was that secret witnesses were the backbone of most *liumang* cases. This reliance on secret witnesses was one of the factors that led to the downfall of the *Liumang* Act. The Constitutional Court held in 2008 that the secret witness system was unconstitutional. The Court qualified this decision by stating that the right to confront and examine witnesses may be restricted by concrete and clear statutory provisions when necessary to protect the witness's life, body, freedom, or property. Debate over what this interpretation would mean in practice was silenced when the Legislative Yuan decided to repeal the *Liumang* Act in its entirety.

Police officers visited other bars in the vicinity and learned that Chen had tabs at several of them that he forcefully refused to pay. He had not punched anyone, though he made repeated threats. Police took witnesses' statements under code names and added them to the expanding file. Some people with evidence supporting the case were unwilling to give statements despite assurances of secrecy. Such reluctance is understandable, especially in smaller communities where people are often clear about who has wronged whom. One investigator explained that witnesses' ability to give confidential statements was a key benefit of using the *Liumang* Act. For example, in one case a man demanded payment from each vendor at a market under the guise of "sanitation" and "public security protection" fees. If the vendor paid, then nothing happened, including none of the services for which the "fee" was named. If the vendor did not pay, then he would be forced out of the market. Although the individual sums extorted were not large—about NT $500–1000 (approximately US $17–34) per month—the money added up when multiplied by a market full of dozens or even hundreds of vendors. The police could have transferred the case to the prosecutor, who could have then brought criminal charges for obtaining money through intimidation, but this was problematic because the vendors were unwilling to speak up for fear of retribution. The government has sought to overcome this reluctance by imposing fines of up to NT $30,000 (approximately US $1,025) when people refuse to serve as witnesses in criminal cases (CPC Art. 193). If no one dares to be a witness despite the fines, it would be pointless to pursue criminal charges. The *Liumang* Act offered another route.

The process of gradually collecting witness statements and other evidence easily could have gone on for weeks or months as the police amassed enough evidence to show that Chen's behavior rose to the level of undermining social order. Collecting evidence for a *liumang* case was not, as a police investigator remarked, a "one or two day or one week" affair, it was often a long-term effort. As part of their investigation, the local police also discreetly looked into Chen's employment status, daily routine, health status, and other information that could have been helpful to the examination of his case (PP Art. 14).

Satisfied that Li and additional witnesses were telling the truth and that other evidence backed up their stories, the police compiled the statements, photocopies, photographs, and other evidence and entered it into the *liumang* investigation materials form 流氓調查資料表 for Chen's case (PP Art. 13, Appdx. 3). The police then sent this form, the related evidence, and the comparative table of code names and real names (PP Art. 12, Appdx. 1)—a listing of all the secret witnesses who gave statements— to the Tainan City Police Department (PP Art. 13).[8] The police at the Tainan City Police Department entered Chen onto the official register (PP Appdx. 4); reviewed the evidence to check that it conformed with the rules (and would have sent the case back for further work if the evidence was improperly collected or had other problems); checked the criminal information system 刑事資訊系統 or database of criminal cases 刑案知識庫 to see whether Chen already a had a *liumang* or criminal record; and formed a recommendation whether to submit Chen's case for a preliminary examination to determine if he was a *liumang* (PP Art. 13).

---

[8] For Taipei and Kaohsiung, the various materials from the investigation were consolidated on the precinct level (PP Art. 13). For all areas under the NPA review committee, this process occurred one level higher, i.e., on the department level (PP Art. 13).

The police also checked with local offices of the Ministry of Justice's Investigation Bureau and the Military Police Command—the "other concerned public security units" 其他有關治安單位 mentioned in the *Liumang* Act[9]—to see whether they had any other information on Chen (PP Art. 14). The investigation was, in theory, a collaborative effort among the three agencies. In reality, the participation of the latter two authorities frequently boiled down to attending preliminary examination meetings and affixing their chop (i.e., their official seal) on case files to evince their approval.

The Tainan police concluded that the evidence was solid and lawfully obtained, agreed that Chen met the requirements in the *Liumang* Act, and recommended that he be treated as a warned *liumang*. Specifically, Chen was alleged to have made a habit of eating and drinking without paying 白吃白喝 and threatening violence when asked to pay, which the police viewed as tyrannizing "good and honest people" 欺壓善良 (LMA Art. 2). In view of the Constitutional Court's determination shortly before the investigation into Chen's behavior began that the latter ground was unconstitutionally vague and would no longer be enforceable as of February 2009, the police decided to pursue only the charges of "eating and drinking without paying." The Constitutional Court had also called on the legislature to consider revising the provision on "eating and drinking without paying," but stopped short of holding it unconstitutional.

Chen's case was now ready for review by the "examination group for eliminating *liumang*" 檢肅流氓審查小組 ("examination group")—otherwise known as the preliminary examination meeting 初審會議. The examination group's sole purpose was to decide whether to make a recommendation that a suspect should be deemed a *liumang* and, if so, which type (PP Art. 15). For all areas outside the special municipalities of Taipei and Kaohsiung, there was an examination group for each police

---

[9] The "other concerned public security units" are further discussed in the Implementing Rules (Art. 3).

department on the county or city level. Tainan City, which had not yet become a special municipality, thus had its own examination group, as did Tainan County because of its separate police department with equal status under the NPA. The examination group's name came from the Police Provisions. The *Liumang* Act simply provided that the police should examine the case with other concerned public security units (LMA Art. 2).

All of the examination group's members were law enforcement authorities of some type. Run by the precinct chief (for Taipei and Kaohsiung) or the chief of the county/city police department (for all other localities),[10] the examination group also included representatives from the local offices of the Investigation Bureau and Military Police Command (PP Art. 15(1); IR Art. 6). Further joining the group were a mix of other police representatives, who were referred to as "superiors from other units" in the Police Provisions (PP Art. 15(1)). A police officer explained that this group included precinct chiefs, commanding officers of the criminal investigation division, and other police officials concerned with *liumang* work. The group met approximately once per month (PP Art. 15(2)).

The examination group received Chen's file and called the local police who worked on the case to give a report at their meeting (PP Art. 15(2)). If unsatisfied with a case, the examination group had the power to send the case back for further investigation. The examination group did not have the power to decide that Chen was a *liumang*. It could, at most, make a recommendation 建議. In making its recommendation, the examination group reviewed the evidence collected by the local police with one notable omission: the precinct would have already sealed up the comparative table of secret witnesses' code names and real names. Once

---

[10] The Implementing Rules provided that the "responsible commanding officer" of the relevant police department was in charge of coordinating the examination with the other concerned public security units (Art. 6).

sealed, the comparative table was for the public security tribunal judge's eyes only. The examination group members were allowed to read the witnesses' statements, but they did not know who these witnesses were other than "A1," "A2," "B1," etc.

The examination group agreed that Chen's case should proceed to the next step: the "deliberation committee for *liumang* cases" 流氓案件審議委員會 ("review committee"), also formally known as the "committee for the deliberation of and objections to *liumang* cases" 流氓案件審議及異議委員會 because it handled objections once a person was determined to be a *liumang* (PP Art. 16). Totally unbeknownst to Chen, who remained firmly rooted on a bar stool, only one step remained before he was officially declared a *liumang*.

B. Wang: Running Guns in Taipei

Meanwhile, far to the north, the Taipei Municipal Police Department had been conducting an ongoing criminal investigation into Bamboo Union's activities in the city. Wang, not exactly the sharpest new recruit in the gang, had become careless and bragged to several friends about his gun-running prowess. One friend talked a bit too loudly at a restaurant, and news of Wang's activities reached the police.[11] As in the case of Chen, the police took witnesses' statements (most of which were taken under code names) and collected photographs and other evidence. Unlike Chen's case, however, as part of their criminal investigation, the police eventually raided an apartment used by the gang. The search turned up Wang's backpack containing three shiny, new handguns; a handwritten note with an address where he was to take the guns; and, unfortunately for Wang, his photo ID. The fleet-footed Wang managed to escape down a back alley.

---

[11] Unlike in the United States, police in Taiwan cannot conduct undercover investigations to bust criminal organizations. A draft Law on Undercover Investigations 臥底偵查法 has been circulating for years, but the legislature has yet to pass it as of this writing and the topic remains contentious.

Had Wang been caught in the apartment, he would have quickly found himself at the police station as a *liumang* suspect caught in the act,[12] as well as a criminal suspect. For *liumang* suspects who were caught red-handed, within twenty-four hours of arrival at the station, the police had discretion in deciding whether to complete the *liumang* investigation materials form and related evidence and send them to the higher-level police agencies, with a copy to the NPA, for their examination and review (PP Art. 15(3)).[13] Rather than wait for the monthly meeting of the review committee, the Police Provisions explained that police should conduct an examination within twenty-hour hours of taking the person into custody and have an official above the criminal unit brigade commander 刑警大隊長 or the commissioner of the Criminal Investigation Bureau 刑事警察局局長 check and ratify their decision to pursue the suspect as a *liumang* (PP Art. 16(3)). Because the police were required to transfer the case to the public security tribunal within twenty-four hours if they decided to treat the suspect as a serious *liumang* (PP Art. 29),[14] in practice, such cases would skip the preliminary examination stage and go straight to the review committee. Yet in these circumstances, even the review committee procedure was truncated. The police conformed to the tight timeline by contacting individual committee members to obtain their approval, rather than having

---

[12] The *Liumang* Act and Police Provisions provided that if the police discovered a person (eighteen or older) who was in the act of engaging in *liumang* behavior, the police should take the person into custody and need not obtain prior court permission (LMA Art. 10; PP Art. 28(6)). This provision is similar to Article 88 of the Criminal Procedure Code, which provides that a person discovered committing a criminal offense, or immediately thereafter, may be arrested without a warrant. In both cases, however, the person cannot be held more than twenty-four hours without court permission.

[13] The Police Provisions further called on the police to fax the materials within sixteen hours of arrival at the station (PP Art. 15(3)).

[14] The twenty-four hour period was calculated by reference to Article 93-1 of the Criminal Procedure Code (PP Art. 31(2)). Travel time to the police station, for example, was not included in the twenty-four hours. Police thus had a longer time to spend with a *liumang* than with a criminal suspect because, in criminal cases, the practice is for the police to have sixteen hours to move the case to the prosecutor, leaving eight hours for the prosecutor before the suspect need be before a judge, who will rule on whether detention is required. As a general practice, a criminal court judge is on-call each night, though not necessarily waiting at the court, and this judge handled both *liumang* and criminal cases.

the committee convene a formal meeting. This simplified procedure was necessary to comply with the twenty-four hour requirement.

But Wang was quick on his feet and escaped. The police started by searching for Wang and pursuing criminal charges for gun possession under the Act for the Control of Firearms, Ammunition, and Weapons[15] 槍砲彈藥刀械管制條例 ("Firearms Act") as well as charges under the Organized Crime Act.[16] The evidence for Wang's case was sent to the prosecutors' office for a decision whether to indict. At the same time, the police decided to pursue Wang as a *liumang*. In a Chinese expression similar to the American cliché about "two bites of the apple," the police could "eat the same fish twice" 一魚兩吃, meaning that a single suspect was subject to both *liumang* and criminal charges for the same offense.

A Taipei police officer explained that *liumang* cases frequently arose out of criminal cases, and the target then became known as a "case reported" *liumang* 案報. He contrasted this with "receiving reports" 收報, whereby someone reported the *liumang* behavior independent of a crime, as seen in Chen's case. Of all the *liumang* cases in Taipei, the officer estimated that 80 percent stemmed from criminal cases. This high number is hardly surprising considering the overlap in the application of the *Liumang* Act and criminal laws. Other policemen and a prosecutor who formerly served on the NPA review committee gave a similar description. The prosecutor noted that there were generally fewer evidentiary problems with *liumang* cases that arose out of criminal cases because the corresponding criminal case would pass through the additional screens of the prosecutors' office and the district court, which entail more rigorous standards than the procedures in *liumang* cases.

---

[15] Unless permitted by the government, it is illegal to manufacture, sell, transport, transfer possession, rent, lend, possess, conceal, or display any of a long list of guns and other weapons (Firearms Act Arts. 4-5). A person convicted of possessing a handgun is subject to a fine and a prison term of five or more years (Firearms Act Art. 7). Transporting weapons is subject to fixed-term imprisonment of seven or more years, a life sentence, or even the death penalty (Firearms Act Art. 7).

[16] A participant in a criminal organization is subject to a fine and a prison term between six months and five years (Organized Crime Act Art. 3).

The incentives for police to report people as *liumang* were complex. As with other police work, in *liumang* cases, police were rewarded for exceptional work and penalized for sub-par work. The latter the police commonly referred to as having "points deducted" 扣分. The specific acts that resulted in individual police officers receiving a positive citation 記功 or commendation 嘉獎 or, on the other hand, being reprimanded 申誡 or receiving demerits 記過 were laid out in the Reward and Punishment Provisions for Police Handling of Cases under the Act for Eliminating *Liumang* 警察機關辦理檢肅流氓條例案件獎懲規定 ("Reward and Punishment Provisions"). The Reward and Punishment Provisions contained detailed tables listing the items for which police were rewarded and penalized during each phase of a *liumang* case from collecting evidence all the way through post-determination guidance. For example, police could be commended for safely transporting *liumang* from the court to the training institute.

Police doing *liumang* work were reviewed on a semi-annual basis and ranked into different categories based on the results. The performance of each city and county police department was also evaluated on a semi-annual basis using intricate point calculations set out in the NPA's Provisions on Examining the Results of Work to Eliminate *Liumang* 執行檢肅流氓工作績效考核規定 ("Examination Provisions"). The Examination Provisions listed the "predetermined standards for credits" 預定積分標準 that each police department was expected to achieve. These standards were based on the size of the population, number of criminals, and size of the police force. The police were expected to iden-tify a certain number of *liumang* every six months. A former public security tribunal judge who spent the first decade of his career in the police force attributed the police's simultaneous pursuit of criminal and *liumang* charges in a single case to an attempt to boost their scores during these periodic evaluations. He maintained that, while serving as a police officer during the martial law period, when the higher-ups in the police called for results in the fight against *liumang*, he witnessed local cops moving into high gear to charge people as *liumang* and even sometimes going so far as to "create *liumang*" to meet the orders from above. The police officers with whom we spoke while the *Liumang* Act was in effect were all aware of the influence that *liumang* cases had on their performance reviews. When asked why the grades mattered, a police officer said that they were very important because the higher-ups, including the NPA, took the reviews seriously.

Police work in criminal cases is reviewed using similar methods, yet the police evinced special concern when dealing with *liumang* cases. This concern was largely due to the many opportunities to be penalized or rewarded in a single *liumang* case. As a police officer told us, *liumang* work involved "heavy rewards and heavy punishments." There was not simply one grade. A police officer carefully explained the various categories: a grade for reporting *liumang* 提報的績效, a second grade for *liumang* appearing at the station and transferring *liumang* 到案移送的績效, and a third grade for *liumang* rulings by the courts 裁定的績效. For example, if a judge ruled not to impose reformatory training, then the police were required to submit a report to the NPA. If the NPA determined that the police did not put forth a good effort when collecting evidence, then points would be deducted. Another police officer started his description of the grading process with the caveat that the assessment was "very complex," and perhaps we would still not understand the system after discussing it for an entire day.

It is, thankfully, unnecessary for our purposes to delve into the calculus behind the grade calculations. What is clear is that a strong motivating factor behind the police's decision to report a person as a *liumang* was the effect that decision would have on their grades. There appears to have been little incentive to report additional *liumang* after a unit had met the goal for a given period because any reported case was a chance for demerits. Two police officers noted that the police sometimes held off on reporting suspected *liumang* when they had already accumulated enough points for the specified period. The police had three years from the time of the behavior to report a *liumang*, and there was no requirement that the police report a suspect as soon as they felt that they had obtained sufficient evidence to support a *liumang* determination. A police group leader put a slightly different spin on this practice by giving the example of a case that arose in May but then was reported in July or August (i.e., during the next six-month review period) because the police were still preparing the dossier. When asked what police do when it is clear that they will not meet the standards for a grading period, he replied, "give up" and prepare to be penalized. He compared it to taking an exam: if it is certain that you will not pass this time, then prepare for next time. We then asked what happened if the police were in a really safe area and there were no *liumang* to arrest, to which the group leader replied, "You can only wait to be penalized." He elaborated that many police officers did not want to do *liumang* work because it could be difficult to meet the semi-annual requirements. Consequently, some police units purposefully rotated people: "After you have been penalized, then I will take over the work! In the next period, perhaps I will be penalized and he will then take over!"

This incentive structure placed police in somewhat of a *Goldilocks and the Three Bears* conundrum. At the end of each review period, they did not want to report too few *liumang* for fear of being penalized, and they did not want to report too many unless they were very confident that all of the suspects would be deemed *liumang*. The structure encouraged them to report a number that was "just right," that is, the number that was needed to meet the required standards. Even if they did hit the projected number on the nose, it is another question whether this number was "just right" for the actual conditions in a given locality. Of course, what is "just right" is a highly subjective determination. One person in the community might think that the police were not pursuing enough suspected *liumang*, whereas another person in the same community might think that the police were excessively harsh in their efforts to crack down on *liumang*. Whether the application of the mathematical equation in the Examination Provisions churned out the optimal number of reported *liumang*—and how the perception of what was the optimal number varied among different groups of people—is a question beyond the scope of this study.

At this point, Wang's *liumang* case took a brief hiatus. The Police Provisions provided that, if a suspected *liumang* was simultaneously transferred to the prosecutors' office for possible indictment under the Organized Crime Act, then a final determination should be postponed on the *liumang* charges. If the prosecutor did not issue an indictment, however, or the court found the person not guilty—and provided that no more than three years had elapsed since the *liumang* behavior occurred— then the police could go ahead and make a decision on the *liumang* charges (PP Art. 18(4)). This practice comported with the Organized Crime Act, which provided that its provisions prevailed in the event of a conflict with the *Liumang* Act (OCA Art. 17). In Wang's case, the prosecutors' office decided that there were problems with the evidence connecting him to Bamboo Union and therefore it was unlikely that the government would be able to obtain a conviction under the Organized Crime Act.[17] It was easier to establish criminal charges for straight-up gun possession, for which the prosecutor issued an indictment. With possible organized crime charges off the table, Wang's case was then kicked back to the police and the *liumang* case could go forward, albeit in a slightly altered form.

A prosecutor's decision whether to indict sometimes influenced the substance of the allegations against a suspected *liumang*. An investigator told us that the police would remove specific incidents of *liumang* behavior from the *liumang* case if the prosecutor decided not to indict,

---

[17] The prosecutor shall issue a ruling not to prosecute if the evidence is insufficient to show that an offense has been committed (Criminal Procedure Code Art. 252(10)).

or the court found the person not guilty, of corresponding criminal charges. For instance, he explained that if the police originally planned to report a suspected *liumang* for four incidents of *liumang* behavior, two of which overlapped with criminal offenses, and the prosecutor decided that there was not enough evidence to issue an indictment on one of them, then that incident got knocked out and only three remained. The same result occurred if the court found the person not guilty or the indictment was revoked because of a settlement.[18] On the other hand, two judges with extensive experience with *liumang* cases emphasized that the criminal and *liumang* proceedings were independent. Despite being familiar with the *Liumang* Act, they were visibly surprised when we pointed out that, under the *Liumang* Act, the bases for a rehearing after the original public security tribunal issued a ruling included a decision not to prosecute or a not-guilty verdict because the evidence that a crime had been committed was insufficient or the crime could not be proven and this decision or verdict was sufficient to influence the *liumang* determination (LMA Art. 16(7)). Apparently, neither had encountered this situation in practice. In Wang's case, although the police initially intended to recommend Wang as a serious *liumang* because he transported and possessed illegal guns *and* participated in a violent gang, they decided to limit the allegations to gun possession because of the lack of evidence substantiating the gang offense.

The decision to list gun possession as Wang's only *liumang* behavior did not change the possible severity of his sentence. The public security tribunal was charged only with deciding whether or not to impose reformatory training. It had no power to decide the length of the reformatory training, nor could the tribunal sentence a *liumang* to multiple sentences.

---

[18] Certain crimes (generally relatively minor ones) fall under the category of "indictable only upon complaint" 告訴乃論罪. For such crimes, although the prosecutor can issue an indictment and conduct an investigation, the victim must file a complaint with the court, otherwise the court cannot issue a judgment. A victim's failure to file a complaint had the potential to influence related *liumang* cases.

Wang would either be declared a serious *liumang* or not; there were no gradations beyond that.[19]

Unlike criminal cases, the decision in a *liumang* case boiled down to a determination of whether or not the person was a serious *liumang*, not simply whether he carried a gun, operated a brothel, or did any other specific act. It was a declaration about the sum total of a person's behavior. It was as if a court declared, "You are a thief," instead of ruling, "You are guilty of stealing X articles on Y date from Z person." There were concrete acts underlying the *liumang* determination, yet it carried more than a whiff of a status crime (i.e., a crime that depends on a person's status more than his or her conduct). At the end of the day, Wang was to be punished for being a *liumang* rather than committing the criminal act of possessing a gun.

What happened if a person pleaded guilty to the criminal charges, or the court found him guilty, but he contested the *liumang* charges? The Implementing Rules listed confessions (IR Art. 4); indictments or disciplinary citations issued by prosecutors; and judgments issued by adjudication agencies as three forms of evidence. It is unclear whether one of these standing alone would have been sufficient to support a *liumang* determination, especially because *liumang* cases required an additional showing that the offense was "sufficient to have undermined social order." In one case, a person admitted that three guns found in his possession were indeed his. He was found guilty of criminal gun-possession charges and did not appeal. He refuted that he was a *liumang*, however, and hired a lawyer to represent him in the *liumang* proceedings,

---

[19] Article 13(2) of the *Liumang* Act provided that it was the function of the public security tribunal to decide whether or not to impose reformatory training, but not to decide the length of the sentence within the statutory one- to three-year period. The actual length of the sentence was left to subsequent determination. In its 2008 interpretation, the Constitutional Court expressed concerns that this provision could result in an excessive deprivation of physical freedom, especially when combined with criminal punishment of less than three years, but it did not declare the provision unconstitutional and instead called for it to be re-examined and amended. The 2009 repeal of the *Liumang* Act rendered this issue a moot point, but it is still relevant to Wang's hypothetical case.

even though he had not done so for the criminal case. Considering that the criminal sentence would have been set off from time spent in reformatory training, the investigator who told us this story attributed the accused *liumang*'s resistance to his fear of the "*liumang*" label and of a stay in a "training institute," which had a lingering reputation for harsh conditions. Several judges echoed this sentiment, saying that criminals usually preferred prison because reformatory training was believed to be strict in comparison and prisons were "relatively comfortable." And a lawyer told us that "reformatory training" sounded relatively harsh (literally "bitter" 苦, meaning that it caused suffering).

As discussed further below, our visits to the training institutes gave no indication that the conditions were worse than in prisons and, indeed, both training institutes housed criminals and *liumang* in the same facilities but in separate living areas. One training institute employee claimed that its facilities had superior training resources to prisons because, as compared with criminal offenders, *liumang* were "lighter" offenders and thus the hope was that they would be able to find jobs upon release. We were told at this same facility that the training resources had been even better when the military was in control because cost was not an issue at that time. This informant's statement fell on skeptical ears. His depiction of the military-controlled "control and training" facilities as amply funded bastions of learning is at odds with the general sentiment—as well as with the personal recollections of one of the authors who visited such a facility in the late 1960s—that they were fearsome places that featured fierce discipline rather than vocational training.

A more readily understandable reason for people to prefer prison over reformatory training is that they would usually be imprisoned closer to home, that is, unless they lived in the vicinity of Taidong, where the prisons that also housed training institutes were located. Although people repeatedly emphasized Taiwan's relatively small size during our conversations, it is still sufficiently large to make travel time-consuming and costly enough that visiting incarcerated friends and relatives in Taidong—located in southeastern Taiwan and isolated from the rest of the island by mountains—could be a major inconvenience, if not prohibitively expensive.

Another reason for an accused *liumang* to vigorously dispute charges was that the sentence for being a *liumang* could have been longer than if the same behavior was treated as a criminal offense. For instance, a prosecutor who formerly served on the NPA review committee explained that the police wanted to use the *Liumang* Act as a means of combating a rising incidence of handbag snatching by thieves on mopeds, a threat that a female member of our team was warned about on several occasions. The police believed that a possible three years of reformatory training—as compared with the often milder criminal sanctions for petty robbery—would act as a deterrent. The prosecutor on the committee was more skeptical about whether purse snatching was behavior that was properly punished under the *Liumang* Act, noting that the courts had traditionally treated purse snatching as a purely criminal act.

After the prosecutor declined to indict on any organized crime charges, Wang's case returned to the hands of the police. Wang's gun possession case was still pending in the criminal courts, but, unlike the Police Provisions' express requirement for cases brought under the Organized Crime Act, there was no requirement that the police must suspend a *liumang* case pending resolution of gun possession charges. Wang's *liumang* case and criminal case thus proceeded simultaneously. For the *liumang* case, the police compiled the evidence against Wang and formulated a recommendation that he be deemed a serious *liumang* on the basis that he possessed three handguns. Next, as with Chen's case, the case moved to the examination group, though the relevant group in Wang's case was on the precinct level (PP Art. 15(1)). The examination group was satisfied with the case and decided to send Wang's case to the review committee with a recommendation that he be treated as a serious *liumang*.

Meanwhile, the police were still trying to figure out where Wang was hiding. Wang was eventually picked up by police in Taoyuan County, which adjoined Taipei County (now New Taipei City) to the north and, not coincidentally, is home to Taoyuan International Airport. Because of Taiwan's size, although it can be hard to hide there for a long time, it also is not particularly hard to leave. One popular option is for suspects to flee to Hong Kong, Macau, Mainland China, or other nearby Asian places. This is especially true for gang members who have well-established connections outside Taiwan. The government is concerned not only about links between organized crime in Taiwan and the Mainland, Hong Kong, and Macau, but also links with Japan, the Philippines, and more far-flung locations. Because Wang's alleged *liumang* behavior and criminal acts were carried out in Taipei and Wang resided there, the Taoyuan police transferred Wang back to the jurisdiction of the Taipei police.

Back at the station, Wang was informed of the pending criminal gun offense for which he had been arrested and told that he may remain silent, retain defense counsel, and request the investigation of evidence favorable to him (CPC Art. 95). Wang, who at this point was only aware of the criminal charge, could hire a lawyer to defend him (CPC Art. 27). The prosecutor meanwhile had applied to the criminal court for a detention order[20] because Wang had vividly demonstrated that he was a flight risk and hence it was necessary to detain him pending trial (CPC Art. 101). The judge agreed, and Wang was shipped off to the detention house 看守所.[21] These procedures happen rapidly in criminal cases because, when a prosecutor seeks pre-trial detention, the police and prosecutor have a total of only twenty-four hours from the time that a suspect is

---

[20] When an accused *liumang* was also a criminal suspect facing a minimum of five years in prison, the accused and their criminal file were required to be transferred to the prosecutor for investigation and the *liumang* case file was to be sent to the public security tribunal (IR Art. 27). Put simply, the prosecutor got dibs on the person. If the accused was not detained pending trial in the criminal case, the court was called upon to notify the transferring police so that they could send the accused to the public security tribunal for a determination regarding confinement (IR Art. 27).

[21] The Detention Law 羈押法 (DL) and its Implementing Rules 羈押法施行細則 contain detailed provisions on the procedures and conditions for detention, such as that detainees are allowed to read (but private books should be examined) (DL Art. 18) and visits are limited to thirty minutes unless special permission is granted by the officials at the detention house (DL Art. 25).

taken to the police station until the time when he must be brought before a court for a determination whether to detain him pending trial.

Just as Chen sat obliviously on a bar stool as his file was passed up to the NPA review committee, Wang sat in the detention house unaware that his file was en route to the Taipei review committee.

III. REVIEW DETERMINATIONS AND COURT PROCEEDINGS

Chen and Wang had passed the preliminary examination stage and were well on their way to being declared *liumang*. Their files were now with the review committees. Chen had only one more step before he was officially declared a *liumang* and began his punishment. Wang, in comparison, had two more steps: a decision by the review committee and then a ruling by the public security tribunal.

A. Chen: NPA Review Committee's Determination

As previously noted, there were three review committees, which covered Taipei, Kaohsiung, and the rest of Taiwan, respectively. Each review committee, like each examination group, met approximately on a monthly basis, with the option of additional meetings when necessary (PP Art. 16). In Chen's case, because he was in Tainan, his file landed before the third review committee, which was under the NPA.[22]

The review committees' operations were laid out in the *Liumang* Act, the Implementing Rules, and the Main Points for the Organization of the Police Committee for the Deliberation of and Objections to *Liumang* Cases

---

[22] Even though the NPA is the central police authority that oversees all police functions in Taiwan, the three review committees operated independently. The NPA review committee was not authorized to tell the Taipei and Kaohsiung committees how to decide a case. The only way in which the NPA review committee could overturn a decision made by one of the other two committees was if a warned *liumang* filed an administrative appeal challenging the determination, all of which were handled by the NPA (LMA Art. 5).

警察機關流氓案件審議及異議委員會編組要點 ("Review Committee Rules" or RCR). The Review Committee Rules called for six to eight committee members (RCR Art. 4), though one member of the NPA review committee with whom we spoke said that it generally consisted of seven members, but there could be anywhere between six and twelve. Members' one-year terms were renewable (RCR Art. 4), and there was no limit on how long members could sit on the committee. Despite the Implementing Rules' provisions that the review committee be composed of police, prosecutors, legal specialists, and impartial people from society (IR Art. 7), the last two groups generally merged into one. These "impartial people from society" were not jury members selected randomly from the general population: they were usually legal scholars. A police official on the review committee said that they generally sought out one administrative law scholar and one criminal law scholar, and the single prosecutor on the committee brought an understanding of criminal procedure. One police officer described the legal specialists' role as representing "reason and law" and said that they tended toward more lenient treatment when a suspect was on the line between receiving a warning and guidance or being sent to the courts as a serious *liumang*. A police official similarly described the legal specialists—and notably the prosecutor as well—as tending toward a "humanitarian point of view." A prosecutor who served on a review committee commented that the scholars often did not attend, which left him alone with the remaining committee members, all of whom were "their people," that is, the police. Of course, even if the scholars and prosecutor attended, the committee was still dominated by the police. The police whom we met were all very professional, candid, and earnest about the review procedures. They gave us no reason to doubt that they conducted a searching review. That does not change the fact, however, that the entire process through the review committee was dominated by the police, who had incentives to increase the numbers of *liumang* cases and could face demerits for failed cases.

The review committee members gathered on the day of the meeting, with a majority of members needed for a quorum (RCR Art. 6). Police from the various examination groups also converged on the meeting place and waited outside, unless called by the committee to report on and answer questions regarding individual cases (RCR Art. 7; PP Art. 16). The Tainan police who handled Chen's case took their place outside among their counterparts from various places in Taiwan. Behind the closed doors, the review committee had already begun to discuss Chen's case. As described by a prosecutor who sat on the NPA review committee, consideration of each case began with an oral report and recommendation by an NPA official, during which the members could raise questions.

The local police were called in when needed. This was followed by a review of the file and a discussion among the committee members. Like the examination group, the review committee could read the witnesses' statements but did not know the secret witnesses' identities. Nor did these secret witnesses attend the review committee meetings. The committee kept minutes of each meeting, but these minutes were not available to the public, nor were they sent to the public security tribunal.

The review committee could reach any of the following conclusions in a case: (1) decide that the person was a serious *liumang* and transfer the case to the public security tribunal; (2) decide that the person was a *liumang*, but not a serious one, and impose a warning and guidance; (3) send the case back for further investigation because the evidence was insufficient; (4) refuse to hear the case because of procedural problems; or (5) tell the police that the reported behavior did not amount to *liumang* behavior. A former member of the NPA review committee noted that the committee members recognized the often lengthy investigations done by the local police and the frustration police felt when their recommendation was turned down. Consequently, he said that to soften such a blow, the review committee would bring in the police responsible for the case and explain the particular points in the case that presented obstacles.

Opinions varied on the level of scrutiny exercised by the review committee. One lawyer who favored abolishing the *Liumang* Act called the committee a mere rubber stamp. This impression is not entirely surprising considering that an investigator who had participated in preliminary examinations estimated that the NPA review committee accepted the examination group's recommendation in 85 to 90 percent of cases. Far from calling the review committee a rubber stamp, however, this investigator attributed the high rate to the strict standards of the examination group, which would send back cases for further evidence collection when deemed insufficient. On this theory, weak cases were weeded out before they reached the review committee. Of the cases sent on to the review committee, he estimated that the examination group recommended that 65 to70 percent be treated as warned *liumang* and the remaining approximately 30 percent be sent to the public security tribunal as serious *liumang*. Another police officer estimated that the Taipei review committee accepted their recommendations in approximately 90 percent of cases, which he also attributed to the stringent examination by the police. According to this officer, 250 cases were sent to the Taipei review committee in 2005, of which the committee determined 129 to be serious *liumang*, determined 122 to be warned *liumang*, and sent five back for more evidence. (The numbers add up to slightly more than 250 people because of some spillover from 2004.) The officer emphasized that these statistics did not reflect the number of cases that the police department sent back to the local police for more evidence prior to sending the cases to the review committee. According to statistics from the NPA's Criminal Investigation Bureau, in 2004, a total of 1,721 people were reported as *liumang* to the three review committees. Of these, the review committees decided that 728 were serious *liumang*, 727 were warned *liumang*, and the remaining 219 were sent back for additional evidence, for a *liumang* determination rate of 86.9 percent.

Even if the review committee agreed that the person was a *liumang*, it could disagree with the examination group's recommendation as to which type. The NPA's statistics do not show the percentage of cases for which the review committee agreed with the examination group's specific recommmendation that a person be treated as a serious or warned *liumang*. When asked whether the local police ever refused to accept the review committee's decision that a person be treated as a warned *liumang* instead of a serious *liumang*, a former committee member confirmed that this had happened and, in such cases, the police generally continued their investigation. The police could report cases a second time, but there was no guarantee that they would fare better the next time around. The review committee could once again decide that the suspect should be treated as a warned *liumang*. There was no formal limit on how many times a case could bounce between the police and the review committee, but the same former member said that at some point the review committee would cease to listen. The three-year time limit on punishing *liumang* behavior also came into play as the process stretched on. It was also possible that the examination group only recommended guidance but the review committee decided instead to treat the person as a serious *liumang*, though the general sentiment of those interviewed was that the more common scenario was the opposite.

In Chen's case, the committee members readily agreed that Chen was over eighteen, the evidence in the file was properly documented, and the behavior in question occurred within the past three years.[23] They also agreed that Chen had been eating and drinking without paying. The thornier issue was whether Chen's behavior rose to the level of being "sufficient to have undermined social order" (IR Art. 4; PP Art. 18(5)). As mentioned in the previous chapter, "eating and drinking without paying" required more than a simple refusal to pay a bill. The Police Provisions emphasized that, to rise to the level of *liumang* behavior, there must have

---

[23] The three-year period was calculated from the time the behavior was established 成立. If the behavior was continuous or ongoing, then the period was calculated from the time the behavior ended (LMA Art. 3).

been some sort of coercion 脅迫, intimidation 恐嚇, or violent behavior 暴力行為 that prompted the victim to refrain from demanding payment (PP Art. 18(8)). When deciding whether Chen's behavior met the legal definition of "undermining social order," the review committee took into consideration the three fundamental characteristics required by law: "unspecific" 不特定性, "offensive violation" 積極侵害性, and "habitual" 慣常性. The committee members were thus thrust into a position of interpreting the law, and their interpretation, made without the benefit of hearing from any defense lawyer, would not be reviewed independently by either a prosecutor or judge before Chen was officially declared a *liumang.*

A prosecutor who spent two years on the NPA review committee told us that the prosecutor played the biggest role on the committee and the police greatly respected the prosecutor's opinion, especially with regard to whether the public security tribunal would view the evidence as sufficient. Given the closed nature of the committee, it is impossible to confirm whether his view of the prosecutor's role was an accurate reflection of intra-committee dynamics. Moreover, he may have been an unusually active prosecutor representative on the committee: quite possible, given his unique background of having also worked as a lawyer and a public security tribunal judge prior to joining the prosecutors' office. While it is therefore possible that an active prosecutor within the committee could have served a function similar to having *liumang* cases proceed through the prosecutors' office, this was highly dependent on the individual composition of the committee.

If the committee members failed to reach a consensus through discussion, the matter would be brought to a vote, though a former NPA review committee member said that this rarely occurred. When a vote was necessary, it was based on majority rule. No vote was required in Chen's case: the review committee members agreed that Chen qualified as a *liumang* who should receive a warning and guidance because there was substantial evidence that he made repeated threats toward several different bar owners after being approached for payment. They sent a written determination 認定書 explaining the facts and reasoning to the Tainan police, with a copy to the NPA (PP Art. 19; IR Art. 25). The determination included Chen's identifying information (name, sex, birth date, occupation, identification card number[24]), a description of the *liumang* behavior, reference to the specific provisions of the *Liumang* Act on which the determination was based, and other relevant information (PP Art. 19). Within ten days of receiving the determination (PP Art. 22(4)), the police delivered a written warning 告誡書 to Chen (IR Art. 8; PP Art. 21).[25] As with the determination, the warning included personal information on Chen (name, sex, birth date, occupation, etc.), the facts and reasons for the determination, the determining agency (i.e., the review committee), and the written determination's document number (IR Art. 8; PP Art. 22).

The first time that Chen had any idea that he had even been under suspicion was when he received this warning. Keeping Chen in the dark obviously helped the police, because he did not know that witnesses had been giving statements against him and, thus, did not threaten the witnesses or pay them to stop talking. It also cut down on flight risk when the target was clueless. Of course, this procedure also foreclosed the possibility that Chen might have stopped his illegal behavior early in the process had he been given some informal warning by the police. It also

---

[24] This identification card number is included on national identification cards along with the holder's photo and other identifying information.

[25] The Implementing Rules provided several methods for serving the warning; the first option being personal service by the police (IR Art. 15; PP Art. 23). A second option was for the police to leave the warning with a parent, spouse, or adult sibling or child who lived with the warned *liumang*. And, if the person's address was unclear, the police could serve the warning by public announcement 公示送達 (IR Art. 17; PP Art. 23(3)). When service by public announcement was necessary because a *liumang* could not be located, then relevant provisions in the Civil Procedure Code 民事訴訟法 were to be used (IR Art. 17). Special methods applied to active military personnel and people in jail or who were otherwise in custody (IR Art. 16; PP Art. 23(2)). Upon delivery, the recipient was supposed to sign the certificate of service (PP Art. 23(4), Appdx. 8). The Criminal Procedure Code contains provisions on serving notices in criminal cases (CPC Arts. 55-62).

meant that Chen did not have a voice in the proceedings. That being said, the Constitutional Court held in 2008 that, in accordance with due process of law, the reported person shall have the right to appear and be heard during the examination procedure. As with other changes called for by the 2008 interpretation, the subsequent repeal of the *Liumang* Act silenced debate over how to revise concrete provisions in the Act.

Chen's case had filtered through several screens since bar owner Li first complained to the police. Any one of these could have stopped the case. The local police might have decided that Li's allegations were un-founded, or that Li was targeting Chen due to an unrelated grudge. The examination group might have tossed aside the case because the local police failed to gather sufficient evidence. Or the review committee might have decided that Chen failed to pay his bills, but this failure was not sufficient to have undermined social order. In rare instances, the review committee might have found the evidence insufficient because of police corruption. A former member of the NPA review committee commented that his committee had come across the problem where, because of the improper relationship between the police and certain local residents, the police would help find people to act as secret witnesses in hopes of getting rid of someone.

Yet repeated review does not necessarily translate into more thorough review. The ability of this multi-tiered system to effectively weed out un-substantiated cases was hindered by the lack of full information. The witnesses were only "heard" through their written statements, and the identities of secret witnesses were known only to the interviewing police officers. Moreover, the accused *liumang* had little or no opportunity to voice his opinion.

B. Wang: Taipei Review Committee's Determination and Court Proceedings

As with Chen's case, Wang's case was sent up to a review committee, but for Wang the proper body was the Taipei review committee. The

NPA would only have a direct role in Wang's case if the Criminal Investigation Bureau or other NPA unit had been involved in the investigation. Otherwise, the entire process was in the hands of the Taipei government authorities.

The Taipei review committee, like the NPA review committee, generally met on a monthly basis[26] and usually consisted of seven members: a prosecutor, two professors, and four members from the police. The committee received the precinct's investigation materials form, the examination group's recommendation, and sometimes supplemental materials from the local police handling the case. Representatives of the local police also were available to field questions as needed. Members did not receive copies of the witnesses' statements in advance of the meeting, but the police would often bring the entire file to the meeting to consult in case there were questions. As with Chen's case, the identities of the secret witnesses were not revealed to the members of the review committee.

The committee members agreed that Wang should be treated as a serious *liumang* because he illegally possessed three guns.[27] There was also evidence that he acted as an intermediary for their sale, but some members questioned whether this evidence would hold up in the public security tribunal because the prosecutor in the criminal case, after viewing the same evidence, indicted only on the possession charges. Despite repeated references in the written rules and our interviewees' statements that a key quality of *liumang* behavior was that it be habitual in nature 慣常性, the officers we interviewed did not use this terminology with respect to cases

---

[26] A Taipei police officer told us in 2006 that the review committee had met about fourteen times in the past year and had heard over 300 cases, or approximately twenty cases per meeting. Each meeting lasted about three hours, with the time spent on each case varying based on its complexity.

[27] Chen's behavior fell within one of the four scenarios in which the circumstances were "certainly" serious according to the Implementing Rules (i.e., a person who illegally possesses firearms), provided that the behavior was sufficient to have undermined social order or to have endangered the life, body, freedom, or property of others (IR Art. 5). The Taipei police with whom we spoke, however, did not refer to this provision of the Implementing Rules directly when discussing the criteria for a serious *liumang*.

of gun possession. The focus instead was on the number of guns. A Taipei police officer said that their standard was to treat a person as a serious *liumang* if he carried two or more working guns, whereas one gun would only result in a warning and guidance. According to this same officer, the NPA review committee required three or more guns for a person to qualify as a serious *liumang*, as did the Kaohsiung review committee.

None of the written rules for the review committees that we saw contained this criterion. And it is unclear whether this criterion was uniformly applied. When a Taipei police official was asked whether the Taipei review committee applied different standards to cases from high or low crime areas, he firmly replied that the standards were uniform. And a police officer who handled *liumang* work in a Taipei precinct gave us a copy of internal police standards that he said were issued by the NPA. The standards provided that a person must possess two or more guns to be a serious *liumang*. On the other hand, a former member of the NPA review committee commented that, in his experience, the NPA review committee considered where the behavior took place, and he agreed that standards were based on society's needs, which varied across Taiwan. The same former NPA review committee member noted that the committee used internal police standards as to how many guns a person need possess before the review committee would send him to the public security tribunal. He recalled that two regular handguns or three refurbished handguns were enough for the committee to treat the accused as a serious *liumang*, a threshold that agreed with the internal standards that we were given by the Taipei police. The former NPA review committee member further noted that, although police policies were not part of the committee's formal rules, the committee members' basic position was to respect these policies. Nonetheless, it is another matter whether the courts agreed or not.

The internal standards used by the police appeared to have little, if any, sway beyond the review committee's door. When we asked a public security tribunal judge whether the courts had standards regarding the number of guns that a person must possess to be deemed a serious *liumang*, he said that their court did not have such standards because it was too crude to simply say that a person was a *liumang* because he had one, or two, or three guns. According to the judge, the public security tribunal should consider the three general criteria to determine whether the behavior was sufficient to have undermined social order.

After the review committee agreed to transfer Wang's case to the public security tribunal, the police prepared a transfer document[28] 移送書 and sent it to the Taipei District Court along with the evidence and other materials in the dossier.[29] The materials were sealed in an envelope marked "To be received personally by the public security tribunal judge" and "Not to be opened or read other than by the public security tribunal judge" (PP Art. 31(1)). The police were also responsible for notifying the accused and his designated relatives and friends, if any, of the transfer (LMA Art. 9; PP Art. 31(4)). Even if the police could not locate the accused or he was already being detained on criminal charges, as in Wang's case, this did not stop the public security tribunal from handling the case. One judge singled out gun and organized crime cases as two instances for which an accused *liumang* was likely to already be detained. Just because the accused was in custody did not necessarily mean that he was aware of the brewing *liumang* charges. At the time of Wang's case, the 2008 interpretation granting a right to be heard during the examination stage had been issued but not implemented.

---

[28] According to the Implementing Rules and Police Provisions, the transfer document should have included details on the accused (name, sex, birth date, occupation, identification card number, registered address, and other differentiating characteristics); concrete facts and evidence; all implicated legal provisions and the reasons for the transfer; the signature and seal of the responsible commanding officer; and the date (IR Art. 25; PP Art. 30, Appdx. 13).

[29] The Implementing Rules provided that the police should send the following to the public security tribunal: the written warning, written decision, written determination, full-body frontal color photograph, and other materials with referential value (IR Art. 25). A public security tribunal judge told us that other documents which may have accompanied the transfer document included witnesses' statements (both secret and not-secret) and injury examination reports.

Consequently, Wang knew of the criminal charges because the prosecutors' office issued an indictment and he was locked up pending trial but, up until this point, no one had ever told him that he was also under suspicion as a *liumang*.

Wang now had a choice to make regarding representation. He could have hired a single lawyer to represent him in both his *liumang* case and his criminal case, hired two different lawyers, or simply gone it alone in one or both cases. Unlike the Criminal Procedure Code, the *Liumang* Act did not provide indigent suspects with publicly funded lawyers in any *liumang* cases.[30] Wang also had the option to hire several lawyers for each case, though the Implementing Rules provided that the accused was allowed no more than three lawyers, which is consistent with the Criminal Procedure Code (IR Art. 38). The problem for Wang was that finding even one knowledgeable lawyer in the field of *liumang* law was a serious challenge. The *Liumang* Act was not part of the standard law school curriculum, and it was not on the bar exam. The *Liumang* Act was only covered on tests to serve as a police officer, with exams asking questions like "According to the rules, what is the time limit to transfer a *liumang* from the police station?"[31]

Few lawyers had experience with *liumang* cases and finding one could take on the air of a snark hunt. Still, there were lawyers who took these cases. When we asked one such lawyer how accused *liumang* located him, he noted that there were basically no lawyers in Taiwan who specialized in *liumang* cases, so usually accused *liumang* sought out criminal lawyers,

---

[30] It is possible that an accused *liumang* could have received pro bono legal services through one of the branches of the Legal Aid Foundation 法律扶助基金會, but we did not hear of any cases where this happened or where a lawyer was provided with other public funds. The Legal Aid Foundation began operations on 1 July 2004, following promulgation of the Legal Aid Law 法律扶助法. The law was enacted to provide legal aid to people who are indigent or otherwise unable to receive proper legal protection, such as the mentally impaired (Legal Aid Law Arts. 1, 14). The Foundation, which is funded by the Judicial Yuan, other governmental entities, and community groups, as of this writing has twenty-one branch offices throughout Taiwan that provide legal aid services (http://www.laf.org.tw).

[31] The answer is twenty-four hours.

often finding them through introductions from other people. Another lawyer concurred that his clients mainly found him through word of mouth.

A public security tribunal judge from Tainan who stopped hearing *liumang* cases in 2005 estimated that only about a third of the accused *liumang* who appeared before him had lawyers. Another judge in Tainan had seen only one case out of ten in which the accused *liumang* had a lawyer. And yet another Tainan judge who served as a public security tribunal judge from the mid to late 1990s estimated that half of the accused *liumang* that came before him had lawyers. He attributed this low number to restrictions on lawyers' access to case files, and thus their lack of ability to counter the government's case, but noted that access had improved. Nonetheless, based on our conversations with lawyers and other judges, it did not appear that the number of accused *liumang* with representation had increased in the final years of the *Liumang* Act. We did not conduct a widespread survey that would illuminate whether the rates differed significantly in urban and rural areas, or whether rates varied based on other geographic or demographic factors.

Criminal and *liumang* cases further differed in that there was no plea bargaining in *liumang* cases. Beginning in 2004, a form of plea bargaining became available to defendants who committed crimes other than those punishable by death, life imprisonment, or imprisonment of at least three years (CPC Art. 455-2). No corresponding provision was added to the *Liumang* Act and we heard of no examples where plea bargaining was extended to *liumang* cases. In view of the fact that the Criminal Procedure Code provides for plea bargaining only for certain crimes, and *liumang* behavior is technically not a crime and subject to criminal sanctions, there was no apparent legal basis on which to extend plea bargaining to *liumang* cases. In addition, because there was no prosecutor in a *liumang* case, it is unclear with whom the *liumang* and his lawyer, if any, would have bargained.

Beyond plea bargaining, another tool that is available to prosecutors in criminal cases but was lacking in *liumang* cases is deferred prosecution

緩起訴 (CPC Art. 253-1, -2). Similar to plea bargaining, prosecutors may opt to use deferred prosecution for crimes other than those punishable by death, life imprisonment, or imprisonment of at least three years (CPC Art. 253-1). The deferred prosecution period lasts from one to three years, during which time the prosecutor can require the defendant to apologize to the victim, provide compensation to the victim, or accept psychological guidance, among other measures (CPC Art. 253-1, -2). The prosecutor will continue with the investigation or indictment if the defendant commits a crime or any other listed transgression during the deferred prosecution period (CPC Art. 253-3). No equivalent to deferred prosecution was available to people accused of being serious *liumang*. For ordinary *liumang*, the warning and guidance imposed on them was similar in spirit. The warned *liumang* had one year of monitoring by the police and, if he was a law-abiding citizen during this time, then he was wiped clean from the *liumang* register. As in a deferred prosecution, however, a return to *liumang* ways would likely land the person in court. Once again, a key difference between the treatment of a *liumang* and a criminal defendant was that the police were making the calls in the former case while the prosecutors' office was in control in the latter.

Wang, who had retained a lawyer for his criminal case, decided to expand his criminal lawyer's representation to encompass the *liumang* charges.[32] The lawyer began by checking the court computer to confirm that Wang's case was pending. Unlike during the martial law period, Wang's lawyer was allowed to read the *liumang* case file, albeit the file was

---

[32] The accused or his legal agent, spouse, lineal blood relative or collateral blood relative within three degrees of relationship, head of household, or family members could select a lawyer to appear in court (LMA Art. 9). A lawyer hired to represent a *liumang* was technically not a "legally appointed" 法定 agent. "Legally appointed" agent indicates that the relationship is created by a legal provision, not the represented person's choice. In a case where the accused was summoned or detained by the police in accordance with Articles 6-7 and then was sent to the court *within twenty-four hours*, a judge at the Taipei District Court told us that the accused was given a "reasonable period of time," which he described as a few hours, to find a lawyer before the hearing. Another judge said that judges usually let the accused call lawyers or relatives who could help him find a lawyer. If the accused was already being held in a detention center because of a pending criminal case, the time limit to retain a lawyer would not be so tight.

of limited use given the redacted names and other secret information. For example, the lawyer was allowed to read the transfer document but the decision whether to let the lawyer read the witnesses' statements rested with the judge. Notably, on the whole, the right to look at the file could only be exercised by a lawyer, not by the accused *liumang* directly. The transfer document itself was often riddled with blanks (or, more specifically, circles) in place of names, dates, and locations that might compromise the witnesses' identities. Still, it was better than nothing. As one lawyer remarked about the changes brought by this reform, "Without [the transfer document] we could only guess wildly, but now at least it is easier to guess." The judge was responsible for maintaining the strict secrecy of the comparative table of code names and real names, ensuring that these were not given to Wang's lawyer when he applied to review the case file (Matters that Courts Should Pay Attention to in Handling Cases under the Act for Eliminating *Liumang* 法院辦理檢肅流氓條例案件應行注意事項 ("Court Matters" or CM) Arts. 20, 21). In comparison, under the Criminal Procedure Code, the defense may examine the file and exhibits and make copies or photographs thereof (CPC Art. 33). The *Liumang* Act did not specify how long or how often a lawyer was allowed to meet with a detained client, though police monitoring of their conversation was permitted in limited circumstances with court approval.[33]

While Wang's lawyer started his work, the case began to make its way through the public security tribunal system. In 2007, district courts closed a total of 2,312 *liumang* cases, with Kaohsiung (333 cases), Taichung (299 cases), Taipei (255 cases), and Banqiao (203 cases) closing the bulk of cases. In contrast, Penghu District Court closed only 5 *liumang* cases in 2007. In 1998, district courts closed a total of 2,971 *liumang* cases, with the number reaching a ten-year low of 1,675 in 2002.

---

[33] Judges could notify officials at the detention house that lawyer-client communication was to be monitored if the judge believed that the lawyer would destroy evidence or collude with his client (CM Art. 19).

Once Wang's case arrived at the district court, the first step was to distribute it to a public security tribunal judge (CM Art. 9).[34] Taipei District Court randomly distributed *liumang* cases among the public security tribunal judges. In Tainan, the chief judge 庭長 of the district court public security tribunal explained that they looked at seniority and who volunteered to hear the cases. A Tainan public security tribunal judge reiterated that his court first called for volunteers to hear *liumang* cases; if too many judges volunteered, then priority went to senior judges. Likewise, if too few judges volunteered to hear *liumang* cases, then the senior judges had an obligation to take the cases.

Once assigned, the judge would begin by checking whether there were any procedural errors. If there were problems, the judge could either return the case to the police for them to supplement and correct the file within a judge-determined period of time or reject the case outright if the errors could not be remedied (LMA Art. 13; CM Art. 14). For example, it would have been an uncorrectable error if more than three years had elapsed between the time of the behavior and the time that the case was transferred to the court (LMA Art. 13).

The judge also checked whether the court had jurisdiction over the case.[35] This could be tricky. Take the example of Datong District and Zhongshan District, two districts in Taipei that are separated by railway tracks. Datong is within the jurisdiction of Shilin District Court, whereas Zhongshan is within that of Taipei District Court. As a result, if a person

---

[34] The Court Matters specified that cases received in the morning were to be distributed that afternoon, whereas cases received in the afternoon were to be distributed on the morning of the following working day (Art. 9).

[35] The Implementing Rules provided that territorial jurisdiction of the public security tribunals was based on the location of the behavior, the accused *liumang*'s registered address, his domicile/residence, or where he was located (IR Art. 21). This provision tracked closely the language on jurisdiction in the Criminal Procedure Code (CPC Art. 5). The Implementing Rules further provided that in the case of concurrent jurisdiction over a *liumang* case, the court that accepted the case first should hear it, except if agreed by the courts that a later accepting court should take the case (IR Art. 24). Public security tribunals looked to the Criminal Procedure Code to settle other questions regarding jurisdiction, such as what to do if several courts disputed jurisdiction.

was picked up in Zhongshan but lived in and engaged in the alleged *liumang* behavior in Datong, then the case should have been transferred to Shilin District Court.[36] In theory, the judge was further responsible for contacting the chief judge of the district court to arrange for a panel hearing if the case was complicated or involved the public interest (CM Art. 10). The usual practice, however, was for a single judge to hear a *liumang* case. Two judges, each with years of experience hearing *liumang* cases, could not recall a single instance where a panel heard a *liumang* case on the district court level, and they were surprised to see this provision lurking in the Court Matters. By way of comparison, in criminal cases, trials are conducted by three-judge panels unless simplified trial procedures are used (CPC Art. 284-1).

The police continued to participate in Wang's case as the tribunal prepared to address the merits. In a criminal case, the police would be out of the immediate loop once the case reached the judge's hands because the prosecutors' office would take the lead. In the *liumang* context, there was no trial prosecutor; instead, the police coordinated logistics with the public security tribunal, such as by providing materials requested by the tribunal and arranging for witnesses to appear. A former public security tribunal judge explained that, if a judge found a procedural error, he should have sent the police a written notice that explained the materials that required corrections. The court could proceed to the substance of the case only after the procedural errors were remedied. The police could also decide to withdraw the case prior to the tribunal issuing a ruling (CM Art. 14; IR Art. 40). After withdrawing the case, the police could try to supplement and correct the problem and then transfer the case back to the court. If the problem could not be remedied, then the police were required to cancel the determination that the person was a serious *liumang*, but the person could still be subjected to guidance as a

---

[36] The Taipei District Court's jurisdiction, which prior to 2010 encompassed parts of both Taipei County and City, is not coextensive with the area under the responsibility of the Taipei Municipal Police Department.

warned *liumang* (PP Arts. 32(4), 33(1)). Moreover, the Police Provisions provided that, if the tribunal failed to issue a ruling within six months, the police should follow up by reminding the tribunal on a semi-annual basis (PP Art. 32(5)), a practice that was confirmed by police with whom we spoke.

In addition to determining that there were no procedural errors, if the accused was not already in criminal detention, the public security tribunal had to decide whether to confine him pending completion of the *liumang* proceedings. This was a non-issue in Wang's case because he was already in the detention house. The power to confine an accused *liumang* while the case was pending rested with the tribunal (CM Art. 5), but the police could recommend that the person be confined because facts indicated that he would flee, tamper with or destroy evidence, or threaten witnesses, among other enumerated reasons (LMA Art. 11; PP Art. 31(5); CM Art. 7).

The usefulness of this temporary confinement was tempered by time limits imposed by the *Liumang* Act. Confinement was limited to one month, with a permissible one-month extension (LMA Art. 11; CM Arts. 12, 24).[37] There were two slight wrinkles in this two-month limit. First, in addition to the initial confinement, the police could later request the tribunal to impose repeat confinement 再予留置 if the accused did not appear when legally summoned and had no valid excuse, violated the terms of his release, or repeatedly engaged in any of the behavior that justified temporary confinement in the first place (LMA Art. 11-2; PP Art. 31(6)). Second, the confinement period was calculated separately for each level of court and thus the public security tribunal in the high court could impose an additional two months if a case reached it on appeal (LMA Art. 11). Because reformatory training generally was not suspended when a *liumang* appealed a ruling, additional confinement by

---

[37] The one-month confinement period was calculated from the date that the confinement warrant was issued (CM Art. 5).

the high court would most likely have arisen only when the police appealed a ruling not to impose reformatory training. A judge with experience on a public security tribunal commented that he had never known an accused *liumang* to be confined for four months pending completion of proceedings.

The decision whether to confine the accused was made at a hearing, which was the first time that the judge met the accused *liumang* and his lawyer, if he had one. If the judge decided that confinement was necessary, then the public security tribunal would issue a confinement warrant 留置票. The Implementing Rules provided that confinement should take place in "confinement houses" 留置所 set up by the Ministry of Justice and, if not established, then people should be held in "detention houses" 看守所 (IR Art. 30). As previously noted, lawyers were allowed to visit their clients while in confinement, but police were allowed to monitor their communications if they had court approval.[38] If the judge subsequently rejected the case because of procedural problems, then the judge was to promptly release the accused (CM Art. 8). If, on the other hand, the case was heard on the merits of the police work that had been done, and the accused was sentenced to reformatory training, then the time spent in confinement would be deducted from the maximum three-year period (LMA Art. 5). This provision did not mean much in practice. Because most serious *liumang* did not serve their full three-year sentences anyway, deducting one or two months would seldom translate into less time at the training institute.

The judges with whom we spoke questioned the usefulness of a two-month confinement period in proceedings that often stretched much longer, a sentiment that was seconded by an employee at one of the training institutes. That the most serious accused *liumang* were often already detained on criminal charges also lessened the need to order

---

[38] See above note 33.

confinement.[39] The aversion to ordering confinement was further attributed to the Taiwan judiciary's tendency to be more reluctant to constrain people's freedom than the police. In this vein, a Taipei police official opined that Taipei judges imposed reformatory training at a lower rate than judges in other parts of Taiwan because they put more emphasis on human rights.

Even if the accused satisfied one of the listed grounds for confinement, judges were to refrain from confining the accused when unnecessary (LMA Art. 11-1). Public security judges most often imposed bail 具保 instead of confining the accused. Judges could also order custodial release 責付 or restricted residence 限制住居, or some combination of these and bail (IR Art. 34). Even if the tribunal initially ordered confinement, the accused *liumang* could request that the tribunal stop confinement and instead impose bail (LMA Art. 11-1). There were no rules specifying bail amounts for *liumang* cases, or criminal cases for that matter. The judge independently decided the amount of bail based on the circumstances of the case, economic means, flight risk, and other factors.

As still used in criminal cases today and previously also in *liumang* cases, custodial release entails turning over the accused to the custody of another person who becomes answerable for the behavior of the accused. The person assuming this responsibility must give a written assurance obligating him to secure the appearance of the accused (CPC Art. 115). This person may be a relative or even the police, and police told us that they were not in a position to refuse a judge's order that they assume this responsibility. Considering that no money was at stake and the person charged with watching the accused *liumang* suffered no repercussions

---

[39] The Criminal Procedure Code states that initial detention of a defendant may not exceed two months during the investigation stage and three months during the trial stage. A single two-month extension is permissible at the investigation stage. At the trial stage, each extension may not exceed two months and, if the maximum punishment is imprisonment of ten or fewer years, then only three extensions are allowed for each of the trial and first appeal and one extension if there is a second appeal to the court at the next level (CPC Art. 108).

if the accused failed to appear (other than perhaps the judge scolding the police for failing to keep an eye on their charge), it is hardly surprising that one judge with whom we spoke described custodial release as less effective than bail in ensuring that an accused *liumang* appeared. Nonetheless, custodial release was useful in situations where the person did not have money for bail—such as in the case of foreign workers with little access to cash—in which case it ensured that there was at least one more person concerned about the accused.

Restricted residence, another alternative to confinement, has two meanings. First, the judge could restrict the accused *liumang* to a certain city or other area and require that he report to the tribunal if he wanted to leave. Second, and more commonly used, the tribunal could restrict the person from leaving Taiwan. At the confinement hearing, the judge could even decide that there was no basis on which to hold the accused and thus release him without any restrictions.

With no need to decide whether to confine Wang, and having determined that there were no procedural errors, the judge then turned to the merits of Wang's case. Wang was well aware that he had done some bad things, yet, at least prior to the trial hearing (there was no temporary confinement hearing), he remained ignorant as to the specific charges. The Court Matters recognized this information vacuum by providing that, at the trial hearing, the judge shall point out necessary evidence to Wang, or at least tell the essential points of the case, in order that he be given an opportunity to defend himself (CM Art. 16). If the accused had already confessed, the judge should have investigated whether the confession was consistent with the facts (CM Art. 16). The Court Matters did not elaborate on what "consistent with the facts" meant, and the judge therefore had to turn to the Criminal Procedure Code for guidance (CPC Art. 156).

When Wang and his lawyer appeared before the public security tribunal for the hearing, they and the judge would likely be the only three people in the courtroom. Usually none of the police witnesses were present in *liumang* cases. Until the Constitutional Court's 2008 interpretation, secrecy was the rule, not the exception, despite the constant refrain that witness identities be kept secret only "if necessary" (LMA Art. 12). For instance, describing the ability to question witnesses in court as a lawyer's "greatest weapon," a lawyer who represented accused *liumang* said he had been hopeful back in the mid-1990s that revisions to the *Liumang* Act following Interpretation No. 384 would give lawyers this weapon but, in reality, there was no change. He added that, when viewed against Taiwan's major criminal procedure reforms, the *Liumang* Act was a "freak." Another lawyer who had handled *liumang* cases said that sometimes witnesses appeared in front of the accused and his lawyer, but not often. Of those who did appear, some were not seen by the defense and may have had their voices altered for protection.

It was only in 2008 that the Constitutional Court held that the secret witness system as then structured was unconstitutional. Yet the Court recognized a need for secrecy in limited situations. The Court explained that the right to confront and examine witnesses may be restricted by concrete and clear statutory provisions when necessary to protect the witness's life, body, freedom, or property.

Returning to Wang's case, when the secret witness system was still in use, the decision whether to refuse Wang's requests to confront 對質 and question 詰問 a witness rested with the judge and was based on a determination whether the witness was at risk of retaliatory acts (LMA Art 12). In order to protect witnesses, the judge was allowed to question them individually in private or use other protective measures, such as voice alteration (CM Art. 18; LMA Art. 12). One technique that a lawyer cited as used by more accommodating judges was to allow the lawyer to question the witness while the witness was out of sight in another room—though this technique still allowed lawyers and their clients to hear the witness's voice, thus leaving open the possibility that they could identify the witness based on voice alone unless the voice was altered. Other judges asked lawyers to give them lists of questions so that the judge could question witnesses on behalf of the lawyers.

Although it was an infrequent occurrence, one judge explained that sometimes a witness's identity was very clear, thus making it unnecessary to maintain secrecy. For example, a witness might have given similar testimony in Wang's concurrent criminal case, in which case it would have been pointless to conceal the witness' identity in the *liumang* case. Even if the witness did not appear in the criminal case, the accused would often be able to guess the witness's identity based on the charges and sometimes, after the fact, by the phrasing used by the judge in his written determination, e.g., "the victim," or "a person present at the scene." The accused was allowed to introduce his own witnesses, in which case their identities were obviously known to him.

The consensus among people we asked was that accused *liumang* generally did not have a hard time figuring out who the witnesses against them were. In a case where a suspect was accused of taking protection fees from hundreds of sellers in a market, it was harder to guess which handful of sellers came forward. On the other hand, the process of elimination worked well in a case where a person was accused of kidnapping pigeons from only three people. Even if the secret witness system did not, in reality, shield many witnesses from being identified, it may at least have given them a false sense of security that made them more willing to cooperate with the police.

Liumang hearings were unusually intimate because there were no prosecutors involved and police appeared only occasionally. Although the judge could call police as witnesses, and the police could request to appear[40] (CM Art. 23), one lawyer with whom we spoke said he had never seen police in the public security tribunal. This observation was seconded by a court clerk who spent four years working for a public security tribunal judge. And the judges with whom we spoke emphasized the police's role as one of bringing witnesses to court, not serving

---

[40] If the judge decided that it was unnecessary for the police to appear and thus rejected the request, the judge was required to provide his reasons for doing so (CM Art. 23).

as witnesses themselves. The police with whom we spoke also agreed with this description. We did find a police officer who said that he had served as a witness in a *liumang* case. He went on to explain that the accused *liumang* usually did not know that police were serving as witnesses because the judge asked them questions one-on-one. Yet he did not agree that it was proper to categorize the police as "secret witnesses." Nor would there be an audience when the judge questioned the accused. *Liumang* cases were closed to the public; our requests for special permission to attend were denied, with one exception. The people that were left at the hearing, then, were Wang, his lawyer, and the judge. The public security tribunals held firm to Taiwan's "inquisitorial" tradition even as Taiwan's criminal courts have adopted adversarial-leaning reforms in recent years.[41] The old system was "inquisitorial" in the sense that it followed the practice common to classical Continental European traditions in which activist judges dominated the trial proceedings, with little participation from either the prosecution or defense. In contrast, the new system, like many of the contemporary Continental systems, is more "adversarial" in that the criminal adjudication process is structured as a supposedly equal contest between activist lawyers who present the competing views of the defense and the prosecution for resolution by neutral, largely passive decision-makers.

Again, the inquisitorial bent was not surprising when there was no prosecutor present to serve as an adversary to the accused's lawyer. The judge questioned Wang directly, though his lawyer was also allowed to question Wang as well as make a statement (IR Art. 38; CM Art. 17). The result was a strange hybrid hearing rather than a classic inquisitorial trial: the accused had a lawyer to help him to a limited extent, but the proceedings were far from adversarial. Because there was no prosecutor, as described by one judge, the triangular relationship among the

---

[41] A modified adversarial system was formally introduced in 2002 through revisions to the Criminal Procedure Code (CPC Arts. 161, 163).

prosecution, defense, and judge that now exists in Taiwan's criminal cases was missing a corner in *liumang* cases. As a result, the judge was concurrently in charge of the judicial and prosecutorial roles.

One should not assume that all judges welcomed the arrival of the adversarial system in criminal trials. The inquisitorial system still has its supporters. A public security tribunal judge described adversarial hearings as tiresome and too long. He preferred serving as a public security tribunal judge because he did not need to sit in court for such a long period of time. Some Taiwan judges have found the new role imposed on them by adversarial proceedings to be difficult, burdensome, and irritating.

Wang's criminal gun-possession case that was proceeding simultaneously was formally independent from the *liumang* case, but there was a certain amount of information sharing that occurred. The public security tribunal judge was allowed to view the case file in a companion criminal case by asking the responsible criminal court judge to transfer the file, the existence of which was readily apparent from the records in the *liumang* file. As a general rule, the criminal file tended to contain a greater variety of evidence than the file for the companion *liumang* case, in part because the investigating prosecutors in criminal cases were in charge of obtaining search warrants. In *liumang* cases, there were no prosecutors to get these warrants, and the police instead tended to rely on the testimony of victims and other witnesses. Indeed, there were no procedures whatsoever for obtaining warrants in *liumang* cases. This is not surprising: why go through the hassle of obtaining a search warrant when little more was needed than testimonial evidence?[42] Furthermore, given the substantial overlap between criminal and *liumang* cases, the evidence for the *liumang* case would likely have been collected under a warrant issued for the companion criminal case.

---

[42] The *Liumang* Act required that the testimony of a secret witness could not be the only basis for the decision to impose reformatory training and police should "investigate other necessary evidence" (LMA Art. 12). This other evidence included, for example, testimonial evidence from non-secret witnesses or physical evidence.

A request by a criminal judge for a *liumang* case file was more complicated because of the confidentiality demanded by the secret witness system.[43] The special envelope containing the secret witnesses' identities was of little use if their names were blurted out in the court down the hall. It is also theoretically possible that the same judge would hear both the *liumang* and criminal cases, though this was especially unlikely in large courts like Taipei where dozens of judges handle criminal cases. It apparently did not occur to either the legislature or the legal officials that it might be improper for a criminal court to consider evidence obtained from a *liumang* tribunal.

For the *liumang* tribunal, the critical issue was whether the judge should decide to impose reformatory training. The Court Matters provided that, when making this decision, in addition to concluding that all procedures from the examination to the transfer were conducted in accordance with legal procedures and that the person had engaged in one of the listed types of *liumang* behavior, the judge should "pay attention to whether the behavior was sufficient to have undermined social order" (CM Art. 25). The judge should not impose reformatory training if he believed that the *liumang* behavior was not "serious" or if it could not be proved that the accused had engaged in *liumang* behavior.[44] What "proved" meant with respect to these requirements is not entirely clear. In criminal cases, the prosecutor bears the burden of proof (CPC Art. 161); "burden" has been interpreted by the Supreme Court to mean meeting the standard of proof beyond a reasonable doubt (Supreme Court, 1987, Taishang No. 4986). There was no prosecutor to bear this

---

[43] The Court Matters specified procedures for when there was a concurrent criminal case, including the rule that the criminal court and prosecutor must maintain the secrecy of witnesses when borrowing the *liumang* case file (CM Arts. 15, 21).

[44] Other reasons for refusing to impose reformatory training included procedural errors (CM Art. 26); the accused was under eighteen or insane; the accused was dead; the three-year period in which *liumang* behavior may be considered had passed; or a public security tribunal had already issued a ruling regarding the same *liumang* behavior or the case had mistakenly been transferred to the courts twice (LMA Art. 13).

burden in *liumang* cases, leaving the judge to search out the truth. Nor was the standard of proof clear in *liumang* cases, though, when asked, a judge with extensive experience handling *liumang* cases showed us one of his rulings in which he incorporated the Supreme Court's "beyond a reasonable doubt" standard. If the judge decided to impose reformatory training, then the next step was to issue an enforcement document 執行書 (CM Art. 30).

In 2005, the Taipei District Court ordered reformatory training in 77 cases, or 57.46 percent of the *liumang* cases for which rulings were finalized.[45] Reformatory training was not imposed in 32.84 percent of the cases, leaving 9.70 percent to fall under "other," which a judge in the court described as cases where the police withdrew the case, the accused died, there were overlapping cases filed in different courts, and other miscellaneous reasons that stopped the case before the public security tribunal issued a ruling. Despite the fact that 57.46 percent in 2005 was that court's highest percentage of people sentenced to reformatory training in at least ten years,[46] the Taipei District Court's numbers were still lower than average for Taiwan generally. According to the Taipei District Court's statistics, for all of Taiwan, public security tribunals ordered reformatory training in 578 cases in 2005, or 64.58 percent cases for which rulings were finalized. Reformatory training was not imposed in 26.03 percent of those cases, leaving 9.39 percent under "other." These numbers had remained relatively stable over the preceding ten years, ranging from a high of 65.56 percent in 1997 to a low of 55.47 percent in 2004. It is curious that the 55.47 percent reformatory-training rate provided by the Taipei District Court for all of Taiwan for 2004 does not agree with the 2004

---

[45] In criminal cases, a case is finalized after the court issues a judgment that the person is guilty or not guilty. In *liumang* cases, the analogous decision was whether or not to submit the accused *liumang* to reformatory training.

[46] During the ten-year period from 1995 to 2005, the percentage of people sentenced to reformatory training by the Taipei District Court fluctuated from over half (55.12 percent in 1997, 55.42 percent in 2000, 57.46 percent in 2005) to a low of 21.43 percent in 1998.

statistics from the NPA. According to the NPA, public security tribunals in Taiwan committed 557 people to reformatory training in 2004 and declined to impose reformatory training in 268 cases, for a reformatory-training rate of 67.5 percent. Neither source provides explanatory notes that might help reconcile the difference. Yet, we can surely conclude that tribunals imposed reformatory training over half the time.

The judge in Wang's case issued a ruling stating his reasons for imposing reformatory training.[47] In a *liumang* case, the "holding" 主文 was a simple decision either to impose reformatory training or not to impose reformatory training, but where no reformatory training was imposed, the judge could recommend whether the review committee should subject the person to guidance or let him go scot-free. For example, in a case from Tainan District Court, the judge ruled that the accused was not a serious *liumang* because his behavior of possessing a gun did not satisfy the conditions for undermining social order. The judge added that the behavior of the accused was also not sufficient to establish him as a common *liumang*, i.e., one subject to a warning and guidance. There was really nothing that a judge could do to make a review committee follow a recommendation, however, and as one police officer said, the judge's decision to tell the review committee what to do was like "drawing feet on a snake." In other words, it exceeded what is necessary.

In contrast to their terse "holdings," judges would set forth the rationale for their decisions in detail in the reasoning portion of their rulings. Indeed, one lawyer commented that usually it was only when he saw the ruling in one of his cases that he finally got a complete understanding of the whole story.

If the judge imposed reformatory training, the Court Matters provided that the judge should send the enforcement document and ruling

---

[47] As previously mentioned, use of a ruling 裁定 rather than a judgment 判決 in *liumang* cases was consistent with the Criminal Procedure Code, which states that decisions 裁判 shall be in the form of a ruling unless a judgment is specified (CPC Art. 220).

to the "original transferring police agencies" (CM Art. 30). A Taipei police officer explained that if the public security tribunal did not impose reformatory training, it would send the ruling directly to the NPA, which then would transmit it to the lower police. If, however, the public security tribunal did impose reformatory training, then the police would coordinate with the tribunal to transfer the person to the appropriate training institute, as described further below. In either case, the court would also mail the ruling to the accused and his lawyer. Absent an appeal, the public security tribunal's role ended at this point.

The time from when a public security tribunal accepted the case to completion varied tremendously. One lawyer described a case that zipped through the district court tribunal, saying it took only five days for the tribunal to issue its decision not to impose reformatory training. The police appealed, and the case was sent back to the tribunal, which then took fewer than ten days to reverse its previous decision. This pace was extraordinary. In 2007, the *liumang* tribunals in district courts took an average of 404 days and nine hours from the date that the *liumang* case entered the court to the date the public security tribunal issued its ruling (not including appeals). By way of comparison, in 2007, district courts spent an average of 62 days and twenty-two hours to close a criminal case. The common practice of holding a *liumang* case pending resolution of the companion criminal case is cited as a major reason for the long processing time in *liumang* cases. If the proceedings seemed to be dragging on, the police could nudge the case along, or at least attempt to do so. As previously mentioned, the Police Provisions provided that, if the public security tribunal failed to issue a ruling within six months, the police should follow-up on a semi-annual basis (PP Art. 32(5)).[48]

---

[48] The police were not to use this process of so-called "coordinating through writing" 具函協調 in certain situations, such as if the case was suspended pending a decision in a companion criminal case (PP Art. 32(5)).

Wang would not necessarily have been free if the public security tribunal had either rejected the case (e.g., due to procedural reasons)[49] or decided not to impose reformatory training. The police had ten days to appeal the decision by filing an appeal with the higher public security tribunal, located within the local high court (LMA Art. 14; PP Art. 32(3), Appdx. 15).[50] According to police and judges with whom we spoke, it was standard operating procedure for police to appeal adverse rulings. One judge remarked that, over several years, he had never seen a case where the police failed to appeal a ruling not to impose reformatory training. And the police told us that not only did internal rules require them to appeal, but also that not appealing would be like contradicting themselves. The police had reported the person because they thought he was a *liumang*, so why change their minds now? Again, the threat of performance reviews was never far from their minds. As with many decisions, the police expressed concern that not appealing would have influenced their grade. They seemed to allow little room for a decision not to appeal on the basis that the reasoning of the judicial tribunal's decision was compelling.

Alternatively, if the tribunal issued an adverse ruling, the police might have decided to give up on the serious *liumang* charges and instead treat Wang as a warned *liumang*. The Police Provisions provided that if the public security tribunal had ruled that Wang was not a serious *liumang* but that he still engaged in *liumang* behavior, then the case would revert to the Taipei review committee, which could have decided to treat Wang

---

[49] As previously mentioned, if there were problems with the application or transfer procedures, the police should first have tried to correct the problem and return the case to the court. If this was not possible, the police were required to cancel the determination that the accused was a serious *liumang*, but the accused could still be subjected to guidance as a warned *liumang* (PP Art. 33(1)).

[50] The police who transferred the case were required to report to the municipal police or NPA, as appropriate, stating the public security tribunal's reasons for rejecting the case or denying reformatory training (PP Art. 33(3), Appdx. 16). Police were also required to report decisions not to appeal the ruling, though we heard of no case where the police failed to appeal (PP Art. 33(3)).

as a warned *liumang*, provided that the three-year period had not expired (PP Arts. 20(2), 33(2)). If, on the other hand, the tribunal determined that there was insufficient proof that Wang engaged in *liumang* behavior or otherwise did not fit the conditions for being a *liumang*, the review committee was required to cancel its determination that he was a serious *liumang* (PP Art. 33(2)). If the person was already a warned *liumang*—presumably as a result of a prior determination—guidance could continue until the standard one-year period expired (PP Art. 33(2)).

IV. SANCTIONS

Chen and Wang were thus both officially declared to be *liumang*. While Chen was back at home in Tainan and subject to relatively modest restraints, Wang headed south to Taidong to begin his reformatory training. Wang's criminal case was still pending in the Taipei District Court. As further detailed below, because of the "first ruling finalized, first enforced" system used when there were concurrent *liumang* and criminal cases, Wang began by serving his time in reformatory training (IR Art. 46). At the same time, as subsequently discussed in Section V.B of this chapter, Wang appealed the district court public security tribunal's ruling to the high court in Taipei.

A. Chen: Warning and Guidance in Tainan

As a warned *liumang*, Chen embarked on his one-year guidance period (LMA Art. 4).[51] Even if Chen challenged the adverse determination, the police-administered guidance would not cease while his administrative

---

[51] As previously mentioned, both warned *liumang* and post-reformatory training *liumang* 結訓輔導流氓 were subject to one-year guidance periods. For warned *liumang*, the one-year period started on the day that the person received the written warning (IR Art. 9; PP Art. 38). For post-reformatory training *liumang*, the one-year period started on the day that the reformatory training concluded, i.e., on the day that the three-year period ended (including set-off time) or a judge agreed to earlier release, depending on the circumstances (IR Art. 48; PP Art. 38).

appeal was pending. Chen may also have decided that challenging the determination was more bother than it was worth and that it was instead simpler to be good for a year, at which point the police would remove him from the *liumang* register.

The Police Provisions provided that the local police where Chen lived—specifically the "principal supervising guidance personnel" 主要監管輔導人員—were in charge of Chen's guidance (PP Art. 38(2)).[52] "Key supervising guidance personnel" 重點監管輔導人員, however, were to take charge of the *liumang*'s guidance when dealing with the following targets: gang leaders or important members; people who were relatively well known in the area, and people whom the police determined required particular attention (PP Art. 38(2)).[53] In practice, the substation police handled the bulk of the guidance responsibilities.

The Police Provisions set out three main components of guidance: interviewing the *liumang* in person 正面訪問, recording indirect findings through observations of the *liumang* 側面瞭解, and engaging in consultation and investigation 諮詢調查. First, the local police visited Chen on a regular basis. The responses we received from police varied when we asked how often the visits took place, some saying once or twice per month and others saying twice per week. According to the Police Provisions, the police were supposed to visit *liumang* once or twice per month

---

[52] For each *liumang* undergoing guidance, a consignment document 交付書 was issued along with a listed-*liumang* guidance supervision card 列冊流氓監管輔導紀錄卡 (PP Appdx. 21, 22). These documents were sent with other materials in the file to the police in charge of the *liumang*'s guidance.

[53] In addition to direct supervision of individual *liumang*, the local precinct was supposed to convene a quarterly analysis and appraisal meeting at which meeting they reviewed each *liumang*'s case and placed each *liumang* into one of three categories (PP Art. 42(4)): Category one 甲類 was for *liumang* who required increased supervision because they did not have regular employment, were hanging out with gang members, or were otherwise engaging in shady dealings. Category two 乙類 was for *liumang* who had regular employment, a fixed residence, and were staying away from gangs and other *liumang* and thus did not require additional supervision. The third category 丙類 was for special circumstances, such as *liumang* who were currently in police custody or were serving in the military (PP Arts. 42-43).

with an additional interview by higher-ups in the department—specifically, investigators from the "criminal investigation beat" 刑責區偵查員 and the key supervising guidance personnel" 重點監管輔導人員—at least once every three months when circumstances required (PP Art. 40(1)). One police group leader stated that, in his area, the practice had been for substation personnel to visit *liumang* at least once per month and the investigators only to visit once every three months. According to the Police Provisions, the police were to call Chen to set up the interview at a time and place that would not adversely affect his job, life, or self-respect (PP Art. 40(1)). The interviews were to be spaced out evenly, unless special circumstances otherwise required, and the substance should have been planned in advance so as to avoid random, aimless questioning (PP Art. 40(1)). At base, the point was to find out where the *liumang*'s money was coming from, with whom he was associating, and how he was spending his time. At a minimum, noted one police officer, the police wanted to know whether the *liumang* was engaging in legitimate work.

The general practice was for police to visit *liumang* at their homes, although one police investigator told us that warned *liumang* were normally required to come to the police substation for these interviews. When making a home visit, the police were to knock and announce their reason for coming, which the Police Provisions explained should be done with attention to proper manners and bearing (PP Art. 40(1)). Likewise, the interview was to be conducted with an attitude that would encourage a *liumang* to better himself, but the interview was not to be long and tedious (PP Art. 40(1)).

These written procedures sound very polite—and it seems as if Miss Manners had a hand in their drafting—but they were not totally without bite. The police would only come knocking for so long. The Police Provisions provided that if the police failed to meet Chen after two attempted visits, the police were to send a notice instructing Chen to appear at the station at an appointed time for his interview (PP Art. 44(4), Appdx. 27).

If Chen failed to appear without proper grounds for doing so, the police should submit a detention request 拘留聲請書 to the public security tribunal (PP Art. 44(5), Appdx. 28).

The second component of guidance was to indirectly observe Chen, literally "indirectly find (through observation)," by methods such as contacting people at work, relatives, and neighbors in order to understand Chen's daily, post-warning life so as to determine whether he was reforming or, instead, still engaging in illegal activities (PP Art. 40(2)). Police told us that they sometimes visited without notice to check up on a *liumang* who was undergoing guidance and see whether he was backsliding into his old *liumang* ways.

The third component—consultation and investigation—involved selecting reliable, appropriate personnel to help investigate Chen's life circumstances, societal background, the people with whom he primarily spent his time, and whether he was engaging in illegal activities (PP Art. 40(3)). The police recorded their observations and investigation results on Chen's listed-*liumang* guidance supervision card 列冊流氓監管輔導紀錄卡 and could take special action if certain events occurred (PP Art. 41). Thus, for example, if Chen moved to another area, the police would transfer his file; and if Chen had died, the police would remove his name from the register (PP Art. 41(1), (4)).

Engaging in *liumang* behavior during the guidance period could have landed Chen in front of the public security tribunal. If the police had discovered that Chen engaged in *liumang* behavior—either the same type for which he was originally deemed a *liumang* or another of the enumerated varieties—the police could have ordered him to appear at the station by sending a written notice 通知書 (PP Arts. 26(2), 27, Appdx. 12).[54] The police would then note the *liumang*'s compliance on the record after questioning him (PP Art. 28(9)). If a person failed to report without

---

[54] In deciding what time the person should appear, police were to consider the restrictions in the Criminal Procedure Code, Article 100-3, against nighttime interrogations (PP Art. 28(8)).

proper grounds for doing so, the police could apply to the court for an arrest warrant 拘票 and arrest him 拘提 (PP Art. 27(2), Appdx. 12.1). Under certain circumstances, the police could first detain the person and then apply to the court for permission after the fact; for example, when the person posed a flight risk and exigent circumstances made it impracticable to wait for court approval. If the application was denied, the police had to release the detained person promptly (PP Art. 27(3)).

If the police claimed that Chen had engaged in *liumang* behavior during his warning period, the public security tribunal could either send Chen to reformatory training or rule that the one-year guidance period should continue. When asked what happened if the police transferred a case in which a *liumang* under guidance engaged in *liumang* behavior but only committed a minor infraction of the kind that would not generally be deemed serious the first time around, an experienced judge pondered for a moment and said that the police always said that the person qualified as a serious *liumang*. Technically, for the police to transfer the case to the public security tribunal, the *Liumang* Act only required that the *liumang* have engaged in one of the types of listed *liumang* behavior during the guidance period (LMA Art. 19). If the standard convention was for police to send recidivist *liumang* to the public security tribunal as serious *liumang*, then the courts did not face the dilemma of what to do with a warned *liumang* who the police claimed had committed only a slight transgression during the warning period. Instead, the police always claimed that the transgression during the warning period was significant enough to warrant changing the person's status to "serious" *liumang*.

A police investigator told us that he thought the recidivist rate during the one-year guidance period generally had been relatively low, but it had been higher for those people without fixed residences. It certainly makes sense that people without fixed residences are less stable and also harder to keep track of. A Taipei police official estimated that, of the approximately 122 warned *liumang* per year in his area, only about five or six were found to have engaged in *liumang* behavior during the guidance period. Plainly, the incentive to avoid reformatory training was substantial.

At least on the books, the police were supposed to provide *liumang* with services and help during the guidance period, such as assisting with problems in finding a job or enrolling in school (PP Art. 44(6)). A police investigator told us that implementation of this duty varied from person to person, with some police using a "brothers" method of helping *liumang* during the guidance period. This prompted us to ask whether "guidance" was basically "keeping a watch on" the *liumang*, to which the investigator replied "yes." Other police agreed the guidance did not entail helping *liumang* find jobs, with one noting, "It's paying attention to his usual behavior, that's it."

This leads us back to Chen, who sat at home reading his warning and waiting for the first police visit. Chen's first option was to accept this guidance and make it through the year without engaging in other *liumang* behavior—at least not any that the police would find out about. In such case, when the year ended, the review committee would first check the police records to confirm that Chen had not engaged in any *liumang* behavior during the one-year period and would then approve the removal of his name from the register (LMA Art. 4; PP Art. 45). Chen would then receive notice that his guidance period was over and that his name was off the register (PP Art. 45(4), Appdx. 31). Nevertheless, a police officer in Taipei commented that their practice was to include *liumang* in the "public security population" 治安人口 for a few years after guidance ended. This group includes people who are known to have "criminal habits" and, thus, are of particular concern to the police, though no guidance or other formal monitoring is involved. Once Chen was formally off the register, if the police discovered that he had again engaged in *liumang* behavior, the entire process would start anew.

Chen, however, decided to take his second option. Instead of quietly acquiescing to a year of guidance, he opted to fight the determination.

B. Wang: Reformatory Training in Taidong

The public security tribunal had ordered that Wang be sent to reformatory training. As with Chen, Wang decided to fight the determination and commenced the appeal process as detailed later in this chapter. Once the public security tribunal issued an enforcement document, the police would coordinate with the tribunal and training institute authorities to execute its terms, which included making sure that, if the person was currently in prison, reformatory training began promptly upon his release (PP Art. 34). Wang received the ruling while being detained on criminal charges awaiting trial.

The fact that Wang first headed to the training institute instead of a prison was a result of the relative speed of his *liumang* proceedings. As previously noted, Wang's criminal and *liumang* cases proceeded simultaneously, with his initial punishment resting on whichever process was faster.[55] Here, the public security tribunal ruling was finalized while the criminal case was still pending, which meant that Wang would begin by serving time in a training institute. If Wang was later convicted and sentenced to time in prison (or to rehabilitation measures 保安處分) for gun possession, he would move to a prison or other required custody following release from the training institute to serve any time that was not set off by his reformatory training. If, on the other hand, Wang had been first convicted and sentenced to time for the criminal charge, then he would have begun by serving that sentence and later moved to a training institute, provided the criminal sentence was less than three years, i.e., the maximum time for reformatory training.

As previously noted, the Constitutional Court expressed concerns in its 2008 interpretation that this practice could result in an excessive

---

[55] The Implementing Rules provided that, if the same behavior for which a *liumang* was sentenced to reformatory training also violated criminal laws, then the first ruling finalized should be the first enforced (IR Art. 46).

128

deprivation of physical freedom, especially when criminal punishment preceded reformatory training. But the Court stopped short of holding the practice unconstitutional, and the legislative decision to repeal the *Liumang* Act ended the debate. Prior to repeal, the actual geographic distance traveled in a move between reformatory training and prison could have been mere footsteps. The two training institutes also housed regular convicts under the same roof, albeit in separate areas of the facilities. The *liumang* and regular convicts did not share sleeping quarters, but they did share certain facilities and classes.

In theory, the public security tribunal's streamlined proceedings moved cases through at a faster clip than proceedings in criminal court. Unlike *liumang* cases, court proceedings for criminal cases in Taiwan often occur in stages, which may be separated by periods of weeks or even months.[56] Oftentimes the judge handling the *liumang* case would wait for the verdict to issue in the criminal case. The *Liumang* Act permitted judges to wait for a judgment in the criminal case, though it was a matter of debate whether it instructed them to do so (LMA Art. 21). The judges with whom we spoke uniformly insisted that it was within the judge's discretion whether to wait for the criminal judgment before proceeding with the *liumang* case. "A judge can wait, and a judge can also not wait," responded one public security tribunal judge. A former public security tribunal judge said that, although it was usually not worth waiting for a decision in a companion criminal case, he waited for the criminal judgment to issue in cases where he expected that his ruling in the *liumang* case might conflict with the outcome in the criminal case. He could then consult the criminal judgment, which was helpful because the criminal hearing was generally more rigorous than that before the public security tribunal.

---

[56] Preparatory proceedings, such as evidentiary hearings, can stretch the case over a long period of time. But Article 293 of the Criminal Procedure Code provides that, if needed, trials are held in successive daily hearings, with proceedings beginning anew if fifteen days lapse between hearings.

Another judge told us that sometimes he waited until the criminal case was completed and sometimes he did not. If he trusted the criminal judge, then he would wait to read the opinion in the criminal case and even copy from it. He was less likely to wait for the judgment in the criminal case if he did not think that the accused should be sent to reformatory training. On the other hand, if he thought that reformatory training was proper but the accused was facing more than three years in prison on the criminal charges, then he would await resolution of the criminal case. In cases where he thought the criminal judgment was too harsh and the sentence might be lightened on appeal, he even waited for the appeal before deciding the *liumang* case. A different judge in the same court said that he did not wait for related criminal cases to finish because the *liumang* and criminal cases were "completely different." Even a not-guilty verdict in the criminal case had no influence on the *liumang* proceedings in his opinion.

The question whether to wait for a judgment in a criminal case was common. Like the police and lawyers with whom we spoke, judges emphasized the tremendous overlap between criminal and *liumang* cases. A Tainan district court judge, who worked as a police officer for about ten years before becoming a judge in 1997 and served a total of four years as a public security tribunal judge after joining the bench, stepped down from the public security tribunal in 2005 because he felt the *Liumang* Act was a waste of judicial resources. In his opinion, the majority of *liumang* cases could have been handled using criminal laws. He estimated that only three of the twenty *liumang* cases that he heard in 2003 did not have a companion criminal case. Another Tainan public security tribunal judge told us that nine out of ten *liumang* cases he heard had related criminal cases. And another Tainan judge who handled *liumang* cases estimated the *liumang*/criminal case overlap at 90 percent.

It was possible that Wang would have been found not guilty of the criminal charge, in which case he would have been subject to only reformatory training. This scenario was unlikely, given the strong evidence against Wang. In the end, whether a person was sent to prison or reformatory training, the important thing to the populace was that those who threatened them were off the street.

The actual process of getting Wang to the training institute was uncomplicated because he was in police custody pending trial on criminal charges. If, in contrast to Wang's situation, the accused *liumang* had been released on bail pending the tribunal's ruling, the tribunal would have summoned 傳喚 the person to report for reformatory training and, if ignored, the tribunal could have arrested him 拘提 (LMA Art. 18; IR Art. 45; PP Art. 34(2)). Ordinarily, the training began immediately, but exceptions did occur. One judge even told us the unusual story of a public security tribunal judge who summoned a *liumang* to appear in court so that he could be sent to reformatory training. When the *liumang* appeared, he told the judge of his family's hardships and how he had just started work a few days ago. The judge gave him some money and told him to go take care of matters with his family before starting his reformatory training.

If the person subject to reformatory training had already begun serving a criminal sentence that was sufficient to set off the entire three-year reformatory training period, the proper procedure was for the tribunal to exempt the person from reformatory training. The police could, however, still impose one year of guidance upon his release from prison, as if the person had served and been released from reformatory training (LMA Art. 19; PP Art. 34(2)). In Wang's case, because he spent several months in detention awaiting trial on criminal charges, he could have applied to set off this detention period from the maximum three years of reformatory training (LMA Art. 21; IR Art. 35). Wang started reformatory training right away because his criminal process had not run its course.

Wang was released from criminal detention and shipped off to the training institute without significant delay, leaving his criminal case to go forward while he began reformatory training (PP Art. 34(2)). Extended delays were sometimes possible, and these could cause snags in the system. Specifically, if reformatory training was not commenced within three years of the ruling, the police had to apply to the public security tribunal that issued the initial ruling to permit subsequent enforcement (PP Art. 34(2)). In such "have not begun enforcement" cases 未開始執行, the police had to provide concrete facts and evidence that the *liumang* had not reformed and reformatory training was still necessary (PP Art. 34(2); CM Art. 33). The *liumang* was then given an opportunity to present favorable evidence and defend himself before the judge, and the judge could subpoena the police to appear if he or she deemed it necessary (CM Art. 33(3)). If the public security tribunal rejected the police's application, the police could appeal the ruling to the higher court within ten days (PP Art. 34(2)). Furthermore, even if the application was rejected, the police could reapply for enforcement within seven years of the original ruling if they had evidence that enforcement was still necessary (PP Art. 34(2)). No ruling imposing reformatory training was enforceable if seven years had elapsed since the date of the original ruling (PP Art. 34(2); CM Art. 33(4)). Delays in enforcement could cause further problems when the *liumang* was still at large and thus able to continue his *liumang* behavior.[57]

No such delays complicated Wang's case. Because Wang was from northern Taiwan, he was sent to Yanwan Training Institute 岩灣技能訓練所 in Taidong. *Liumang* from southern Taiwan were sent to Dongcheng Training Institute 東成技能訓練所,[58] which, curiously, was also in Taidong. The few female *liumang* were all sent to Hualien Prison. The number

---

[57] The Police Provisions addressed the specific situation where a *liumang* engaged in illegal activity while his case was pending before the public security tribunal or the court had already issued a ruling imposing reformatory training but it had not yet been enforced—the bottom line being that the local police should transfer the listed-*liumang* guidance supervision card and other materials to the principal supervising guidance personnel and key supervising guidance personnel for enforcement (PP Art. 41(3)).

[58] Dongcheng also housed *liumang* from Penghu, Kinmen, and Lienchiang counties.

of facilities holding *liumang* dwindled after the Ministry of Justice took charge of reformatory training in 1992. Most famously, the feared "Green Island" 綠島, which in dictatorial days was also the most prominent destination for political dissidents, closed its doors. The Ministry of Justice also stopped housing *liumang* at Hualien Prison, Taichung Prison, and Taiyuan Training Institute 泰源技能訓練所, with the minor exception of the smattering of female *liumang* who were housed at Hualien Prison. The decrease in facilities over time was only natural given the sharp decrease in the number of incarcerated *liumang* toward the end of the *Liumang* Act's life.

The number of *liumang* undergoing reformatory training dropped dramatically from a high of several thousand in the early 1990s to around 400 by the early 2000s. According to Ministry of Justice statistics, there were 627 *liumang* undergoing reformatory training at the end of 2000. This number dropped to 443 by the end of 2001 and further decreased to 320 in 2002. The numbers then crept back up, landing at 398 by the end of May 2005. In the waning years of the *Liumang* Act, *liumang* were fairly evenly split between the Yanwan and Dongcheng training institutes. According to Yanwan's internal statistics, in January 2004, the facility housed 723 inmates, 198 *liumang*, and 525 criminals serving prison terms. By December 2005, these numbers had shifted slightly: the total number of inmates dropped to 712, with 203 *liumang* and 509 criminals. After repeal in 2009, the Ministry of Justice announced that it had released 393 incarcerated *liumang*, of whom 176 reentered society. The other 217 incarcerated *liumang* remained in custody because of criminal charges (Ministry of Justice 2009). Another 1,063 people had been sentenced to reformatory training but had not begun their sentences.[59]

---

[59] 流氓條例廢了 191人將出牢籠 (*The* Liumang *Act was abolished: 191 people will be released from prison*), *Nownews* (6 January 2009) (Chinese only).

The last statistic demonstrates that the number of *liumang* at the training institutes did not reflect the full number of people sentenced to reformatory training. Some never made it to the training institute. If the criminal sentence in a companion case exceeded three years in prison and was decided first, then there was no need to execute reformatory training. Others eventually ended up at the training institute after they finished their criminal sentences of less than three years. As one judge emphasized, although there were only about 400 *liumang* undergoing reformatory training, he estimated that there were at least as many who had been sentenced to reformatory training but were first serving prison sentences on criminal charges.

One institute employee attributed the modest number of inmates compared with pre-1992 numbers to the shorter time spent in reformatory training (minimum of one year and a maximum of three years as compared with the pre-1992 term of seven years, which was subject to extensions). At Dongcheng, we were told that the Ministry of Justice even considered consolidating all *liumang* into a single facility. We heard no compelling argument why *liumang* from the north and south were separated into two training institutes in the same city, with each group sharing their building with ordinary prisoners. Perhaps there was an implicit belief that consolidating *liumang* from all over Taiwan in a single training institute would have given them an even better networking opportunity. In fact, the notorious Celestial Alliance gang owes its beginnings to criminals from all over Taiwan getting together at Green Island in the mid-1980s after a number of big brothers in gangs from different places were locked up there following a crackdown on crime.

The divided training institutes structure was not based on a difference in training opportunities with, for example, one facility focusing on automotive skills and another on computers. The main difference between the facilities that we noticed after visiting both was one of attitude. The employees at Dongcheng readily engaged in broad discussions about the role of reformatory training—and the *Liumang* Act in general—in maintaining social order. At Yanwan, on the other hand, we encountered a more narrow focus on the job at hand. As one official responded, "We don't know about public security in society; we just handle enforcement."

Statistics regarding the number of *liumang* who were in the training institutes at any one time do not account for recidivism, and thus cannot simply be added up to determine the total number of people who were ever inmates. Because *liumang* sentences varied between one and three years, available statistics also do not fully reflect how many different individuals passed through the training institutes: if a hundred people were inmates for each year 2001, 2002, and 2003, this could mean the same hundred people all serving the maximum three-year term, or it could mean three hundred people, each serving the minimum one-year term. At one training institute, we were told that they had a number of repeat visitors, including one six-timer. This prompted wry remarks about how well-trained this *liumang* must be after so many years of carpentry, computer skills, and other classes. It also suggests what some others have concluded: at the training institute, many inmates also learned how to be more effective *liumang*. To be sure, the six-time inmate did not learn how to avoid getting caught. Answering the question of how many *liumang* "graduates" of the institute became recidivists is complicated, because some may have left the training institute and then committed a crime that landed them in prison rather than back at the training institute. Just because a former inmate never returned to the training institute does not mean that he reformed into a model citizen. He may have even become worse. Perhaps he did not reform but instead simply got better at not getting caught. More than one police official expressed the thought that the chances of *liumang* reforming in reformatory training were not great; often, the *liumang* simply became smarter. There was always the complex question whether reformatory training truly improved someone's behavior. We do not know how many serious *liumang* again committed *liumang* behavior after their release and simply did not get caught.

In Wang's case, he was dropped off at Yanwan. Along with delivering Wang himself, the police also sent a file with copies of the court ruling, writ of execution, and investigation materials form (PP Art 35). The training institute was allowed to refuse a person for reformatory training 拒絕收訓 in limited circumstances, such as a serious mental or physical disability. In such a case, the police were responsible for getting the person to a hospital or other appropriate location (Measures for Enforcing the Punishment of Reformatory Training 感訓處分執行辦法 ("Enforcement Measures" or EM) Art. 5; PP Art. 34(3)). If the reason for refusal disappeared, then the police could apply to the public security tribunal to have the person once again committed to reformatory training (PP Art. 34(3)). Upon arrival at the training institute, Wang's health inspection showed that he was of sound mind and body (EM Art. 5). He was admitted to the training institute and began his journey toward eventual release.

The purpose of reformatory training as stated in the Enforcement Measures was for the *liumang* to repent and become good and fit for life in society (EM Art. 2). To this end, the Enforcement Measures charted a three-level structure whereby the inmates'[60] training changed as they proceeded from life training through technical training and finally to professional training (EM Art. 8). Taiwan instituted this three-stage process in 2001 following a rather belated decision by the government to differentiate the treatment of *liumang* from that of criminal offenders. Prisoners serving time for criminal sentences do not undergo this three-stage process.

Each of the three stages was further broken down into several components that accounted for varying percentages of the *liumang*'s evaluation

---

[60] The phrasing was literally "person receiving the sanction of reformatory training" 受感訓處分人 in the Enforcement Measures. We refer to a *liumang* in the training institute by the more succinct and realistic term "inmate."

grade. An inmate could move to the next stage only after receiving a passing grade in his current stage. Life training consisted of general legal knowledge, physical training, moral education, life education, and labor services (EM Art. 10). This first stage initially lasted three months, at which point the inmate's progress was assessed and, if he did not pass the test, the time was extended for a maximum of an additional two months (EM Art. 9). The inmate next underwent technical training, upon completion of which he underwent a technical examination and certification process (EM Arts. 11-12). The final stage, professional training, focused on the inmate's moral character and knowledge education (i.e., as distinct from life or moral education), and took into account his educational background, namely high school, middle school, or elementary school (EM Arts. 14-15). The Enforcement Measures did not clarify exactly how "knowledge education" differed from "technical" or "moral" education, leaving the reader to wonder how distinct the three stages really were in practice.

Generally, the educational level of *liumang* was not high; one counselor at Dongcheng estimated that most had only graduated from middle school. An employee at Yanwan said that he had not come across any college graduates, though there were many who had attended high school. Materials used by Dongcheng personnel, which were shown to us by a counselor there, described the usual timing for each phase: three months for life training, three months to one year for technical training, and three months for professional training. This information was told to incoming *liumang*. The officials at Dongcheng also gave us a blank logbook like the ones they filled in for each *liumang*, which consisted of nearly thirty pages of blank, neatly lined charts on which counselors filled in individual items detailing the *liumang*'s progress.

In light of this emphasis on training, we asked whether the training institutes found inmates jobs after their release. We were told that institute personnel could contact *liumang* after release to see whether they had found suitable work. They stopped short of saying that the institute personnel actively helped former inmates find employment. During the meeting, the officials provided us with a table of the employment rate for graduates of various classes in the training institute from 2003–2005. The rates varied tremendously, though the percentages are of questionable value considering the small sample size. The lowest employment rate was 17 percent (7 out of 39 people who left the facility after completing a given class) for the class in making "Western-style clothes" and the highest was 83 percent (5 out of 6) for the auto mechanics class. Other classes, like skills involving plumbing and electricity, fell in between, with rates ranging from 27 percent to 50 percent. In total, 31 percent of the 259 former inmates who were tracked found jobs.[61]

The training institutes also offered religious services (EM Art. 17). We visited classrooms where Buddhist and Christian gatherings were held—and religious symbols were posted—and chatted with the resident Buddhism instructor as we toured the grounds of one facility. He commented good-naturedly that the inmates were receptive to the religious offerings, if for no other reason than that it gave them something to do. Reading books borrowed from the library provided another means of passing time. The library we visited at Dongcheng consisted of a sterile, but pleasant, one-room selection ranging from novels to legal texts, and featured Taiwanese pin-up posters on the wall that perhaps extended the library-going experience beyond merely intellectual stimulation.

The training institutes' grounds were landscaped, had flowers, and included basketball courts, though access to outdoor activities was strictly limited to a few times per week. Inmates were not allowed alcohol, but they were allowed to smoke at set times (EM Art. 21). And the training institute officials told us that inmates were generally allowed to keep small, self-provided televisions in their cells, though we did not see any. The classrooms that we saw varied: some contained rows of computers, others

---

[61] The table did not specify for what period the released inmates were tracked. The booklet in which the statistics appear, however, was dated March 2006.

half-constructed fireplaces as inmates learned to lay bricks, and others were workshops devoted to auto mechanics or sculpted miniatures, decorative canoes, and other handicrafts. Institute personnel emphasized the inmates' artistic accomplishments and gave us colorful, cross-stitch pouches as souvenirs along with a list of items that were available for purchase.

Computers in the classrooms and flowers in the yard do not alter the fact that inmates were deprived of their liberty and had to conform to a harsh, regimented schedule under austere conditions. Although advance planning for our visit allowed ample time for officials to spruce up the facilities, neither institute could be mistaken for a college campus. Cramped, windowless cells that often held five inmates, an exposed toilet, and little else offered one of the most vivid images of the inmates' hardships. Still, the training institutes were far from the gulags of Stalin and they were not inferior to any but the best of Taiwan's contemporary prison conditions. As expected, our visits did involve a certain amount of show, such as an elaborate and delicious lunch prepared and served by inmates at Yanwan who learned their impressive culinary skills while incarcerated. The reformist sentiment of this gesture was tempered, however, by the conversation at lunch, which included the head of the institute singing the praises of Singapore's extremely strict justice system and bemoaning that he was not even allowed to use a few whacks with a rod to keep inmates in line. Yet perhaps these remarks were designed to underscore the humanitarian environment of his institute. Other details—such as the institute-wide English lessons at Dongcheng that consisted of displaying English phrases across electronic bulletin boards and classroom blackboards—were less contrived and at least appeared to be part of the daily routine, though we cannot confirm that our presence—the institute's first foreign guests—had no influence on this practice.

Our visits left no doubt that conditions had improved dramatically since the days when the military was in charge and political dissidents were harshly confined alongside genuine *liumang*. What we do not know is whether these improved conditions did a better job of reforming *liumang.* We were left with the question whether the changes to reformatory training were reminiscent of a Chinese idiom invoked by a staff employee at one of the training institutes: "change the soup but not the medicine" 換湯不換藥. The "soup" of *liumang* reform definitely had been changed, but was the "medicine" *more* effective than it used to be? On a bright note, there were no reports of a new gang of the magnitude of Celestial Alliance having emerged from either Dongcheng or Yanwan, so perhaps the better conditions did lead to better results. Without extensive empirical social science research, we can only speculate.

Wang could have been any of the buzz-cut inmates we saw at Yanwan sitting in class, reclining in their cells, or cleaning up the grounds as part of the inmates' responsibility for chores (EM Art. 23). Once at the institute, in addition to commencing his life training, Wang was placed in one of four groups, with the fourth one being the group subject to the most restrictive conditions (EM Art. 30).[62]

In general, inmates began in the fourth group and advanced gradually, but there was room for flexibility (EM Art. 30). The institute affairs committee 所務委員會—the highest decision-making body within the training institute—made an individual determination based on an examination of each *liumang* (EM Art. 30).[63] If the institute affairs committee decided that the incoming *liumang* had a sense of responsibility and was

---

[62] The Enforcement Measures provided that inmates should wear insignia with colors that indicated their group: red for one, blue for two, yellow for three, and white for four (EM Art. 20).

[63] A Dongcheng employee explained that below the institute affairs committee were the discipline group 管教小組 and progressive treatment examination committee 累進處遇審查會. The discipline group met monthly and submitted recommendations to the progressive treatment examination committee for the addition and deduction of points. The progressive treatment examination committee then reported to the institute affairs committee for final approval. At Yanwan, we were similarly told that counselors raised matters with the progressive treatment examination committee (though they did not specifically mention a "discipline group"), which then reported to the institute affairs committee. The institute affairs committee was made up entirely of training institute personnel, who, an employee pointed out, were different from the parole examination committee 假釋審查委員會, whose members had begun to include scholars and specialists in recent years.

fit to live together with the other inmates, then, after a report to the Ministry of Justice was approved, the incoming *liumang* could enter directly into group three (EM Art. 30). Once inside the training institute, the staff informed all incoming *liumang* as to how this system worked. An inmate's class within this system of progressive treatment shifted as responsibility points were added or deducted based on the inmate's behavior.

The Enforcement Measures set forth a detailed scheme for adding and subtracting points under the "reward and punishment" system. Reasons for adding points include, among others, reporting another inmate who was plotting to escape or committing a violent act; receiving excellent grades on work; making a special contribution to the technology or equipment; and exhibiting such good behavior that he was considered a model inmate (EM Art. 36). Such positive behavior was not merely rewarded with points. Institute officials could also reward inmates by giving them public praise, issuing certificates of merit or prizes, increasing visits or correspondence privileges, and conferring other awards (EM Arts. 37, 39). On the flip side, negative behavior could lead to a deduction in points and other punishments, such as an admonishment, temporary suspension of visitation or letter writing, one to five days of forced labor (limited to two hours per day), or temporary suspension of outdoor activities (EM Arts. 38, 39). These punishments might have been insufficient to rein in an inmate's behavior. If an inmate sought revenge, stirred up trouble, or engaged in other unsuitable behavior, the Enforcement Measures permitted officials at the training institutes to apply to the Ministry of Justice for the transfer of the inmate to another place for reformatory education (EM Art. 24). The destination of the transferee was constrained by the fact that there were only two facilities in operation in the *Liumang* Act's final years and the transferee was already in one of them. Alternatively, the head of Dongcheng told us that, to avoid tensions, they could put inmates into solitary confinement for up to two months. He further said that the institute personnel were careful when selecting roommates. Just as close living conditions can bring the inmates closer together, they can also exacerbate tensions.

Wang was somewhat atypical in that he was a member of a large, organized gang. One institute official explained that the more common inmate was a young member of a local gang. Whether one speaks of large gangs or local ones, it was unusual for higher-ups in the organizations to be confined as *liumang*. In part this is a question of evidence. The big brothers were generally smart enough to keep their hands clean of *liumang* behavior or traceable crimes. One judge told us that police did not dare send the "real big *liumang*" to either the public security tribunal or the regular courts. And another judge remarked that the Organized Crime Act was used for big *liumang*. He had not seen a big *liumang* in the public security tribunal. While what qualifies as "big" or "small" is subjective, still the sentiment among judges was clear and institute officials seemed to share it: in its waning years, the *Liumang* Act was used overwhelmingly to put small-scale offenders behind bars.

A serious hurdle to having local police go after larger criminals is that it is not unusual for these figures to hold considerable sway in the local community, and some even hold elected office. This presents a problem because the local police budget is primarily funneled through the local government. When asked why not reform the payment structure to create a direct channel from the national government to the local police, an official at the Criminal Investigation Bureau replied that the local police and government would still need to live together. To alleviate this problem in high-profile criminal cases, the Criminal Investigation Bureau sometimes brings in special task forces to take the pressure off local police. This is only a partial solution, because it is often difficult for central police to find evidence in the local areas due to police corruption and other impediments. Still, having central government intervention is sometimes more effective than relying on purely local work. A member of the Tainan City police force acknowledged the problem of big *liumang* who had "special status" in the community, and noted the benefit of using NPA-dispatched police because "they do not have local pressure on them."

Wang gradually worked his way up the institute's group ladder, losing a point here, gaining a few there. Upon reaching group one, he was nearly eligible for early release. To be considered for release prior to the end of the three-year period, the Enforcement Measures provided that a *liumang* must complete a minimum of one year at the institute and maintain his group-one status with 26 points for at least three consecutive months (EM Art. 40).[64] While the personnel at Dongcheng emphasized these requirements as the conditions for release, those at Yanwan described the requirements in more abstract terms, with one person stating that there was no formal prerequisite and it was up to the individual committee members. The committee looked at a variety of factors, such as whether this was the inmate's first time undergoing reformatory training, whether he had received awards, and whether he was relatively young (with more lenient treatment for the young).

Once Wang satisfied the applicable prerequisites and the officials at the training institute recommended that he be released, his case passed to the Ministry of Justice for approval. According to statistics from Yanwan, in 2004 the Ministry of Justice approved the release of 98 out of 99 of the people recommended for early release by the institute. In 2005 the Ministry of Justice was less deferential and approved 129 out of 148 cases. The Ministry of Justice approved Wang's application. It was then up to the same judge who had heard the original case to make the final decision (EM Art. 40). The Court Matters instructed judges to examine whether the *liumang* met the provisions of the Enforcement Measures and decide whether there was a continuing need for reformatory training (CM Art. 34). In practice, this was a swift, perfunctory review of the file. It was almost unheard of for a judge to reject a request for early release. One judge explained that judges always agreed to early release because the

---

[64] Points were determined on a monthly basis (EM Art. 32). The minutiae of the point system calculations were laid out in an appendix to the Enforcement Measures (EM Art. 31).

public security tribunal received only a single piece of paper without any other materials to review.

If the public security tribunal were to reject the application, then the institute officials could reapply after three months, though this restriction was not applicable if the rejection was based on a procedural problem (EM Art. 40). Alternatively, Wang would be released at the end of three years even if he never satisfied the conditions for early release (EM Art. 41). Few *liumang* served full three-year terms, according to officials at the institutes. One training institute employee reported in 2002 that the average length of stay was two years and one month. Institute officials told us that it generally took about one year and three months to reach class one and then the inmate needed to maintain that classification for three months. Considering that not every inmate was on a fast-track to class one, and further that a drop to class two required the inmate to regain his class one status and retain it for another three months, it is not surprising that the average stay would reach two years. Another employee estimated off the top of his head that inmates were generally released after approximately 1.5 years.

Wang's time behind bars did not end after he left the training institute. While Wang was in the training institute, he was sentenced to five years for the gun possession charges, the minimum sentence allowed by law. Consequently, the news that he had completed his reformatory training gave him limited reason to celebrate. His time spent at Yanwan was deducted from his five-year sentence and he was transferred to a prison to complete his prison term. If Wang had been found not guilty on the criminal charges, he would have been released after receiving judicial approval and then commenced his one-year guidance period. In such case, within three days of release, Wang would have been required to register his residence with the local census agencies and to report to the police for guidance (EM Art. 44). It would have been as if he were in the same position as Chen when he sat at home reading the notice that he had one year of guidance ahead of him.

V. CHALLENGE TO THE *LIUMANG* DETERMINATION

Chen and Wang had two entirely separate channels to challenge their respective *liumang* determinations. Chen's path began with agency review and eventually led him to an administrative court, whereas Wang had to fight the ruling in the public security tribunals within the general court system.

A. Chen: Administrative Challenge to the Review Committee's Determination

Chen's prospects for reconsideration were found in administrative channels, first with the review committee and police and, finally, with the administrative courts. Specifically, the successive layers of review were filing (1) an objection 異議 with the NPA review committee, (2) an administrative appeal 訴願 with a different committee within the NPA,[65] and (3) an administrative lawsuit 行政訴訟 with the administrative courts (LMA Art. 5). Chen first looked to the *Liumang* Act and Implementing Rules for the applicable deadlines and procedures when navigating the appeals system. His challenge also brought into play provisions in the Administrative Appeal Law 訴願法, the Administrative Litigation Law 行政訴訟法, and supporting rules. For example, the Police Provisions expressly provided that, where the *Liumang* Act and Implementing Rules were silent with respect to the procedures for

---

[65] According to the *Liumang* Act, a warned *liumang* was required to file a second administrative appeal with the NPA before proceeding to the courts—literally an "administrative re-appeal" 再訴願 (LMA Art. 5). In contrast, a 1998 revision to the Administrative Appeal Law abolished the re-appeal requirement, thus removing one step from the process. This discrepancy on paper did not translate into a difference in practice. It was standard practice for the committee that heard administrative appeals to allow *liumang* to proceed directly to an administrative lawsuit rather than first file an administrative re-appeal. A lawyer who served on the committee that heard administrative appeals in *liumang* cases told us that administrative re-appeals had stopped being used in *liumang* cases. Another lawyer who handled *liumang* cases confirmed that the practice changed and that his clients did not have to submit re-appeals.

administrative relief, the police should look to the Administrative Appeal Law (PP Art 25(5)).

Based on interviewees' statements, Chen's decision to fight the review committee's determination was unusual. But Chen was determined. Within ten days of receiving the warning, Chen filed a written objection 異議書 with the NPA review committee, stating the reasons for his appeal (LMA Arts. 5).[66] For the appeal process, Chen had the option either to go it alone or hire a lawyer. Other than financial restraints, there were no restrictions on his ability to hire a lawyer to help with his appeal. The review committee then had thirty days from receipt of the objection to issue a decision (IR Art. 12), and the NPA had fifteen days from that date to deliver the review committee's written decision 決定書 to Chen (PP Art. 25). Although in some ways it may seem pointless that Chen had to submit his objection to the exact same body that named him a *liumang* in the first place, this process allowed the review committee to reflect on and correct its own mistakes: essentially a "do over." A police official noted that he had seen the Taipei review committee overturn its ruling when it mistakenly used the wrong name, but he added that cases of mistaken identification were exceptional and few objections succeeded. A former member of the NPA review committee gave a more optimistic view of a *liumang*'s ability to have a determination overturned. He estimated that at least ten to twenty percent, and perhaps even twenty to thirty percent, of the objections were successful during his time on the committee.

---

[66] The *Liumang* Act provided that the warned *liumang* should raise his objection with the "original determining agency" 向原認定機關聲明異議. The wording in the Implementing Rules was slightly different: the warned *liumang* should raise the objection with the "determining police agency" 向認定之警察機關提出 (Art. 8). The Implementing Rules further provided that the *liumang* who raised an objection should sign the objection and send it in duplicate to the "warning police agency" 告誡之警察機關 (Art. 11). The Police Provisions clarified that once the police received the objection, they had five days to send it, along with copies of the warning and certificate of service, to the "original determining policy agency." The police also included their opinion regarding what the reply should be to the *liumang*'s stated grounds for the objection (Art. 25(1)). Despite the slight variance in wording, the bottom line was that the objection ended up before the review committee.

Even though the people reviewing the objection were usually identical to those who made the original determination, Chen now had a voice, unlike at the time when they made that determination. In addition to identifying information (e.g., Chen's name, date of birth, etc.) and the document number of his warning, Chen could now state the facts and reasoning for contesting the determination (IR Art. 11). Chen's reasoning—that he refused to pay Li because of the unacceptable quality of the food and that he had paid the other owners but did not have receipts to back up his story—did not sway the review committee in light of the evidence of Chen's threats and that he continued to frequent Li's bar, hardly a sign of displeasure. The review committee notified Chen of its decision in a written objection decision 聲明異議決定書 (IR Art. 12; PP Art. 25, Appdx. 10). If the review committee had instead determined that Chen's objection was well-grounded, then the proper relief would have been to cancel the warning and issue a written "warning cancellation" 撤銷告誡書 (LMA Art. 5; IR Art. 12).

Undeterred, Chen proceeded up to the next level of review: an administrative appeal. The administrative appeal process was not unique to *liumang* cases. Even today, it is a standard process through which aggrieved citizens may challenge decisions by government agencies. What differed, however, was the body to which the appeal was addressed. For *liumang* cases, the NPA was charged with creating and supporting a "deliberation committee for administrative appeals" 訴願審議委員會 ("appeals committee"). An aggrieved *liumang* had thirty days from receipt of the review committee's rejection of his objection to file an administrative appeal with the appeals committee (IR Art. 12).[67]

---

[67] The final sentence on the form for decisions made in response to a *liumang's* objection 聲明異議決定書 (objection decision), which was attached to the Police Provisions as an appendix, read, "If the person making the objection is not satisfied with this decision, he should raise an administrative appeal with the National Police Agency within thirty days of receipt of this decision" (PP Art. 25, Appdx. 10).

The required contents of the administrative appeal were not set forth in the *Liumang* Act or Implementing Rules. For this, Chen turned to the Administrative Appeal Law (AAL Art. 56). Chen's administrative appeal, like his objection, contained basic identifying information on him and his case and further set forth the facts and reasons for his appeal. Unlike the initial objection procedure, the Administrative Appeal Law also allowed Chen to attach evidence (AAL Art. 56).

The composition and workings of the appeals committee that heard *liumang* cases were laid out in the Administrative Appeal Law and the cumbersomely named Deliberation Rules of the Deliberation Committee for Administrative Appeals of the Executive Yuan and All Levels of Administrative Agencies 行政院及各級行政機關訴願審議委員會審議規則 ("Deliberation Committee Rules" or DCR) and related Organizational Rules of the Deliberation Committee for Administrative Appeals of the Executive Yuan and Administrative Agencies under the Executive Yuan 行政院及各級行政機關訴願審議委員會組織規程 ("Deliberation Committee Organizational Rules" or DCOR). The Administrative Appeal Law provided that the committee should be composed of the agency's high-level staff members, impartial people from society, scholars, and experts. Moreover, non-agency members could not make up less than one-half of the total members (AAL Art. 52). The succinct six-article Deliberation Committee Organizational Rules[68] expanded on the structure set forth in the Administrative Appeal Law by specifying that the appeals committee should have between five and fifteen members, one of whom would serve as the committee director (DCOR Art. 4). The agency chief was charged with assigning a deputy chief or other high-ranking personnel with special knowledge of the legal system to serve as the committee director (DCOR Art. 4). The agency chief was further responsible for assigning other

---

[68] The Deliberation Committee Organizational Rules were issued by the Executive Yuan as allowed for under Article 52 of the Administrative Appeal Law (AAL Art. 52(3)).

high-ranking agency personnel to serve on the committee, as well as selecting the non-agency members (DCOR Art. 4). The Deliberation Committee Organizational Rules reiterated that at least half of the members must be non-agency personnel (DCOR Art. 4). Applying these general rules to *liumang* cases, even though the appeals committee was set-up by the NPA, made clear that the committee was intended to have a high level of independence from the agency.

We spoke with a lawyer who had served on the appeals committee for *liumang* cases, which took a bit of hunting because this little-known committee had a very low profile. There were relatively few *liumang* cases—especially as compared with criminal cases—and administrative appeals of *liumang* cases were very rare. An NPA official working on *liumang* cases described the number of appeals as "very few." The committee member's statements agreed with this depiction. He described the committee composition as generally ranging from seven to nine people, with three people from the police and about four or five lawyers and professors. Because of the small number of administrative appeals, which he estimated as no more than twenty per year, he said the appeals committee met when it had cases, rather than on a rigid schedule. According to law, and confirmed by interviewees, the appeals committee had three months from the NPA's receipt of the appeal to issue a decision, with the possibility of a two-month extension when the appeal needed to be supplemented (AAL Art. 85; DCR Art. 27).

A decision in Chen's case by the appeals committee required the agreement of a majority of members who were present at the meeting, and a majority of members must have been present for a quorum (AAL Art. 53). Such administrative determinations (whether for a *liumang* case or today for other types of administrative appeals) are generally based on the written documents alone (AAL Art. 63). When an appeals committee deemed it necessary, the committee would notify the appellant *liumang* to appear and state his opinion (AAL Art. 63). The appellant could also apply to appear. The law specified that the appellant *liumang* should be given an opportunity to appear if he had good reason 有正當理由, leaving the appeals committee to determine whether good reason existed (AAL Art. 63). If a hearing was held, the Administrative Appeal Law and Deliberation Committee Rules provided specific procedures regarding the order of appearance by the appellant and the agency with jurisdiction, here the NPA (AAL Arts. 65, 66; DCR Arts. 14, 15).

Provided that there are no procedural problems with an appeal (e.g., filed after the thirty-day appeal period had expired), the appeals committee's decision boiled down to whether the appeal was well-grounded.[69] If so determined for a *liumang* case, the appeals committee would cancel the review committee's decision that the person was a *liumang* (AAL Art. 81). Chen was not so lucky and was once again denied relief. As with the previous level of review, the NPA was required to send a written decision to Chen within fifteen days of the determination with copies to the original determining police agency (i.e., the review committee), the police agency that issued the warning, and the local police for the area covering the *liumang*'s registered address (PP Art. 25; DCR Art. 28). If the full time was taken for each step in this process, then approximately six months would have elapsed since the initial determination, leaving half of Chen's one-year guidance period. Guidance was, as a general rule, not suspended while appeals were pending, although the review committee had the power to suspend it (LMA Art. 5).[70] Chen's last avenue for review was the courts.

---

[69] Even if there was only a procedural error, the Deliberation Committee Rules still provided relief in limited cases. If a *liumang*'s appeal was filed past the legal time limit and the agency's decision was clearly in violation of the law or improper, then the appeals committee was required to specify in its decision that the agency should cancel or revise its decision (DCR Art. 25).

[70] A *liumang* could apply for suspension or the review committee could stop guidance *ex officio* 職權 (LMA Art. 5). In the unlikely event that guidance was suspended pending appeal, the period for which guidance was suspended did not count toward the warned *liumang*'s one-year guidance period (IR Art. 13.1).

Chen once again had thirty days to appeal, this time to the administrative courts (LMA Art. 5). By this point, however, he had already served the majority of his one-year guidance period and he was not particularly thrilled at the prospect of spending more in legal fees when there were doubtful prospects for success. Chen decided to simply ride out the remaining few months. Appeals to the administrative courts were exceedingly rare in *liumang* cases. The time, money, and effort involved in mounting an appeal—and slim chances for success—made the decision not to appeal totally rational. Nonetheless, if Chen had instead decided to pursue his appeal, he would have requested the high administrative court to cancel his *liumang* determination on the basis that it injured his rights or legal interests (LMA Art. 5; ALL Art. 4). A further appeal to the Supreme Administrative Court was also theoretically possible. At the time the *Liumang* Act was in effect, administrative courts used a two-tier system in which the high administrative court was always the court of first instance. Since 6 September 2012, the administrative courts have switched to a "three-tier, two-instance" system in which some cases start at the first tier and others at the second tier. The Supreme Administrative Court hears appeals based solely on issues of law, not fact (ALL Art. 242–243), and a party has twenty days to appeal a decision to the Supreme Administrative Court (ALL Art. 241).

B. Wang: Appeal to the High Court

Wang's appeal route was strikingly simple when viewed against Chen's circuitous path. Wang had ten days from receipt of the district court public security tribunal's ruling to file an appeal with the public security tribunal in the high court (LMA Art. 14), after which the district court public security tribunal would transfer the file to the high court reviewing tribunal (CM Art. 28).[71] The public security tribunal on the high

---

[71] The Criminal Procedure Code only allows five days for a party to appeal a ruling (CPC Art. 406) but allows ten days to appeal a judgment (Art. 349).

court level generally limited its review to the documents in the case file without holding a hearing.[72] Included with these documents was the ruling-appeal form 抗告書狀 from Wang that stated the reasons for his appeal (LMA Art. 14). As in Chen's case, Wang could hire a lawyer or go it alone.

It was up to a three-judge panel to evaluate the appeal. If the panel decided the appeal was groundless, the panel would reject the appeal. If the panel decided the appeal was well-grounded, the high court tribunal would cancel the lower tribunal's ruling (LMA Art. 15). If the panel had questions about the evidence, the common scenario was to send the case back to the district court tribunal for a new ruling or for further investigation. Although not formally stated in court rules, we were told that the policy was for a different district court public security tribunal judge to hear the case on remand. In Wang's case, however, the evidence was solid and the district court public security tribunal's ruling carefully spelled out the reasons why reformatory training was proper in his case. The high court thus rejected the appeal. This marked the end of Wang's appeals because *liumang* cases used a system where "the decision of the second-level court is final" 二級二審制, whereas criminal cases can be appealed up one more level to the Supreme Court.

Wang's last hope was to apply for rehearing of his case 重新審理 on the basis that there was a serious factual error, such as that the evidence on which the ruling was based was fabricated or tampered with or the witnesses' statements were false (LMA Art. 16; PP Art. 36).[73] A *liumang* who sought rehearing had to apply to the "original ruling court whose ruling becomes finalized," meaning that if the case went up to the public security

---

[72] The higher court was required to return the case file to the lower court for handling following issuance of its ruling (CM Art. 29).

[73] The Criminal Procedure Code provides similar grounds for retrials (Art. 420). In a criminal case, the defendant may also seek an extraordinary appeal 非常上訴 in limited circumstances where there is an alleged legal error in the court's ruling (CPC Art. 441 et seq.). This procedural route to remedy a legal error was not available in *liumang* cases.

tribunal in the high court on appeal, the *liumang* should apply to the high court (LMA Art. 16). If, on the other hand, the case never reached the high court and was only heard by the public security tribunal in the district court, the application should be lodged with the district court.

Wang had thirty days from when the ruling was determined to request a retrial, with one caveat: if he became aware of the reasons for the retrial only at a later date, then the thirty-day period would be calculated from when he learned of these reasons (LMA Art. 16). A person was not allowed to reapply for a rehearing based on grounds that were already rejected by the public security tribunal (LMA Art. 16), though a person could apply repeatedly on different grounds, and some *liumang*'s persistence was admirable. A judge at the Taipei District Court told us of one *liumang* who had been petitioning for a rehearing for nearly twenty years. The judge reviewing the incoming appeal could immediately tell from the file that the person had filed repeated applications, and the judges with whom we spoke understandably were not amused about being bombarded with repetitive applications.

It was extraordinary, but not unheard of, for a *liumang* case to be granted a rehearing and overturned. One such case was reported in the press in 2005.[74] In 1998, Lin Wei-wen began reformatory training after the public security tribunal on the high court level upheld the Taipei District Court tribunal's ruling that he was a serious *liumang*. But a certain Mr. Wen, a jilted ex-boyfriend of Lin's current companion, had fabricated reports of Lin's alleged *liumang* behavior—eating and drinking without paying, using a gun for intimidation and extortion, and collecting "protection money." Wen went so far as to cajole five other people into giving testimony as secret witnesses.

The court had sentenced Lin to reformatory training, where he served one year and ten months. Thereafter, he applied for rehearing and further filed a criminal complaint alleging that the secret witnesses had committed

---

[74] 一場畸戀 男子被打入冤獄 (*Bizarre love story leads to a man's wrongful conviction*), *Liberty Times* (30 July 2005) (Chinese only).

perjury and raised false accusations.[75] Following the conviction of several of the secret witnesses, the high court public security tribunal (i.e., the "original ruling court whose ruling becomes finalized") agreed to rehear Lin's case (LMA Art. 16).[76] Lin first erroneously applied to the public security tribunal in the district court for rehearing, but the court rejected the application because it was not the "original ruling and determining court" and his relief instead rested with the high court. Once before the proper court, the public security tribunal ruled on rehearing that there was no evidence to prove that Lin engaged in the alleged behavior, rescinded the prior ruling, and ruled that Lin should not have been subjected to reformatory training. Lin was further awarded NT $2,736,000 (approximately US $93,500) in compensation under the Wrongful Detention Compensation Law, calculated at NT $4,000 per day times a total of 684 days of reformatory training and pre-enforcement confinement.[77] Although this modest sum is cold comfort for Lin's incarceration and years of legal proceedings, it is heartening to see that wrongfully convicted *liumang* could use a rehearing to obtain official vindication.

VI. LIFE AFTER BEING A *LIUMANG*

Chen and Wang were finally back on the streets and off the *liumang* register. Yet this did not spare them from the long-term impact of having been branded *liumang*, even after the *Liumang* Act was repealed. This label is not so easy to lose. One lawyer succinctly stated, "Being called a *liumang* is for a lifetime; it is too severe."

---

[75] The *Liumang* Act allowed for criminal charges to be pursued against witnesses who committed perjury or made false accusations in *liumang* cases (LMA Art. 17; IR Art. 43). Perjury and false accusation charges, however, could only be raised after the police determination or court ruling that the person was a *liumang* was finalized (LMA Art. 17).

[76] Although Lin had applied for rehearing at the same time that he pursued criminal charges against the secret witnesses, the public security tribunal refused to rehear his *liumang* case until the witnesses were convicted.

[77] Article 3 of the Wrongful Detention Compensation Law provides that wrongful detention or imprisonment will be compensated at a rate between NT $3,000 and NT $5,000 per day.

In one case, the lawyer quoted above represented an eighteen-year-old high school student who got in a brawl with friends at a bar, at which point they rushed out, leaving the bill unpaid. Because it was only a one-off, mild offense of eating and drinking without paying, the lawyer attributes the determination that his client was a *liumang* to the close relationship 關係 of the pub owner to the police. His parents were frightened to death when they heard of the charges and hired the lawyer to pursue an appeal. As the lawyer reemphasized, "In Taiwan, being called a *liumang* is a very serious matter. This kind of record and label can follow you for a lifetime."

Indeed, most people did fear having "*liumang*" tattooed on their reputations for life, but for some this label—and, more importantly, time in reformatory training—gave them sought-after street prestige. The same lawyer who told of the negative lifelong impact of a *liumang* determination also noted that "fake *liumang*" became "real *liumang*" under the tutelage of seasoned *liumang* while housed together in the training institutes. For some gang members, being sent to reformatory training provided a certificate that they were the real thing. Beyond the official education provided by the training institute, one police officer described an example of the results of the unofficial education. After release, a *liumang* who originally was able to steal only motorcycles was also able to steal cars. Such was the case with Wang. His big brothers in Bamboo Union welcomed him back with open arms and newfound respect. Chen, on the other hand, renounced his *liumang* ways. He continued to hang out in bars, but he started paying his bills.

CHAPTER 4:
THE END OF THE *LIUMANG* ACT

I. THE *LIUMANG* ACT'S TWILIGHT YEARS

There is no question that the *Liumang* Act was increasingly anachronistic when viewed against Taiwan's Criminal Procedure Code. As Taiwan's criminal justice system cruised forward to embrace sweeping reforms, the *Liumang* Act somehow fell off the bandwagon and was left stumbling to catch up. For years, the *Liumang* Act remained an aberration, but unique is not the same as unconstitutional. The Constitutional Court heard challenges to the *Liumang* Act in 1995 and 2001, yet both times declined to strike down the Act in its entirety. The Legislative Yuan, in turn, revised the *Liumang* Act in response to each constitutional interpretation, but the main substance of the Act remained intact. After the Court's 2001 interpretation, reformers became concerned that momentum behind abolishing the *Liumang* Act had all but ceased.

Then, in the fall of 2007, the Justices solicited opinions from legal experts on two additional petitions challenging the constitutionally of the *Liumang* Act that had been long-pending before the Court.[1] The hope among critics of the Act was that the Court would finally hold that the entire Act was unconstitutional. Instead, in Interpretation No. 636 issued on 1 February 2008, the Court held only that the *Liumang* Act had to again be revised in a piecemeal fashion, as it had done in 1995 and 2001 in Interpretations Nos. 384 and 523, respectively. In its capacity as the guardian of the ROC Constitution, it was not the Court's job to

---

[1] As previously noted, petitions for constitutional interpretations are not publicly available, which means that people either learn their contents through the legal grapevine or only when the Constitutional Court publishes its decision to accept or reject the petition.

demand repeal of the entire *Liumang* Act if more modest action was sufficient to solve the constitutional infirmities. The petitions that prompted Interpretation No. 636 primarily addressed specific provisions in the *Liumang* Act. The Justices were persuaded by several of the petitioners' constitutional arguments, but called for only targeted repeal of unconstitutional provisions and other relatively limited revisions. As a result, the fate of the *Liumang* Act once again shifted to the legislature, which had to decide whether to repeal the Act or keep it alive, albeit in an increasingly altered form.

Interpretation No. 636 apparently persuaded Taiwan's political elite that the *Liumang* Act was proving to be more trouble than it was worth. After President Ma Ying-jeou took office in May 2008, the Executive Yuan recommended its abolition. In January 2009, the legislature took the unexpected, dramatic step of repealing the *Liumang* Act in its entirety.

We were thrilled by this action. Our major goal in undertaking this study was to investigate the extent to which detailed implementation of the *Liumang* Act was out of step with Taiwan's impressive reforms to other aspects of its criminal justice system. We also sought to assess concerns that repealing the *Liumang* Act would lead to a significant deterioration in social order. By early 2009, our research had confirmed the belief that repeal would be in the best interests of Taiwan. During the legislative debate preceding abolition, several legislators raised concerns over the possible impact on public safety if they repealed the *Liumang* Act, resulting in closure of the vocational training institutes and release of incarcerated *liumang* who did not have concurrent criminal sentences. In the more than four years that have elapsed since repeal of the Act, we have seen no sociological data that supports the view that abolition has threatened public safety.

Moreover, as predicted by many, the tremendous overlap between *liumang* and criminal cases provided assurance that people who are threats to society have not fallen through the cracks of the criminal justice system in the absence of the *Liumang* Act. Specialized laws, such as the Organized Crime Act and the Social Order Maintenance Law, also help fill any void created by repeal of the *Liumang* Act. If existing laws are deemed insufficient for the task, the legislature is fully capable of amending the Criminal Code or passing new, separate laws to rein in conduct that undermines social order. To date, the legislature has not felt compelled to do so. The key consideration is that suspects who would previously have been pursued as *liumang* are now being afforded the full protections of Taiwan's Criminal Procedure Code before possibly being locked away for years.

The decision to jettison the *Liumang* Act is also important for bringing Taiwan closer in line with international legal norms. Admittedly, Taiwan's engagement with the international human rights community and its ability to bind itself to international instruments are severely hampered by its unique, and precarious, status. Nevertheless, although Taiwan's political community is divided on many subjects, there is general recognition that its government should comply with relevant international rules regarding the administration of criminal justice.

Taiwan signed the International Covenant on Civil and Political Rights (ICCPR)[2] in 1967 while still holding a seat at the United Nations. (Taiwan was excluded from the United Nations in 1971 following a General Assembly resolution that recognized the PRC as the only legitimate representative of China.) Among other protections, the ICCPR requires that state parties afford people charged with crimes a "fair and public hearing by a competent, independent and impartial tribunal established by law" and that they be allowed to examine witnesses against them (Art. 14). A jurisdiction cannot skirt ICCPR protections by calling a proceeding that plainly results in restrictions of physical freedom "administrative" in nature, rather than "criminal." We believe that the harsh

---

[2] Adopted and open for signature, ratification, and accession by General Assembly resolution 2200A (XXI) of 16 December 1966, and entered into force on 23 March 1976.

character of the sanctions applied to *liumang* plainly placed them within the scope of Article 14 of the ICCPR. The *liumang* system's failure, even as amended, to allow meaningful examination of witnesses and other procedural protections plainly violated this provision.

Taiwan did not ratify the ICCPR prior to its exclusion from the United Nations.[3] It was only on 31 March 2009 that the legislature, shortly after repealing the *Liumang* Act, finally took the pragmatic route of incorporating the ICCPR into domestic law. Although the legislature adopted the ICCPR, Taiwan cannot deposit official ratification documents with the United Nations. Taiwan's status is a barrier to creating a formal, binding promise under international law, but it does not prevent the Legislative Yuan from effectuating the content and spirit of the ICCPR. President Ma declared the adoption of the ICCPR "a historic milestone in Taiwan's democratic development in regard to human rights protection."[4] We completely agree.

Importantly, Taiwan has not treated its adoption of the ICCPR as a mere symbolic milestone. Because Taiwan cannot participate in the formal review process for ICCPR parties, in 2013, Taiwan invited a group of independent experts from ten countries to review government-prepared reports on its implementation of the ICCPR. In their concluding observations, the experts stated that they were "deeply impressed by the dramatic progress that has been made since 1987, when Taiwan began to emerge from a long and dark period of martial law. Developments in recent years have greatly accelerated this progress towards a society

---

[3] Even in the absence of ratification, Article 18 of the Vienna Convention on the Law of Treaties provides that states that have signed but not yet ratified a treaty are obliged to refrain from acts that would defeat its object and purpose. Of course, Taiwan's lack of clear "state" status under international law throws a wrinkle into the mix.

[4] Ma Ying-jeou, The Taiwan Relations Act: Turning a New Chapter. Speech presented at the Center for Strategic and International Studies (22 April 2009); see also President Press Release, The President Signed the "International Covenant on Civil and Political Rights" and "International Covenant on Economic Social and Cultural Rights" instruments of ratification, 14 May 2009.

governed by human rights and the rule of law."[5] As with the repeal of the *Liumang* Act, Taiwan's embracing of the ICCPR is a long-overdue step towards protecting the rights of the accused, and would not have been persuasive had the *Liumang* Act not been repealed.

The repeal of the *Liumang* Act and adoption of the ICCPR are two concrete examples of the Taiwanese government's vocal commitment to "build a human rights state," as explained at length in the Executive Yuan's 2002 Human Rights Policy White Paper.[6] This White Paper was issued by the then-new administration of President Chen Shui-bian's Democratic Progressive Party (DPP), the first genuine opposition party to the Kuomintang (KMT) regime in Taiwan's ROC history. The White Paper cited "civil rights in the legal system" as an "important area" and reported that, "after experiencing the national judicial reform conference and vigorous monitoring by NGOs, there has been some progress, but there remain deep rooted problems with the judicial system that are well known by the people, and judicial reform still faces many challenges."

In October 2000, President Chen established a Presidential Advisory Group, with the Vice President as the chairperson, to advise him on human rights issues. The following year, the Chen administration established a Human Rights Protection and Promotion Committee. The 2002 White Paper, a product of their labors, firmly pronounced, "[I]t is the responsibility of a democratic, constitutional country to be fully aware of domestic human rights conditions, to identify problems, and to find solutions." Although the White Paper was written under President Chen, President Ma's KMT administration, prodded by opposition politicians and

---

[5] Review of the Initial Reports of the Government of Taiwan on the Implementation of the International Human Rights Covenants, Concluding Observations and Recommendations Adopted by the International Group of Independent Experts Taipei, 1 March 2013. The experts also reviewed implementation of the International Covenant on Economic, Social and Cultural Rights (ICESCR).

[6] Development and Evaluation Commission Research, Executive Yuan of the Republic of China, 2002 Human Rights Policy White Paper of the Republic of China (Taiwan): Human Rights Infrastructure-Building for a Human Rights State (2002).

public opinion, fortunately has continued to identify human rights problems and to attempt to find solutions. In Taiwan, human rights are an issue that is neither exclusively DPP nor KMT, despite continuing and fierce controversies over details, history, and implementation.

In 2009, all of Taiwan's imprisoned *liumang* who did not have concurrent criminal sentences were released. Yet the significance of the Act's repeal stretches far beyond its immediate, obvious impact on this small group of people. It is a victory for legal reform in Taiwan. The path toward abolition—albeit winding, long, and complex—is a glowing example of the judiciary, executive, and legislature carrying out their respective duties in a democratic, cooperative, and relatively transparent manner. This chapter discusses the concrete process by which judges, officials, and legislators—spurred by civic groups—brought about abolition of the *Liumang* Act. Crucial to this process were the series of judicial interpretations, the sustained efforts by law reform groups, and a gradual realization by the legislative and executive branches that the *Liumang* Act could no longer be justified as compatible with the values of post-martial-law Taiwan.

II. STRUCTURE OF CONSTITUTIONAL REVIEW

To understand the importance of the three relevant constitutional interpretations for the demise of the *Liumang* Act, it is first necessary to take a step back and to understand the structure of constitutional review in Taiwan.

The Constitutional Court is the final arbiter in questions that require interpretation of the ROC Constitution 憲法 (Cst.) and is further charged with unifying the interpretation of laws (Cst. Art. 78).[7] Unlike

---

[7] Although not of importance in the *liumang* context, the Constitutional Court also holds the power to dissolve political parties that are deemed in violation of the Constitution (Constitutional Interpretation Procedure Law Arts. 19–33).

ordinary judges in Taiwan, who have lifetime appointments subject to limited exceptions,[8] a Justice on the Court is limited to an eight-year term. The shift from lifetime to eight-year terms—and a reduction in the number of Justices from seventeen to fifteen—occurred in 2003.[9] In order to facilitate this transition and create a staggered appointment system, eight of the fifteen Justices were appointed to four-year terms in 2003, with the other seven serving eight-year terms. A Justice's term may not be renewed. Nevertheless, because of the newness of the eight-year term system, it remains to be seen whether the Additional Articles of the Constitution will be interpreted to allow a Justice to be reappointed a few years after stepping down from the bench. If a future president decides to nominate a person who has previously served as a Justice, it could result in a protracted battle because the nominee not only would need to pass through the mud-wrestling politics of the Legislative Yuan but also would need an interpretation from the Court holding that the Additional Articles of the Constitution allow for such a reappointment.

Justices are drawn from five categories: (1) Supreme Court judges; (2) members of the Legislative Yuan; (3) distinguished professors; (4) judges from international courts or other public or comparative law specialists; and (5) people who are highly reputed in the legal field and have political experience (Art. 4(1), Organic Law of the Judicial Yuan).[10] According to the Organic Law of the Judicial Yuan 司法院組織法 (Art. 4(2)), no more than one-third of the Justices shall qualify under any single one of these five categories. Yet an early study notes that the Constitutional

---

[8] Article 81 of the Constitution provides for lifetime tenure except if the judge has been found guilty of a criminal offense, subjected to disciplinary action, or declared to be under interdiction.

[9] Despite not taking effect until 2003, these changes were adopted in 2000 as part of revisions to the Additional Articles of the Constitution of the ROC 中華民國憲法增修條文 (Additional Articles) (Art. 5). The Additional Articles were last amended in 2005.

[10] These general categories only set forth the minimal qualifications. For example, not every Supreme Court judge is qualified to serve on the Constitutional Court: the judge must have served on the Supreme Court for more than ten years and have a distinguished record during that time of service.

Court is dominated by academics and career judges.[11] As of 2005, the Court was composed of seven Justices from the judiciary, seven from academia, and one from government (Huang 2005, 8). Notably, twelve of these Justices were educated abroad as well as at home.[12] It is unclear how the Taiwanese government reconciled this composition with the statutory one-third rule. Roughly half of the Justices' terms expired at the end of 2007. By March 2008, there were only eleven sitting Justices; the four vacancies resulted from a failure of the KMT-controlled Legislative Yuan to approve the nominees of then President Chen. These vacancies were filled after Ma Ying-jeou assumed office and, by May 2009, the Court was back up to its full bench of fifteen and remained at fifteen as of July 2013.

Petitions for constitutional interpretations reach the Court through several channels, many of the details of which are set forth in the Constitutional Interpretation Procedure Law 司法院大法官審理案件法 (CIPL)[13] and its Implementing Rules 司法院大法官審理案件法施行細則 (Art. 5). Central and local government agencies may file a request when they are uncertain about how the Constitution pertains to the exercise of their powers or when they are uncertain about the constitutionality of a particular law or order that affects their work. For example, government agencies may apply when there is a dispute among them about the meaning of the Constitution. Natural persons, legal persons, and political parties may also apply for constitutional interpretations when they believe that their constitutional rights have been infringed. In this case, there is a requirement that all other judicial remedies be exhausted before the request is filed, and the request must be directed at the constitutionality of the law or order that

---

[11] Huang 2005, 8 ("Despite the guidelines for selecting Justices, the statistics show that the Constitutional Court has been dominated by academics and professional judicial careerists.").

[12] Huang 2005, 8 (explaining that statistics "show that Justices have overwhelmingly been educated abroad, particularly in Germany, Austria, and the United States").

[13] This law is more directly translated as "Law Governing the Hearing of Cases by the Grand Justices, Judicial Yuan," but we use the generally accepted translation in this study.

was applied by the court of last resort. When reviewing petitions filed by natural or legal persons, the Constitutional Court does not decide individual cases as does the US Supreme Court. Rather, it examines the constitutionality of a law or order divorced from the concrete case that gave rise to the request for an interpretation. For example, in Interpretation No. 636, there is no mention of the particular facts of the *liumang* cases that prompted the petitions.

Members of the Legislative Yuan may also request an interpretation when they are uncertain either as to the application of the Constitution itself or the constitutionality of a particular law. In this situation, at least one-third of the members of the Legislative Yuan must agree to the petition's filing.

Finally, with respect to judges, in 1995 the Constitutional Court held in Interpretation No. 371[14] that a judge may suspend proceedings *sua sponte* (i.e., by the judge's own volition) and apply for a constitutional interpretation when the judge believes that a statute or regulation that is before the court is unconstitutional. Indeed, the first time a judge used this procedure was to question the constitutionality of the *Liumang* Act, and this same procedure was used in the petitions that led to Interpretation No. 636. Interestingly, this judge-initiated procedure is the only means of filing a petition that is not provided for in the Constitutional Interpretation Procedure Law.

Turning to the substance of the petition, the Constitutional Interpretation Procedure Law provides that a petition must include the following components: (1) purpose of the petition; (2) issues and facts, and the related constitutional provisions; (3) grounds for the petition, position adopted by the petitioner, and arguments; and (4) list of exhibits attached (CIPL Art. 8). These general requirements are clarified on the

---

[14] Interpretation No. 371 was issued on 20 January 1995. The Constitutional Court's decision to allow judges in all lower courts to adjourn proceedings and refer constitutional questions to the court was significant in that it indirectly broadened citizens' access to obtain constitutional interpretations early in the litigation process.

Judicial Yuan's website, along with clerical issues such as the size of paper that petitioners must use.

The first step when the petition comes in the door is for a panel of three Justices to review it, determine whether the petition meets the above procedural requirements, and, if the requirements are met, pass it along to the full Constitutional Court for further discussion (CIPL Art. 10).[15] If the petition is denied by the full Court after review by the three-Justice group, the Court will issue a "decision not to accept the petition" 不受理決議. Neither the Constitution nor the Constitutional Interpretation Procedure Law expressly authorizes the Constitutional Court to pick and choose cases based on their perceived importance. In practice, we were told that the Court sometimes rejects petitions if the Justices think that they have no constitutional importance. To avoid criticism, the Court might not clearly state the reason for rejection and instead note that the petition fails to state which provisions of the law in question violate specific constitutional articles or that the petition simply does not raise constitutional issues. The Court may also delay acceptance for long periods, as was seen in the case of the petitions addressed in Interpretation No. 636.

Constitutional Court decisions, which are consecutively numbered, are made publicly available and are conveniently posted on the Judicial Yuan's website. For example, in Decision No. 1269, issued on 30 July 2005, the Court announced its decision to reject 37 petitions, one of which addressed the *Liumang* Act. In a few paragraphs, the Decision describes that petition and the reasons why the Court rejected it. The petitioner had been committed to reformatory training by the public security tribunal of the Taipei District Court, and the public security tribunal of the Taiwan High Court had rejected his appeal.

---

[15] From conversations with people familiar with the workings of the Constitutional Court, we were told that the fifteen Justices are divided into five subgroups, and petitions are assigned by rotation.

The Constitutional Court denied his challenge to the constitutionality of several provisions in the *Liumang* Act and its Implementing Rules 檢肅流氓條例施行細則 (IR) because the petition failed to meet the requirements of the Constitutional Interpretation Procedure Law, namely, the public security tribunal did not rely upon the challenged provisions in the *Liumang* Act when making its decision (CIPL Art. 5(1)). Albeit cold comfort for the petitioner, the decision was at least helpful to future petitioners in that it provided guidance regarding arguments that the Court found inadequate.

The rejected petitioner in the above example is far from being in the minority. The Court accepts only a tiny percentage of petitions for constitutional interpretations. As reported in an introductory brochure issued by the Court, from 1 July 1948, to 30 September 2003, the Court received 7,640 petitions and issued only 566 interpretations. Among the 7,640 petitions filed, 815 (10.67 percent) were filed by governmental agencies, whereas 6,825 were filed by individuals (89.33 percent). The pattern of only accepting a small number of cases has continued in recent years. Since 1998, the number of interpretations announced in any one year has ranged from a high of 28 in 1998 to a low of 13 in 2007. According to the Judicial Yearbook, in 2007, the Court dismissed 348 cases and issued interpretations in only 13, with 176 cases listed as pending (Judicial Yuan 2007, table 2). In 2009, the Court dismissed 412 cases and issued interpretations in only 16, with 246 cases listed as pending (Judicial Yuan 2009, table 3).

If a petition is among the rare few that are accepted, the Justices will proceed to analyze the merits and select a Justice to draft an opinion, which the designated Justice will circulate among all the Justices for discussion prior to voting (CIPL Art. 11). Standard practice is for Justices to meet three times per week, with extra sessions held "when necessary" (CIPL Art. 15). Oral arguments giving petitioners and others an opportunity to be heard in person are seldom convened, though the Court may call for them "when necessary" (CIPL Art. 13). There is no elaboration regarding what this vague "when necessary" provision actually means in practice. When one of the authors of this study visited the Constitutional Court's elegant courtroom, the judge showing it joked that this was probably one of the few times that the room's lights were turned on that year—an exaggeration, but there was more truth than jest in his observation. Our research team was pleasantly surprised when the Court convened a hearing to discuss the petitions that led to Interpretation No. 636 and called on one of our Taiwanese research colleagues to appear as an expert.

Once the draft opinion is ready for a vote, to adopt an interpretation regarding the constitutionality of a statute, two-thirds of the Justices must be present to constitute a quorum, and the agreement of two-thirds of those Justices present is required. The two-thirds quorum requirement is the same for an interpretation when a government order is at issue, but the agreement of only a majority of those Justices present is required (CIPL Art. 14). The author of the majority opinion is not disclosed, though Justices may issue individual concurring and dissenting opinions, which can be quite colorful and impassioned. The majority opinion itself is composed of the "holding" of the interpretation and a separate "reasoning" section that, true to its name, details the bases for the Constitutional Court's holding (CIPL Art. 17(1)).

The Constitutional Interpretation Procedure Law provides that the interpretation may instruct relevant agencies of the need to execute the interpretation and, further, determine the types and means of execution so required (CIPL Art. 17(2)). This general provision is the basis for the Constitutional Court's power to go beyond a mere declaration that a law is unconstitutional and actually order other government bodies to take action. As an alternative to telling other government bodies the means by which the interpretation shall be executed, the Court may simply declare a law, regulation, or order null and void and leave the other bodies to decide what action to take. A modified approach sometimes preferred by the Court is to declare that the law, regulation, or order will become null and void after a specified period. For example, in Interpretation No. 384, issued on 28 July 1995, the Constitutional Court held that five articles of the *Liumang* Act were unconstitutional and declared that the articles would become null and void on 31 December 1996, well over a year after the Interpretation issued. This goaded the Legislative Yuan into action, albeit not sufficient action to cure the problem. The revisions to the offending articles did not fully remedy concerns about the *Liumang* Act's constitutionality. Interpretation No. 523 thus followed in 2001, which necessitated further legislative action. The Court once again used this power in Interpretation No. 636 by giving the Legislative Yuan one year to revise unconstitutional provisions.

III. CONSTITUTIONAL CHALLENGES TO THE *LIUMANG* ACT

As previously noted, the Constitutional Court addressed the *Liumang* Act in three interpretations, all of which commanded legislative action to fix constitutional infirmities. Critics of the *Liumang* Act challenged its constitutionality on a number of different grounds, showing how the broad language in the Constitution can be used to attack concrete provisions in a law. Here we briefly review the first two interpretations and then turn to the last constitutional challenge in more detail.

The Constitutional Court first addressed the *Liumang* Act in 1995. In Interpretation No. 384, the Court declared that five articles of the *Liumang* Act were unconstitutional. First and foremost, the Court held that Articles 6 and 7, which empowered the police to force people to appear without any judicial approval, violated the right to physical freedom of the person 人身自由, as provided in Article 8 of the Constitution. Article 8 requires that, except in the case where a person is discovered while committing a crime or immediately thereafter (i.e., in *flagrante delicto*), no person shall be arrested or detained other than by judicial or police agencies in accordance with "procedures prescribed by law." The Court further emphasized that any law used to deprive people of their physical freedom must be proper in substance "其內容更須實質正當" and comply with Article 23 of the Constitution, which provides that freedoms and rights enumerated in the Constitution shall not be restricted by law except as may be necessary to prevent infringement upon the freedoms of other persons, to avert an imminent crisis, to maintain social order, or to advance public welfare. After stating these constitutional bases, the Court held Articles 6 and 7 of the *Liumang* Act unconstitutional because, as then written, they authorized the police to force people to appear before them without following any judicial procedures. In accordance with this Interpretation, the legislature revised the articles that addressed the police's authority to force suspected *liumang* to appear for questioning. The revised articles required that police first obtain judicial approval or, when exigent circumstances required immediate action, that there be prompt judicial review after the fact.

Second, the Constitutional Court held in Interpretation No. 384 that the secret witness system as then set forth in Article 12 of the *Liumang* Act deprived the accused of the right to defend oneself and hampered the truth-finding function of the court. As discussed in Chapter 3, however, the resulting revisions that allow for secrecy only "when necessary" did little in reality to increase the transparency of the witness system.

Third, the Court struck down the practice of requiring people to serve time in prison followed by time in reformatory training, or vice versa, for the same act. The Justices began by noting that, as then written, Article 21 of the *Liumang* Act allowed the imposition of reformatory training after execution of a criminal punishment for the same act, without regard to whether there was a special preventive necessity to do so. This practice, the Justices explained, could result in the loss of bodily freedom 身體自由. The legislature revised Article 21 to provide that, if the *liumang* behavior for which the accused was committed to reformatory training was also the basis for criminal punishment, time spent serving the criminal punishment and time spent in reformatory training would be mutually set-off 相互折抵 on a one-day-for-one-day basis.

Finally, the legislature expanded the relief channels available to *liumang* in response to the Court's holding that Article 5 failed to protect the constitutional right to lodge administrative appeals and institute administrative litigation (Cst. Art. 16).

Interpretation No. 523, issued in 2001, precipitated more modest reforms than its predecessor. This time, the Justices held that the procedures used for confining suspected *liumang* under Article 11 of the *Liumang* Act violated Articles 8 and 23 of the Constitution: "This confinement . . . is a serious restraint on people's physical freedom. Nevertheless, the Act does not explicitly provide the conditions upon which a court may base its imposition of confinement. . . . The Act grants the court discretion to decide the accused's confinement without regard for whether he is continuing to seriously breach social order, or if he will obstruct the court's hearing of the case by fleeing, destroying evidence, or threatening informants, victims, or witnesses." The Constitutional Court held that the offending provisions would become null and void one year from the date of the Interpretation. Within that year, in 2002, the legislature revised Article 11 by including specific criteria for determining whether confinement was required and by adding two new articles (Arts. 11-1 and 11-2) that detailed procedures for canceling 撤銷, stopping 停止, and repeating 再予留置 confinement.

Several years passed with no action from the Constitutional Court, despite reported calls for further judicial review.[16] Then, on 28 January 2005, Judge Guo Shu-hao, a public security tribunal judge from Taichung District Court, applied for an interpretation (the "Taichung Petition"). Judge Guo suspended proceedings in a *liumang* case pending before him because of doubts about the constitutionality of the *Liumang* Act. In December 2005, a similar petition was submitted by a second public

---

[16] As noted in Chapter 2, the influential Judicial Reform Foundation 民間司法改革基金會 formed a group to study the *Liumang* Act. The group suspended its efforts, however, after its petitions failed. Further Constitutional Court petitions supported by the group and other efforts to repeal the *Liumang* Act were similarly unsuccessful.

security tribunal judge, Judge Qian Jian-rong of Taoyuan District Court (the "Taoyuan Petition"). Nearly two years of silence followed. Eventually, in the autumn of 2007, the Constitutional Court convened a hearing to address the issues raised in these two petitions. Interpretation No. 636 followed on 1 February 2008.

In the Taichung Petition, Judge Guo presented a targeted challenge to the definition of "*liumang*," arguing that several of the enumerated categories of *liumang* behavior violated the constitutional principle of legal clarity 法律明確性原則. Although Judge Qian also raised this argument, he mounted a more sweeping attack on the *Liumang* Act, ranging from the constitutionality of the secret witness system to the practice of imposing both reformatory training and criminal punishments for the same act. The main constitutional arguments raised in the petitions are discussed below, along with the Court's responses thereto.

A. Definition of "*Liumang*" and the Principle of Legal Clarity

The two petitions vigorously challenged the constitutionality of the statutory definition of "*liumang*." In the Taichung Petition (the narrower of the two), Judge Guo focused on two categories in the definition and argued that the descriptions therein violated the constitutional principle of legal clarity. Sections 3 and 5 of Article 2, as then written, listed the following types of *liumang* behavior:

> 3) People who occupy territory; commit blackmail and extortion; force business transactions; eat and drink without paying; coerce and cause trouble; tyrannize good and honest people; or manipulate matters behind the scenes to accomplish the foregoing.
>
> . . .
>
> 5) People who are habitually morally corrupt or who habitually wander and act like rascals and the facts are sufficient to believe that they have undermined social order or endangered the life, body, freedom, or property of others.

Judge Guo honed in on the following four types of behavior, though his petition indicated that other parts of the definition possibly also failed to pass constitutional muster: coercing and causing trouble 要挾滋事; tyrannizing good and honest people 欺壓善良; being morally corrupt 品行惡劣; and wandering and acting like rascals 遊蕩無賴. According to Judge Guo, it violated the right to physical freedom, as provided for in Article 8 of the Constitution, to incarcerate people based on these descriptions.[17] Quoting the Constitutional Court's holding in Interpretation No. 384, Judge Guo contended that these sections failed to satisfy the requirement that any law used to deprive people of their physical freedom must be proper in substance. Moreover, he asserted that the provisions failed to comply with Article 23 of the Constitution, which provides that freedoms and rights enumerated in the Constitution shall not be restricted by law except as may be necessary to prevent infringement upon the freedoms of other persons, to avert an imminent crisis, to maintain social order, or to advance public welfare.

Judge Guo explained that one aspect of laws being proper in substance is the principle of *nulla poena sine lege*, i.e., the principle that there be no punishment without a law authorizing it 罪刑法定主義. This requirement is a basic component of what is broadly known as the principle of legality—the foundational principle that laws be clear and ascertainable. In the criminal context, this requires that people be able to determine what acts are being criminalized.[18] Otherwise, the law does

---

[17] As previously discussed, Article 8 of the Constitution provides, in part, that "physical freedom shall be guaranteed to the people. In no case except that of *flagrante delicto*, which shall be separately prescribed by law, shall any person be arrested or detained other than by a judicial or police organ in accordance with procedures prescribed by law."

[18] As described by one American scholar (Decker 2002, 244–245):

The most fundamental tenet of criminal law is the principle of legality, which today means that criminal liability and punishment can only be predicated on a prior legislative enactment that states what is proscribed as an offense in a precise and clear manner. This is a concept that is reliant on various doctrines, most significantly the "void for vagueness" doctrine and the doctrine of "strict construction."

not serve as an effective guide and people are left without understandable rules to which they can conform. The Constitutional Court explicitly addressed the principle of legality in Interpretation No. 384, in which it wrote that "substantive due process of law covers both substantive law and procedural law and, for substantive law, it must comply with the principle of *nulla poena sine lege*." Likewise, as part of the Taoyuan Petition's more broad-based attack on the *Liumang* Act, Judge Qian contended that the definition of *liumang* violated "the principle of *nulla poena sine lege*" 罪刑法定主義 and "the principle of clarity of crimes and punishments" 罪刑明確性原則.[19]

Although not apparent in the text of the *Liumang* Act, the principle of legal clarity—specifically *nulla poena sine lege*—is explicitly provided for in the Criminal Code. Article 1 provides that, to be punishable, behavior must be clearly stipulated as punishable by law at the time of the act. This provision, however, is of no concrete guidance in the *liumang* context because the Criminal Code is freestanding. A challenge to the

---

[19] Judge Qian wrote that "the principle of clarity of crimes and punishments" is an important component of *nulla poena sine lege* 罪刑法定原則重要的內涵之一就是罪刑明確原則. Exact phrasing aside, this is a "void for vagueness" argument. In the same section of his petition, Judge Qian further raised the principle of equality 平等原則, namely that people should be treated equally under the law and they should not be subject to unreasonable disparities in treatment 均應平等對待, 不得有不合理的差別待遇. Yet, the fact that there was great disparity in the application of the *Liumang* Act appears to be more a result of the vagueness problem than a separate ground on which to challenge the Act. Judge Qian introduced various aspects of inequality that were raised by the *Liumang* Act's application. First, for people who committed a criminal act and who were also determined to be *liumang*—as compared with pure criminal defendants (i.e., those not simultaneously targeted as *liumang*)—there was an unreasonable disparity in treatment. Second, within the realm of *liumang*, various categories of people (i.e., as described by Judge Qian, warned *liumang*, serious *liumang*, recidivist *liumang* after a warning, recidivist *liumang* after reformatory training, and serious *liumang* who are caught in the act) received significantly different treatment, and it was difficult to articulate the criteria for making the distinctions (Qian 2005, 11). That similarly, or in some cases identically, situated people were in jeopardy of being subject to unequal treatment was vividly demonstrated by the case discussed in Chapter 2 in which a district-court public security tribunal judge ruled that two people who bird-napped pigeons were not serious *liumang*. On appeal, one panel took the position that the accused was a serious *liumang*, and the other ruled that the behavior did not have the requisite characteristic of being an offensive violation. The exact same factual scenario thus led to two contrasting outcomes.

liumang definition thus had to be rooted directly in the text of the Constitution. The problem is that it is less than clear as to how "clear" a law must be to satisfy constitutional concerns. The very contours of the principle of legal clarity are hard to pin down.

To give shape to this abstract principle, Professor Jaw-perng Wang of National Taiwan University School of Law advocated looking outside Taiwan. In commentary on the constitutionality of the *Liumang* Act that Professor Wang gave at an academic conference and later submitted to the Constitutional Court,[20] he explained that the principle of clarity for criminal laws 刑法明確原則 is equivalent to the American constitutional principle of "void for vagueness" (Wang 2006, 9; Wang 2008, 121). Professor Wang cited the writings of an American legal scholar, John Calvin Jeffries, Jr., in explaining the principle's theoretical underpinnings (Jeffries, Jr. 1985, 189). Jeffries draws upon three intertwined doctrines: first, the principle of legality, which "stands for the desirability in principle of advance legislative specification of criminal misconduct" (Jeffries 1985, 190). Simply put, the principle condemns judicial crime creation (Jeffries 1985, 189). Second, Jeffries addresses the vagueness doctrine, which he describes as "the operational arm of legality": "It requires that advance, ordinarily legislative crime definition be meaningfully precise—or at least that it not be meaninglessly indefinite" (Jeffries 1985, 196) (internal citations omitted). The third doctrine, the rule of strict construction, provides that criminal statutes be strictly construed against the state.[21] Jeffries describes this rule as "[t]he second doctrine said to implement the ideal of legality" (Jeffries 1985, 198). Professor Wang centered his argument on the vagueness doctrine, as did Judges Guo and

---

[20] The commentary was presented at the conference "Taiwan's System for Dealing with *Liumang*: Constitutionality, Criminal Justice, and Broader Implications," which was held at National Taiwan University School of Law on 14 December 2006. It was later published in 2008. In November 2007, Professor Wang was asked by the Constitutional Court to present his views on whether the *Liumang* Act was constitutional.

[21] This rule that ambiguity in a criminal law be resolved against the government and to the advantage of the accused is also known as the "rule of lenity."

Qian. In view of the extremely mushy wording of the contested provisions in the *liumang* definition, it is hard to see how the rule of strict construction would be of any help. The definition reaches far beyond ambiguous to be hopelessly vague.[22] How can one strictly construe the phrase "wandering and acting like rascals"?[23]

In his commentary, Professor Wang explored three reasons raised by Jeffries as to why an unclear provision in the criminal law should be void for vagueness (Wang 2006, 11). First, a vague provision violates the separation of powers principle. In those circumstances, the legislature has essentially abandoned its responsibility to define crimes, leaving the courts to take the legislature's rightful place (Jeffries 1985, 202). In *liumang* cases, the courts were left to flesh out abstract phrases, such as "habitually morally corrupt," with no legislative guidance. The overarching legislative requirement that the conduct in question be "sufficient to have undermined social order" raised similar concerns because it forced judges into the shoes of legislators. The Implementing Rule's further paltry guidance that conduct be "unspecific," an "offensive violation," and "habitual" was of little, if any, help (IR Art. 4).

Second, a vague provision violates the doctrine of notice because the government fails to give people fair notice of what constitutes criminal behavior. As explained by the United States Supreme Court, "[A] statute

---

[22] In his article "Addressing Vagueness, Ambiguity, and Other Uncertainty in American Criminal Laws," John F. Decker, explains: "A relative of vagueness, ambiguity appears where otherwise understandable legislation lends itself to two or more equally plausible interpretations." Despite being two distinct concepts, it is not always clear when legislation tips from being ambiguous to vague, or vice versa: "[A]t what point is it permissible to conclude the legislation contains sufficient specificity that it can be described as ambiguous rather than vague?" (Decker 2002: 243).

[23] Neither Judges Qian nor Guo pursued what would be called an "overbreadth argument" in American jurisprudence. As John F. Decker explains, "If a party challenges an enactment based on the assertion that one cannot determine whether the regulation intrudes upon otherwise 'innocent terrain' then the complaint is one of vagueness. On the other hand, if a challenge is based on an objection that the regulation does, in fact, intrude into territory where it does not belong, then the claim is one of overbreadth" (Decker 2002, 266) (internal citations omitted). For example, neither judge contended that the *Liumang* Act could be used against people who were staging peaceful demonstrations outside Taiwan's Presidential Palace, a not infrequent occurrence.

which either forbids or requires the doing of an act in terms so vague that men of common intelligence must necessarily guess at its meaning and differ as to its application, violates the first essential of due process of law."[24] Did the *Liumang* Act give fair warning as to when a person's behavior crossed the line between being merely unsociable and rude and instead being downright unlawful? Could a person of common intelligence determine at what point he transformed himself from a contemptible but legal louse to a *liumang*?

In the Taichung Petition, Judge Guo asserted that people were unable to predict when the *Liumang* Act would apply to their conduct because of the lack of clarity in the definition of *liumang*. Judge Guo pointed out that, not only were the aforementioned types of *liumang* behavior unclear, but also there were no supplemental criteria that made them more concrete. While acknowledging that absolute clarity is impossible, Judge Qian emphasized the need for people to be able to predict what conduct the law proscribes and, for this reason, he argued that the individual requirements of a crime's components must be concretely described. Like Judge Guo, he attacked the definition of "*liumang*" because it failed to provide the necessary guidance for people to understand what exactly was proscribed. As discussed at length in Chapter 2, the Implementing Rules' listing of three characteristics of behavior "sufficient to have undermined social order" was stunningly unhelpful in providing concrete guidance both to individuals who might be deemed *liumang* and, as explained further in the following paragraph, to judges who needed to interpret the law. Indeed, both petitions were written by public security tribunal judges whose jobs were to apply the abstract criteria to specific cases on a daily basis. No one was better suited to give a candid appraisal of how the *liumang* criteria worked in practice, or did not work, as the case appeared to be.

Third, unclear criminal laws are unable to control the indiscriminate exercise of power by the authorities because there is no ascertainable

---

[24] Connally v. General Construction Co., 269 US 385, 391 (1926).

standard of guilt. In other words, there is a threat of arbitrary and discriminatory enforcement because people enforcing the law can essentially base decisions on personal likes and dislikes (Jeffries 1985, 212). Of course, a modicum of discretion is unavoidable, and often desirable, in any criminal justice system. The question is when discretion tips from being a positive force into one that creates an enforcement free-for-all. Professor Wang contended that this third rationale was the strongest basis for the Constitutional Court to hold that certain provisions in the *liumang* definition were unconstitutionally vague (Wang 2006, 12). In particular, he argued that the following proscribed behaviors listed in Article 2(3) and (5) were unconstitutional because people enforcing the law ended up doing so in an arbitrary and discriminatory manner: occupying territory 霸佔地盤; eating and drinking without paying 白吃白喝; tyrannizing good and honest people 欺壓善良; being morally corrupt 品行惡劣; and wandering and acting like rascals 遊蕩無賴 (Wang 2006, 12). Furthermore, as Judge Qian pointed out, in addition to problems with the inherent lack of clarity in the criteria upon which police identified warned *liumang* and serious *liumang* (Wang 2006, 13), there was also the concern that police in different areas of Taiwan took divergent views regarding what qualified as "serious" behavior, as compared with behavior that only warranted "warned" *liumang* status (Wang 2006, 11). Because the less you see something the stranger it is, police in areas with fewer *liumang* were said to be more likely to pursue someone as a serious *liumang* than in areas where *liumang* were more prevalent.

To illustrate this point, we should recall the heuristic example of Chen in Chapter 3. The review committee determined that Chen was a *liumang* on the basis that he was "eating and drinking without paying." At least in Chen's case, "eating and drinking without paying" fairly clearly described his behavior: Chen ate and drank, refused to pay, and even threatened the bar owner who requested payment. What if Chen had paid his bills and never threatened the bar owner directly but the rest of his behavior remained the same? Chen was unemployed and spending his days loafing around in bars, frequenting gambling dens, and behaving aggressively toward people. Was his behavior "morally corrupt," or merely "morally astray" without rising to the level of being *liumang* behavior? Could the review committee have found that he was coercing and causing trouble; tyrannizing good and honest people; being morally corrupt; or wandering and acting like a rascal? The police and judges were left to make this judgment with extremely limited guidance. It is this specter of arbitrary and discriminatory enforcement that had Professor Wang and Judges Guo and Qian concerned.

This argument regarding the lack of legal clarity in the definition of *liumang* partly won over the Constitutional Court. In Interpretation No. 636, the Justices parsed the definition of *liumang* and declared the following two clauses unconstitutional because they violated the principle of legal clarity: the act of "tyrannizing good and honest people" (Art. 2(3)) and "people who are habitually morally corrupt or who habitually wander and act like rascals" (Art. 2(5)). The Court further held that the acts of "occupying territory," "eating and drinking without paying," and "coercing and causing trouble" were constitutional but problematic, and the Court thus called on relevant authorities to evaluate the possibility of concretely describing these acts. The Justices addressed several other aspects of the definition and found no constitutional problems.[25] The Court's decision to pluck out discrete offending provisions and leave the definition of *liumang* largely unchanged was

---

[25] Interpretation No. 636 (holding, para.1):

The provision of Article 2, Section 3, of the [*Liumang* Act] regarding the acts of "committing blackmail and extortion, forcing business transactions, and manipulating matters behind the scenes to accomplish the foregoing"; the provision of Section 4 of the same Article regarding the acts of "managing or controlling professional gambling establishments, establishing brothels without authorization, inducing or forcing decent women to work as prostitutes, working as bodyguards for gambling establishments or brothels, or relying on superior force to demand debt repayment"; and the provision of Article 6, Paragraph 1, regarding "serious circumstances" do not violate the principle of legal clarity.

consistent with its prior measured approach when reviewing the constitutionality of the *Liumang* Act.

An attack on the substantive definition of "*liumang*" was but one of several challenges to the *Liumang* Act. The following sections address criticisms that were aimed at various procedural aspects of the Act. When analyzing the various challenges, it is important to bear in mind the fundamental bifurcated scheme that distinguished warned *liumang* from serious *liumang*. Chapter 3 illustrated the vast disparity in procedures and sanctions applied to warned *liumang* and serious *liumang*. The comparatively severe ramifications of being classified as a serious *liumang* were underscored by Judges Guo's and Qian's challenges to the *Liumang* Act, which overwhelmingly focused on serious *liumang*.

B. Power of the Police to Force Suspected *Liumang* to Appear

In the Taoyuan Petition, Judge Qian looked again to Article 8 of the Constitution, this time to challenge the police's ability to force people to appear, as provided for in Articles 6, 7, 9, 10, and 11 of the *Liumang* Act. Prior to Interpretation No. 384, Article 6 of the *Liumang* Act provided that, if a person was found to be a *liumang* and the circumstances were serious, the police had the power to summon the person without prior warning and, if the summoned person did not comply, to force him to appear at the police station. Article 7 similarly provided that, if a person reengaged in *liumang* behavior within a year after a determination that he was a *liumang*, the police had the power to summon him; and, if the summoned person did not comply, the police could force him to appear at the station. For people caught while engaging in *liumang* behavior, the police could take them directly into custody without any prior summons. In Interpretation No. 384, the Constitutional Court concluded that the *Liumang* Act's failure to differentiate between people caught in the act and people apprehended at a later time violated Article 8 of the Constitution, which clearly distinguishes between the two situations and prescribes different procedures. As a result of this Interpretation, the legislature revised the *Liumang* Act to require that police first obtain judicial approval or, when exigent circumstances required immediate action, that there be prompt judicial review after the fact. Judge Qian contended that these revisions did not go far enough.

Judge Qian argued that the procedures and criteria in the *Liumang* Act were constitutionally lacking when viewed against the procedures for arrests under exigent circumstances in the Criminal Procedure Code. For example, he pointed to the comparatively "strict reasons and requirements" for emergency arrests 緊急拘捕 in Article 88-1 of the Criminal Procedure Code,[26] which in part permits emergency arrests when the person is a potential flight risk, provided that the alleged offense is punishable with the death penalty, life imprisonment, or a minimum prison sentence of not less than five years (Qian 2005, 15). Here, "emergency arrest" means an arrest made by the police unilaterally under exigent circumstances. The *Liumang* Act did not have an equivalent restriction and, indeed, the punishment for *liumang* could never reach five years because reformatory training was statutorily capped at three.

Judge Qian further pointed to the differences between the procedures for arresting a person caught in the act of committing *liumang* behavior 實施中 and a person caught in the act of committing a crime 現行犯 (LMA Art. 10; CPC Art. 92). Under the Criminal Procedure Code, an emergency arrest is subject to immediate review by a prosecutor (Art. 92). The *Liumang* Act, in contrast, skipped prosecutorial review and the

---

[26] Although Judge Qian used the term "emergency arrest" 緊急拘捕 in the Taoyuan Petition, Article 88-1 uses slightly different terminology, namely "discretionary arrest" 逕行拘提. In general, the Criminal Procedure Code uses different terms for arrest with a warrant 拘提 and without a warrant 逮捕. In practice, "arrest without a warrant" means arrest under exigent circumstance, such as when a person is caught in the act. Neither a "discretionary arrest" nor an "arrest without a warrant" requires a warrant at the time that the person is physically taken into custody. They are different, however, in that after a "discretionary arrest," the police must obtain a warrant (issued by a prosecutor, not a judge) or the arrestee must be released. In contrast, after a straightforward "arrest without a warrant," the police need not obtain a warrant and may simply send the arrestee to the prosecutor.

case proceeded to the court directly, which Judge Qian argued was insufficient as compared with the advanced review provided to criminal suspects. These and other examples raised by Judge Qian highlight aspects where the Criminal Procedure Code provides different, and convincingly more stringent, limitations on the police's ability to arrest suspects. In Interpretation No. 636, the Constitutional Court agreed, to a certain extent, that the *Liumang* Act's procedural requirements were not only less stringent, but also unconstitutional.

The Court began the reasoning section of Interpretation No. 636 by emphasizing the fundamental right to physical freedom that is contained in Article 8 of the Constitution. The Court went on to quote Article 6 of the *Liumang* Act regarding arrests without warrants, but did so to announce only that the phrase "circumstances are serious" did not contradict the principle of legal clarity.[27] Interpretation No. 636 failed to address squarely the issue of arrests under exigent circumstances. That being said, the Court did declare that procedures for transferring an accused *liumang* to court against his will were unconstitutional (LMA Art. 9).[28] The Court added that procedures for requiring warned *liumang* to appear if they committed another *liumang* act should be interpreted in the same manner (LMA Art. 7). The Constitutional Court declined to vindicate other

---

[27] Interpretation No. 636 (reasoning, para. 6):

When a person is determined to be a *[liumang]* and the circumstances are serious, the police precinct of the directly governed municipality or police department of the county (city), with the consent of the directly supervising police authorities, may summon the person to appear for questioning without prior warning. If the summoned person does not appear after receiving lawful notice and does not have proper grounds for failing to appear, then the police may apply to the court for an arrest warrant. However, if the facts are sufficient to believe that the person is a flight risk and there are exigent circumstances, then the police may arrest him without a warrant. . . . So-called "serious circumstances" shall be determined according to the common societal conception of this provision and shall take into consideration the means used to carry out the act, the number of victims, the degree of harm, and the degree to which social order was undermined when examining the totality of the circumstances to determine whether the circumstances are serious. This provision does not contradict the principle of legal clarity.

[28] Interpretation No. 636 (reasoning, para. 9): "If a person voluntarily appears before and is questioned by the police but does not wish to be transferred to the court, the police may not compel him to be transferred to the court. Doing otherwise would violate due process of law."

challenges to Articles 9, 10, and 11 on procedural as well as substantive grounds.[29]

Formal constitutional arguments aside, we see no compelling reason why the procedures for summons and transfers in *liumang* cases should have been different from, and indeed less protective than, those in criminal cases. Nor could we find any persuasive, or even cogent, evidence that *liumang* suspects were inherently more dangerous or flight-prone than criminal suspects. Moreover, in view of the huge overlap between criminal and *liumang* cases, it made practical sense to have consistent procedures: The police were likely to summon a suspect for both purposes. The legislature's decision to repeal the *Liumang* Act thus strikes us as infinitely reasonable from a procedural standpoint.

C. Right to be Heard by the Review Committee

A second procedural challenge addressed in Interpretation No. 636 was the right of accused *liumang* to be heard by the review committee, which held the power to declare a suspect to be a warned *liumang* or transfer the suspect to the court for a determination whether he was a serious *liumang*. At the time of Interpretation No. 636, accused *liumang* had no opportunity to participate in this determination process, with the first indication that they were even under suspicion usually coming in the form of official notice of the committee's decision.

---

[29] Interpretation No. 636 (reasoning, para. 15):

As for the petitioners' position that the constitutionality of the provisions of Article 2, Section 1, and Articles 10, 14, and 15 of the Act are in doubt, they are not the legal provisions that the judge in the case at hand shall apply. The constitutionality of these provisions does not influence the results of the court's ruling. In addition, the petitioners allege that the constitutionality of Article 2, Section 2; the proviso of Article 6, Paragraph 1; the proviso of Article 7, Paragraph 1; and Articles 9, 11, 22, and 23 are in doubt, and further question the constitutionality of the Act as a whole. The grounds raised by the petitioners in support of the unconstitutionality of the foregoing provisions are insufficient to constitute concrete reasons for an objective belief that the statute is unconstitutional. These two parts of the petition do not meet the requirements set forth in this Constitutional Court's Interpretations Nos. 371 and 572 and are therefore dismissed.

For the first time, in Interpretation No. 636, the Constitutional Court declared that an accused *liumang* was entitled to a voice before the review committee. The Court noted that the diverse membership of the review committee—including police, prosecutors, legal specialists, and impartial people from society—was conducive to promoting objective decision-making. Nonetheless, in order to comply with the constitutional guarantee of due process of law, the accused must have the right to be heard during the proceedings, in addition to the right to obtain relief after receiving an unfavorable decision (Interpretation No. 636, reasoning, para. 8). This newly articulated right was never implemented because of the decision to repeal the *Liumang* Act, but we nonetheless applaud this belated recognition that accused *liumang* should have been allowed some form of earlier participation in the committee's proceedings.

D. Serious *Liumang*: Procedures at the District Court Level

Challenges to procedural aspects of the *Liumang* Act were not limited to the stages when the case was in the hands of the police. Judge Qian and other critics raised weighty concerns regarding the constitutionality of procedures used once cases reached the district courts for handling by public security tribunals. Concerns were focused on the use of a secret witness system, the lack of prosecutorial involvement, and the denial of a public hearing.

1. The Secret Witness System and the Right to Confront and Examine Witnesses

The Constitutional Court dealt an initial blow to the secret witness system in Interpretation No. 384, in which it held that the unfettered use of secret witnesses, as then allowed by Article 12 of the *Liumang* Act, deprived the accused of the right to defend himself and hampered the truth-finding function of the court. As discussed in Chapter 3, however, the resulting revisions that allowed for secrecy only "when necessary" did little to increase the transparency of the witness system because in practice secrecy was deemed necessary almost without exception. This raised the question whether the system of using secret witnesses "when necessary" passed constitutional muster in view of the reality that the exception of secrecy had swallowed the general rule of transparency and confrontation. Judge Qian answered "no" and, in Interpretation No. 636, the Constitutional Court agreed.

Also, in the Taoyuan Petition, Judge Qian contended that, even as revised, Article 12 of the *Liumang* Act deprived the accused of his right to confront and examine witnesses in violation of the right to physical freedom as it relates to the principle of "proper legal procedures," which is commonly translated as "due process." Here again, Article 8 of the Constitution was the primary constitutional basis, though the argument also rested on the right to institute legal proceedings in Article 16 of the Constitution. For concrete support, Judge Qian looked to Interpretation No. 582, issued in 2004, in which the Court addressed whether out-of-court statements made by a criminal co-defendant against another co-defendant should be admissible in court. Prior to Interpretation No. 582 and the adoption of hearsay rules in the Criminal Procedure Code, *all* out-of-court statements by one co-defendant were admissible against another co-defendant, regardless of the context. In Interpretation No. 582, the Court began its holding by stating that Article 16 of the Constitution guarantees people the right to institute legal proceedings 訴訟權. As far as a criminal defendant is concerned, this guarantee includes the right to defend oneself adequately in a legal proceeding. Crucial to Judge Qian's argument was the Court's statement that a criminal defendant's right to examine a witness is a corollary of the right to defend oneself and is also protected by the principle of due process. Judge Qian argued that this reasoning in Interpretation No. 582 should be extended to accused *liumang*. He posited that legislation can "restrict," but not "deprive" people of, the right to confront witnesses because a deprivation violates the proportionality principle 比例原則—the principle that measures

184

must be reasonable, the least restrictive possible, and not excessive (Qian 2005, 18).[30] Judge Qian continued that Article 12 of the *Liumang* Act crossed the line between a constitutionally allowable restriction and a flat-out deprivation because it allowed judges to "refuse" an accused *liumang's* request to confront and examine witnesses. This stark deprivation stands in contrast to Taiwan's more creative Witness Protection Law 證人保護法, which emphasizes the use of voice alteration and other protective measures as alternatives to cutting off all questioning of the witness by the accused. Judge Qian thus continued, while a criminal defendant may have had access to an adverse witness under the Witness Protection Law, in a companion *liumang* case, the witness suddenly underwent a "metamorphosis" and became a secret, unavailable witness. Not only did this difference in treatment of criminal defendants and accused *liumang* violate the principle of equality 平等原則 according to Judge Qian, the use of secret witnesses in *liumang* cases was further pernicious because it acted as a tool for people (and, most alarming, police) who harbored grudges and sought retaliation.

The Constitutional Court agreed that the secret witness system was constitutionally deficient. Specifically, the Justices explained in Interpretation No. 636 that Article 12 of the *Liumang* Act restricted the accused's rights to confront and examine witnesses and to access court files without requiring the tribunal to take into consideration whether, in view of the individual circumstances of the case, other less intrusive measures were sufficient to protect the witness's safety and the voluntariness of his testimony. For instance, the Court cited the use of masks, voice alteration, and other protective measures as possible alternatives. The Court held that Article 12 was clearly an excessive restriction on the accused's right

---

[30] The Constitutional Court stated in Interpretation No. 471 that this principle is enshrined in Article 23 of the Constitution, which provides that freedoms and rights enumerated in the Constitution shall not be restricted by law except as may be necessary to prevent infringement upon the freedoms of other persons, to avert an imminent crisis, to maintain social order, or to advance public welfare.

to defend himself in a legal action and was inconsistent with the principle of proportionality. The Court further held that procedures violated the principle of due process of law under Article 8 of the Constitution and the right to institute legal proceedings under Article 16 of the Constitution. The secret witness provision as then written in the Act was to be null and void one year from the Interpretation's date of issuance.

The Legislative Yuan, in response, could have adopted a modified "when necessary" formulation. In Interpretation No. 636, the Constitutional Court qualified its critique of the secret witness system by stating that to protect witnesses from endangering their lives, bodies, freedom, or property as a result of being confronted and examined, the rights of the accused and his lawyer may be restricted by concrete and clear statutory provisions that comply with the principle of proportionality under Article 23 of the Constitution. The decision to repeal the *Liumang* Act rendered this issue moot. Today, the primary law regulating access to witnesses in criminal cases remains the Witness Protection Law. As noted above, the Court went further in Interpretation No. 636 than only addressing confrontation of live witnesses: the Court further held that the *Liumang* Act unconstitutionally restricted the accused's access to court files.

Professor Wang, who appeared in front of the Constitutional Court to address the merits of the two judicial petitions, extended his critique to notification procedures. He contended that the procedures used to notify accused serious *liumang* that they were so accused violated the right to defend oneself. When the police transferred a *liumang* case to the public security tribunal pursuant to Article 9 of the *Liumang* Act, they were required to notify the accused *liumang* and his designated friends or relatives of this action. The police, however, were not required to provide the accused *liumang* with a copy of the transfer document 移送書. In a criminal case, the indictment (the equivalent to the transfer document in a *liumang* case) must be given to the defendant and must contain the items listed in Article 264 of the Criminal Procedure Code, including descriptions of the facts and evidence alleged (Wang 2006, 16). The indictment is required to list the allegations so that the defendant can defend himself in a meaningful way. Professor Wang argued that accused serious *liumang* were not given this same opportunity, and there was no legitimate reason for treating them differently from criminal suspects.

The Constitutional Court did not address notification procedures in Interpretation No. 636, but we agree with Professor Wang that the difference in treatment between criminal and *liumang* suspects rose to the level of unconstitutional treatment. Put simply, failure to notify the accused in advance of the details on which charges are based denies him an adequate opportunity to answer the charges. This right is enshrined in the ICCPR, which provides that everyone charged with a criminal offense shall be entitled "[t]o be informed promptly and in detail in a language which he understands of the nature and cause of the charge against him" (Art. 14(3)). The punishment dispensed to those adjudicated to be serious *liumang* was the substantive equivalent of criminal punishment, so this right should have been applicable to those accused of being serious *liumang*.

2. Lack of Prosecutorial Involvement

Witnesses were seldom seen in the courtroom during *liumang* cases, but prosecutors were never present. Judge Qian asserted that the *Liumang* Act violated the principles of the separation of prosecution and adjudication 審檢分離之控訴原則 and the division of powers and functions 權能區分原則 because no prosecutor was involved in the proceedings. Most tribunal hearings had only the judge and the accused *liumang* as participants, which forced judges into roles unlike those seen in criminal cases. In criminal proceedings, after the initial police investigation, the prosecutors take a lead role with the police being subject to their direction. The prosecutor makes the crucial decision whether to prosecute. In *liumang* cases, the police made the decision whether to recommend that the accused be sent to confinement, with the only prosecutorial involvement being that a lone prosecutor sat on the review committee.

No prosecutor took part in the judicial hearing. Nor were the police a "party" in *liumang* court hearings. The law did not require that police attend the hearing and, in practice, the police did not fulfill the prosecutorial role in court. Clearly, the involvement of a prosecutor would have heightened professional and public confidence in the fairness and accuracy of the *liumang* adjudication system, but did the Constitution require it?

We stop short of Judge Qian's position that the absence of prosecutors during the actual court hearing was unconstitutional under either principles of the separation of prosecution and adjudication or the division of powers and functions. In *liumang* cases, the judge at least had the transfer document, which was prepared by the executive branch. The hearing itself closely resembled prior inquisitorial practices but this alone is not sufficient to hold the related provisions of the *Liumang* Act unconstitutional. We do agree with Judge Qian that procedures under the *Liumang* Act did not comport with the spirit of recent reforms to Taiwan's Criminal Procedure Code. Specifically, Judge Qian targeted Articles 22 and 23 of the *Liumang* Act, which addressed the composition and functions of the public security tribunal, as well as Articles 18 to 24 of the Implementing Rules, which elaborated the relevant provisions of the *Liumang* Act. We agree that he rightly questioned the wisdom of the public security tribunals' inquisitorial method, specifically the practice of having public security tribunal judges play the dual role of questioning accused *liumang* and then deciding whether confinement was warranted. This practice stood in stark contrast to the modified adversarial system used for criminal proceedings today. The practice of having a judge serve in effect as both prosecutor and sole adjudicator in the courtroom before sentencing someone to three years in conditions that were virtually identical to a prison was arguably inconsistent with contemporary standards of due process in Taiwan. Procedures that may be permissible before merely imposing a fine or a short stay in a detention cell take on a different gloss when applied to a significant prison sentence. We will never hear the Justices' official views on this issue because the Constitutional Court declined to address the relevant articles of the *Liumang* Act on procedural grounds.

3. Lack of Public Hearings

Another issue that is absent from Interpretation No. 636 is Professor Wang's critique regarding the constitutionality of barring the public from the courtroom. Although the Constitutional Court did not address this argument in Interpretation No. 636, we believe that it deserves consideration.

In his argument to the Court, Professor Wang maintained that the constitution requires public hearings before the public security tribunals on the district court level. The system under the *Liumang* Act involved only the judge, the accused *liumang*, and sometimes his lawyer and witnesses, even if the accused *liumang* did not get to see and question them. It was a closed trial. Although Taiwan's Constitution does not expressly grant people the right to "a speedy and public trial" as the 6th Amendment to the US Constitution does,[31] Professor Wang explained the reasoning for this right in Article 16 of the Constitution (the right to institute legal proceedings), and Article 8 (the right to physical freedom) (Wang 2006, 13). For support, Wang looked to Justice Wu Geng's concurring opinion in Interpretation No. 368, in which he stated that the right to institute legal proceedings 訴訟權 in Article 16 includes the right to a public hearing.[32] As a caveat, Interpretation No. 368 did not address a *liumang* case, but Professor Wang proposed that the reasoning be extended to the *liumang* context. The Constitutional

---

[31] In 2010, Taiwan passed a Speedy Trial Act 刑事妥速審判法. Although this Act is a notable step forward in decreasing the time that a case can be pending, as noted by the independent experts reviewing Taiwan's implementation of the ICCPR, it still fails to meet international standards: "Article 5 of the Speedy Trial Act 2010 further stipulates a maximum period of eight years of pre-trial detention, which, in the opinion of the Experts, violates the 'reasonable time' limit of Article 9(3) ICCPR." Review of the Initial Reports of the Government of Taiwan on the Implementation of the International Human Rights Covenants, Concluding Observations and Recommendations Adopted by the International Group of Independent Experts Taipei, 1 March 2013.

[32] The majority opinion did not address this point, but it did note that the right to institute legal proceedings in Article 16 of the Constitution means that people have the right to demand through legal procedures a judicial remedy for the final disposition of disputes over jural relations.

Court later flatly stated in the reasoning section of Interpretation No. 482 that the right to institute legal proceedings includes a public hearing, though this also was not in the context of a *liumang* case.

In the context of *liumang* cases, however, the Court had interpreted Article 8 of the Constitution to require due process and, in Interpretation No. 384, the Court noted that this encompassed the principle that trial proceedings should be open to the public. Therefore, Professor Wang explained, whether Article 8 or Article 16 was used as a basis, accused *liumang* should have a constitutional right to a public hearing. In view of the seriousness of the punishment involved, we support this view. Moreover, as previously noted, the ICCPR requires that state parties afford people charged with crimes a "fair and public hearing by a competent, independent and impartial tribunal established by law" (Art. 14).[33]

E. Serious *Liumang*: Punishment by Reformatory Training

Critics of the *Liumang* Act forcefully criticized the manner in which serious *liumang* were punished. Challenges to the reformatory training system focused on the use of indeterminate sentences and the method of setting off time spent in reformatory training and serving criminal punishments.

1. Indeterminate Sentences to Reformatory Training

Under Article 13 of the *Liumang* Act, the public security tribunal decided whether or not to impose reformatory training, but the tribunal did not decide the actual length of the sentence. Article 19 provided the standard duration: reformatory training was set at between one and three

---

[33] The ICCPR provides for an exception in limited cases: "The press and the public may be excluded from all or part of a trial for reasons of morals, public order (*ordre public*) or national security in a democratic society, or when the interest of the private lives of the parties so requires, or to the extent strictly necessary in the opinion of the court in special circumstances where publicity would prejudice the interests of justice" (Art. 14(1)). Similarly, the Court Organic Act 法院組織法 provides that court hearings shall be open to the public (Art. 86), though Taiwanese law allows limited exceptions, such as for trials involving juveniles (Juvenile Proceedings Act 少年事件處理法, Art. 34).

years with the possibility of release after one year, provided that the original ruling court agreed. In Judge Qian's view, a public security tribunal's ruling to commit a person to reformatory training violated the principle of clarity 明確性 because the tribunal failed to state a definite sentence within the one- to three-year window (Qian 2005, 20). In other words, Judge Qian asserted that the indeterminate sentence left the *liumang* agitated and in fear all day (Qian 2005, 20). This, he argued, was constitutionally unacceptable.

For support, Judge Qian relied on Interpretation No. 471 in which the Constitutional Court struck down a mandatory provision in the Firearms Act 槍砲彈藥刀械管制條例 that required three years of forced work 強制工作處分 when a person was convicted of specified offenses,[34] without considering the necessity of the three-year sentence in view of the defendant's particular situation. The Court explained that the failure to consider individual circumstances violated the proportionality principle (Cst. Art. 23). The Court held that judges may sentence people to three years of forced work but are not required to do so. The Court did not directly address indeterminate sentences in Interpretation No. 471. Judge Qian contended that the reasoning of this Interpretation should be extended to reformatory training and, accordingly, judges should be required to mete out definite sentences in *liumang* cases based on individual circumstances. Judge Qian further questioned the constitutionality of having the actual length of a *liumang*'s reformatory training decided by the administrative agencies that supervised the training. He argued that this practice violated the institutional protections of the constitutional right to institute legal proceedings and also violated the separation of powers principle (Qian 2005, 21).

Although Judge Qian threw a number of weighty constitutional principles at the practice of indeterminate sentencing under the *Liumang* Act, the Constitutional Court did not address them in Interpretation

---

[34] The article at issue, Article 19, has since been repealed.

No. 636. Unlike the mandatory three-year-sentence provision that the Court held unconstitutional in Interpretation No. 471, the revised *Liumang* Act allowed for release from reformatory training after one year, subject to certain conditions. Nor did Judge Qian provide clear support for his position that it was unconstitutional for administrative agencies to recommend early release. Moreover, the determination of how much of their sentences prisoners should serve and which institution should decide when prisoners can be released in individual cases should be left to the legislature and the executive, respectively. That said, those determinations should be made under sufficient constraints such that there is not unfettered discretion. For example, the parole provision in the Criminal Code provides that, subject to certain limitations, parole 假釋 is available for criminal offenders after they have served half of their term of imprisonment, or 25 years of a life sentence (Criminal Code, Art. 77).

2. Setting Off Reformatory Training and Criminal Punishments

Prior to Interpretation No. 384, Article 21 of the *Liumang* Act allowed the imposition of reformatory training either before or after execution of a criminal punishment for the same act, without regard to whether there was a special preventive necessity to do so. In Interpretation No. 384, the Constitutional Court held that this practice violated the constitutional guarantee of physical freedom, and it gave the legislature until the end of 1996 to fix the problem. Article 21 of the revised *Liumang* Act provided that, if the *liumang* behavior for which the accused was committed to reformatory training was also the basis for criminal punishment,[35] time spent serving the criminal punishment and time spent in reformatory training would be mutually set off on a one-day-for-one-day basis. Judge Qian

---

[35] Specifically, time spent serving a fixed-term imprisonment 有期徒刑, detention 拘役 (as punishment, as compared with pre-trial detention 羈押), and rehabilitation measures 保安處分 was set off from reformatory training.

argued that this legislative fix did not solve the constitutional problem. In Interpretation No. 636, the Constitutional Court agreed, to a limited extent. In order to alleviate concerns that the physical freedom of a person subject to both criminal punishment and reformatory training might be excessively deprived, the Court called on relevant authorities to re-examine and revise the phrasing in the *Liumang* Act.

As background, in Interpretation No. 384, the Court explained that one aspect of due process is that people not be punished for the same act twice. Thereafter, in Interpretation No. 604, the Court clarified that multiple punishments may be imposed for multiple violations and this does not give rise to any issue of double punishment. Judge Qian did not contest this position. Instead, he contended that the "setting off" system had other flaws. Most notably, if a person was imprisoned for one year and then, for the same conduct, began reformatory training upon release from prison, he would still have one to two years left after the one-year deduction. For people sentenced to both prison and reformatory training, only those who were sentenced to three or more years in prison thus avoided having to undergo reformatory training. As a result, a *liumang* might as well have committed an act that landed him in prison for three years rather than a lesser offense that would have resulted, for example, in two years of prison and one year of reformatory training.

To highlight the confusion over this practice, Judge Qian raised an example from the 2003 Legal Symposium of the High Court of Taiwan and its Subsidiary Courts. Judges discussed the following scenario at the symposium: if reformatory training and a ten-month prison sentence were proposed for the same act and the prison sentence was finalized first, what should the courts do? One position was that the prison sentence should commence and be completed first based on the "first finalized, first enforced" principle. Another view was that the person should not be sent to prison but only to reformatory training because, as a result of the short length of the prison sentence, to first send the person to prison would effectively result in double punishment (i.e., ten months in prison followed by a minimum of one year in reformatory training). The very purpose of setting off sentences was to avoid such scenarios. Despite the logical force of the second viewpoint, the discussion ended with a decision to side with the first position—"first finalized, first enforced"—regardless of the length of the criminal sentence, highlighting that illogical is not the same as unconstitutional.

Under the *Liumang* Act, reformatory training could last up to three years. If a person served a ten-month prison sentence and then began reformatory training, the total time behind bars thus would exceed the three-year maximum only if he spent more than two years and two months in reformatory training. Nonetheless, we agree with Judge Qian's position that this would always constitute "double punishment" no matter how long the duration of reformatory training, and surely anyone whose reformatory training was about to exceed two years and two months, having served ten months in prison for the same act, would have had an even stronger claim for legal relief. That dual imposition of reformatory training and prison time constituted "double punishment" is buttressed by the reality that the two reformatory training facilities also housed regular convicts under the same roof, albeit in separate areas of the facilities, and that both types of inmates often shared the same training classes. The difference between prison and reformatory training was thus quite blurred.

In Interpretation No. 636, the Constitutional Court quoted Article 19 of the *Liumang* Act, which provided in part, "The term of reformatory training is set at more than one year and less than three years. After completion of one year, if the executing authorities believe that it is unnecessary to continue reformatory training, they may report, with facts and evidence, to the original ruling court for its permission and exempt the person from further reformatory training." The Court pointed out that when criminal punishment or rehabilitation measures were first carried out for more than three years, there was no need to then commence reformatory training because of the mutual set-off provision. In other words, the punishment for the corresponding criminal case already exceeded the maximum allowable sentence to reformatory training. Accordingly, this situation did not raise doubts regarding excessive restrictions on people's physical freedom.

The Justices therefore focused their attention on the situation when criminal punishment or rehabilitation measures were first carried out for less than three years. Because public security tribunals did not sentence *liumang* to a fixed term of reformatory training, a *liumang* could serve anywhere between the statutory minimum and maximum (i.e., one to three years) and that determination was made based on the *liumang's* progress at the training institute. As a result, the exact amount of time that the *liumang* should serve in reformatory training following completion of criminal punishment or rehabilitation measures was unclear. For example, if a person already served two years in prison, did he then still have to complete the minimum one year in reformatory training for a total time behind bars of three years? Alternatively, could the training institute personnel agree to release him immediately because he had already spent more than the minimum one-year term behind bars? If the *Liumang* Act was interpreted as meaning that reformatory training should be enforced for a minimum of one year beyond the criminal sentence, the Court cautioned that the physical freedom of the person subject to reformatory training might be excessively restricted. In Interpretation No. 636, the Court commanded the relevant authorities to re-examine and revise the *Liumang* Act to alleviate this concern.

In a partial concurring opinion, three Justices faulted the majority for not addressing whether the *Liumang* Act violated the principle of *ne bis in idem*, which translates from Latin as "not twice for the same," and means that no legal action can be instituted twice for the same cause of action.[36] Namely, this concern arose because of the substantial overlap between offenses in the Criminal Code (and specialized criminal laws) and *liumang* acts, an issue also raised by Professor Wang. As discussed in previous chapters, it was standard practice for suspected *liumang* to face concurrent criminal charges stemming from the same acts. The concern that people were thus being tried in court twice for the same underlying acts was very real even though the Constitutional Court failed to address this issue head-on in Interpretation No. 636.

F. The *Liumang* Act as a Second Criminal Procedure Code

The most fundamental question according to Judge Qian was whether Taiwan needed to have a "second Criminal Procedure Code," which resulted in the accused being subject to two proceedings and the concomitant waste of judicial resources. This, however, is a policy argument more properly directed at the Legislative Yuan. As expected, the Constitutional Court declined to address this issue.

The argument that the concurrent use of the *liumang* and criminal justice systems squandered resources may not be a constitutional one, but it is a compelling one. Judge Qian argued that the *Liumang* Act, in its entirety, contradicted the proportionality principle because there were alternative

---

[36] According to Judge Qian's view, the principle that people not be punished for the same act twice is also called "the principle of the prohibition against double jeopardy" 雙重危險禁止原則. This statement is misleading because the two concepts are not necessarily coextensive. This highlights a vexing problem in comparative law terminology and translations. Some of Taiwan's terminology comes from Germany, some from Germany via Japan, some from the United States, and still other terminology is unique to China/Taiwan. The principle of *ne bis in idem* is varyingly translated in Taiwan as "do not punish the same behavior twice" 一行為不二罰, "do not punish the same act twice" 一事不二罰, "do not punish the same act again" 一事不再罰, "prohibition against repeat punishments" 禁止重複處罰, and "prohibition against double punishments" 禁止雙重處罰. In Interpretation No. 604, the majority opinion used "do not punish the same behavior twice" 一行為不二罰, but concurring and dissenting opinions by justices in this same interpretation used other formulations. Judge Qian also argued that the *Liumang* Act violated the principle that the "same matter not be tried twice" 一事不再理 because the criminal and *liumang* cases arising from a single act were tried before different courts in different proceedings. In addition to constitutional concerns, Judge Qian argued that this practice wasted judicial resources and was unnecessary, a critique shared by judges whom we interviewed.

means to obtain the same legislative purposes as the *Liumang* Act but with less harm.[37] Judge Qian raised this paramount question in the final pages of the Taoyuan Petition. He asserted that there were still a number of unconstitutional provisions—singling out the secret witness system as a particularly egregious constitutional violation. Put simply, he drew the Constitutional Court's attention to how glaringly antiquated the *Liumang* Act had become. Like Judge Qian, over the course of our research we recognized the *Liumang* Act's historical role in combating the criminal underworld, yet we seriously questioned the continuing need for it under Taiwan's present-day legal system. Thankfully, the executive and legislative branches finally conceded that the time to retire the *Liumang* Act had arrived.

IV. FROM INTERPRETATION NO. 636 TO REPEAL

In Interpretation No. 636, the Constitutional Court gave the Legislative Yuan one year to fix the constitutional infirmities in the *Liumang* Act, or the offending provisions would become null and void.[38] The countdown to 1 February 2009 had begun.

Based on experience with the first two constitutional interpretations that addressed the *Liumang* Act, conventional wisdom expected that the legislature would once again revise the Act in a piecemeal fashion in order

---

[37] For support, Judge Qian invoked Interpretation No. 544, in which the Justices cited the availability of other alternative means to attain the same purposes with less harm as a component of whether a law is consistent with the proportionality principle (Qian 2005: 31).

[38] Interpretation No. 636 (reasoning, para. 14):
In light of the fact that amending the law requires a certain period of time—and so that the relevant authorities can conduct a comprehensive analysis of the Act by taking into consideration both the need to protect people's rights and the need to maintain social order—those parts of the following provisions that are inconsistent with relevant principles of the Constitution shall become null and void no later than one year from the date of this Interpretation: Article 2, Section 3, regarding the act of "tyrannizing good and honest people," Section 5 of the same Article regarding "people who are habitually morally corrupt or who habitually wander around and act like rascals," and Article 12, Paragraph 1, which excessively restricts the transferred person's right to confront and examine witnesses and to access court files.

to meet only the minimal requirements laid down by the Constitutional Court. As the year wore on, it also looked increasingly likely that those revisions would come at the final hour, as was done with previous amendments. Although the Legislative Yuan had always held the power to abolish the *Liumang* Act, that scenario was deemed unlikely, both because the Court had called for only limited revisions and because there is no political capital to be gained by looking soft on crime, in Taiwan or elsewhere. Prospects for repeal were further dampened in light of the insistence on keeping the *Liumang* Act even after the Court declared part of the Act unconstitutional in 1995 and 2001. Following these earlier interpretations, the legislature emphasized that the Act was an efficient weapon to crack down on crime 掃黑利器.

Adding another obstacle to reform, whether well-founded or not, police and other officials with whom we spoke repeatedly stated that the common people supported the *Liumang* Act because they were afraid of *liumang*. This is not to say that all police were against revising the *Liumang* Act. A National Police Agency (NPA) official told us that he supported revisions done through the people's representatives in order to improve the Act. This same official emphasized that people need to consider the victim's perspective because there are times when the criminal law alone is insufficient. For example, what if upon leaving a restaurant you find a man standing next to your car who politely tells you that he has watched your car so that it would not be stolen, and shouldn't you give him a little money to buy something to drink? The threat is implicit but easily understood. Opponents of the *Liumang* Act countered that the Criminal Code is sufficient to deal with these kinds of situations, such as through Article 304, which covers crimes of coercion 強制罪. There is also the Social Order Maintenance Law, which authorizes detention 拘留 for up to five days for various types of injurious conduct (Art. 19). For example, a person may be punished by such detention for using another person's identifying documents or for deceiving by carrying a toy gun that looks like a real gun and thereby endangering safety (Arts. 66(2) and 65(3)).

Then, in the autumn of 2008, the new administration of President Ma Ying-jeou unexpectedly broke the political stalemate. On 17 November 2008, the Executive Yuan submitted a proposal to the Legislative Yuan for abolition of the *Liumang* Act. In the proposal, the Executive Yuan set forth five reasons in support of its position. First, as pointed out in the concurring opinion to Interpretation No. 636, even if the legislature revised the Act, there would still be lingering questions regarding the constitutionality of reformatory training. The Executive Yuan even borrowed the language in the concurring opinion when arguing that it was difficult to make the *Liumang* Act compatible with the Constitution no matter how it was revised. Second, the legal nature of the Act was unclear because it contained components of both administrative law and criminal law. The Executive Yuan bluntly asked whether provisions in the Act actually belonged to administrative law or criminal law, and it further pointed out that the unclear nature of the Act made it difficult to protect the rights and interests of the accused. Third, the overlap between the *Liumang* Act and criminal laws resulted in needless duplication. Fourth, enforcement of the amended Act would have created administrative difficulties; after noting the Constitutional Court's holding that an accused *liumang* had a right to be heard during the proceedings before the review committee, the Executive Yuan advised that this would impose a further burden on the committee's work. Finally, times had changed and, not only was the Act no longer necessary, it was contrary to Taiwan's increasing embrace of human rights. The Executive Yuan briefly traced the Act's history since 1955 and concluded that criminal laws and the Social Order Maintenance Law were sufficient for society's current needs. To underscore this point, the Executive Yuan attached an appendix with a table setting forth the different types of *liumang* behavior and how criminal laws and the Social Order Maintenance Law could be used to address the same behavior.

Legislative debate ensued in December 2008, and representatives of the Executive Yuan, Judicial Yuan, and NPA testified before the Legislative Yuan.

Legislators raised concerns that criminal laws alone would be insufficient to protect the public and further inquired about the impact of releasing incarcerated *liumang*. One legislator estimated that, of twenty-three county and city police departments, sixteen supported repeal—to which the NPA representative replied that left seven police departments which supported only revising the Act.[39] This majority police support for abolishing the Act might seem odd at first glance, given that the Act provided police with an additional tool to remove troublemakers from the street. We can only speculate because the legislative record does not clarify why the vast majority of police departments reportedly supported repeal. Perhaps it was because the police too were embracing a more human-rights friendly approach. It might also have been because police were eager to be rid of the rigid point system described in Chapter 3 that led to demerits if *liumang* quotas were not met. Despite some legislators' concerns, the voices for abolition prevailed by assuaging fears that repeal would lead to a deterioration in public order and by emphasizing the antiquated nature of the *Liumang* Act. On 23 January 2009, the Legislative Yuan officially voted to repeal the Act. Because most incarcerated *liumang* had concurrent criminal sentences, only 176 *liumang* were actually released upon repeal, persuasive evidence that the Act had become superfluous.

The retirement of the *Liumang* Act is a testament to the spirit of legal reform in Taiwan. The judicial, executive, and legislative branches all deserve credit for recognizing that the Act had outlived its time and for carrying out their respective duties in a democratic, cooperative, and transparent manner. Reform-minded scholars and lawyers also deserve praise for pushing the debate forward even when it was politically unpopular to do so. The *Liumang* Act is now a remnant of history, and that is exactly what it should be.

---

[39] *Legis. Yuan, 7th Term, 2nd Sess., 2nd Meeting Rec., 98 LEGIS. YUAN GAZ. 501 (2008).*

CHAPTER 5:
CONCLUDING THOUGHTS

The existence and gradual demise of the *Liumang* Act is a story that needs to be told in both English and Chinese. Surprisingly little attention has been paid to this story despite its major political, legal, and practical implications in Taiwan and beyond.

I. THE *LIUMANG* ACT'S ABOLITION AND TAIWAN'S "SOFT POWER"

In recent years, during democratic Taiwan's fierce domestic political debates, opposition parties have often accused the government of President Ma Ying-jeou of failing to fully respect human rights. One thus might have thought that President Ma would have trumpeted the abolition of the *Liumang* Act as one of the significant accomplishments of his first term.

Perhaps the failure to emphasize the importance of the accomplishment reflects how little public concern abolition has generated. As we have noted, contrary to the dire predictions of those Taiwan politicians and police who sought to retain this harsh administrative punishment, abolition seems to have created barely a ripple in the social order. The abolitionists appear to have been correct in predicting that the regular criminal justice system would be sufficient to deal with the anti-social conduct the *Liumang* Act was designed to address.

Surely the Ma Administration should have more widely advertised this accomplishment abroad. Some foreign critics have unfairly condemned the current KMT government as merely a more attractive, updated version of Chiang Kai-shek's Kuomintang "police state." Ma's government could have made much more use of abolition to reject the charge and gain the appreciation and good will of foreign democracies. By contrast, Generalissimo

Chiang and his American-educated wife, Soong May-ling, had a great talent for making propaganda abroad. Chiang presided over a genuine dictatorship—one of the harshest, authoritarian, Leninist-type regimes in history. Nevertheless, he succeeded in persuading many Americans and other Westerners that his government was the embodiment of "Free China," ostensibly in vivid contrast to the Maoist regime on the Mainland.

President Ma presides over the freest political system ever produced by a Chinese political-legal culture. Yet he has not boasted of putting an end to the last vestige of the island's former police state. Nor, during its first term, did the Ma Administration do a great deal to bring a generation of broader human rights improvements in Taiwan's Criminal Procedure Code and related laws to the world's attention. The recent welcoming of foreign experts to review Taiwan's implementation of international human rights instruments is a promising step toward engaging the world in Taiwan's marked improvement in protecting human rights. Chinese modesty is a virtue, but it should not be indulged to excess. In the quarter-century since the end of martial law—a relatively short period in terms of meaningful legal reforms—Taiwan, under both KMT and DPP administrations, has implemented systemic reforms to its criminal justice system that were unimaginable under the KMT's former police state. (Acronyms are defined in the Appendix, starting on page 209.)

Taiwan now has a powerfully appealing product to sell in the market-place of world opinion. It needs to make the most of its potential "soft power" in the contest to attract foreign support against an uncertain future. Certainly, at a time when the PRC is again struggling with the complex problems of what to do about "re-education through labor" (RETL) and police abuses generally, Taiwan should be shining a light on its abolition of the notorious *Liumang* Act. Abolition provides further evidence to refute the nonsense raised by some Mainland advocates that due process of law and protection against arbitrary official detention do not interest people of Chinese descent. Moreover, as a growing number of Taiwan scholars, lawyers, and officials have observed, until the PRC makes conspicuous further progress in subjecting its police to the rule of law, cross-strait relations between the Mainland and Taiwan will continue to be constrained.

Indeed, President Ma proposed that the subject of human rights be placed on the cross-strait agenda for his second term. It is increasingly clear that stronger cross-strait relations cannot be built on economic ties alone. A meaningful discussion of how each side treats people who face criminal, or quasi-criminal, sanctions is an important next step in exploring prospects for the greater mobility of people between the PRC and Taiwan. Although the PRC has generally been careful not to impose RETL on visitors from Taiwan, the PRC's abolition of that administrative punishment would send the island's people a strong signal of legal progress. It would be especially comforting to business personnel and other Taiwanese people who reside on the Mainland.

II. RETL REFORMERS AND TAIWAN'S *LIUMANG* ACT EXPERIENCE

Despite the major political, legal, economic, and social differences between Taiwan and the PRC, Taiwan's example can be of great assistance to those Mainland law reformers concerned with RETL. This is particularly true for those currently discussing what detailed reforms to enact if, as many expect, RETL is to be abolished in name but retained in substance in some modified way. In China, legal reforms on paper have often failed to strengthen significantly the ability of people accused of criminal or quasi-criminal violations to challenge the government's case in practice. Thus there is reason to question whether reforms to RETL will merely change the soup but not the medicine 換湯不換藥 or, in terms more familiar to English readers, put old wine in new bottles.

Taiwan's experience offers a tested roadmap for gradually reducing arbitrary police powers. For example, knowledge of Taiwan's former bureaucratic procedures for determining who should be deemed a *liumang,* and to what extent, may prove useful as the PRC considers how to improve the criteria and the procedures for deciding who should be subject to RETL's successor. Indeed, the Taiwan precedent of classifying offenders into two categories and subjecting only those in the second, more serious category to incarceration may stimulate new Mainland thinking about how to reduce the numbers of those who are to suffer administrative detention, numbers that have been far larger in the PRC than in Taiwan.

Now that the heads of the local public security apparatus in China appear to be playing at least a slightly diminished role in the extremely powerful political-legal committees that control the administration of justice, the time might finally be right to start making inroads into the overwhelming police influence over decisions when to deprive people of physical liberty because of allegedly dangerous behavior.

As we have suggested, Taiwan's former administrative procedures left much to be desired in terms of their fairness to potential targets of the system. Yet Mao himself once exhorted "We have had a good many teachers by negative example." We hope that Mainland legislators will regard Taiwan's now-abolished procedures not as favorable precedents to be followed indefinitely but rather as negative examples to be increasingly avoided. The predecessor of the *Liumang* Act was first promulgated in 1955, a repressive era under Chiang Kai-shek's iron-fisted rule. By the time of the *Liumang* Act's abolition, it was deemed a remnant of the past that no longer fit Taiwan's impressive progress toward the rule of law. RETL, similarly, was officially established in a turbulent, nightmarish era of the PRC's history. Now it, too, has come to be viewed by many in China as seriously inappropriate in light of their country's social and economic progress and heightened awareness of the importance of protections against arbitrary police conduct. Such an evolving consensus adds to the reform momentum, as has been demonstrated in Taiwan's case.

The very inadequacies of the *Liumang* Act spurred an early generation of Taiwan reformers to insist upon some form of judicial review of the relevant administrative decisions, leading to the establishment of the "security tribunals" in the local district courts. One of the key questions confronting those Mainland legislators and officials who wish to retain long-term administrative detention but in some modified form is whether the present system of allowing judicial review in principle, albeit restricted in practice, should be replaced by a system of compulsory judicial review in every case. If so, they will have to determine the nature of that judicial review. Should it take the form of the existing review prescribed by China's Administrative Litigation Law? If all administrative incarceration decisions are to be reviewed, that would add substantially to the burdens of the court system unless the number of targets is substantially reduced. Or should some specially adapted, more abbreviated, procedures be devised to help the courts discharge the expanded duties contemplated?

In this respect also, the Taiwan experience would be very relevant. Knowledge of the origins, operation, advantages, disadvantages, and demise of the "security tribunals" should prove highly instructive. Again, the special court procedures used for *liumang* cases, if properly assessed in accordance with rule of law values, should be regarded as a negative example. Despite the authorized participation of defense counsel, the failure of the "security tribunals" to provide accused *liumang* with other procedural protections provided to accused criminals gave them much of the appearance and reality of the very inquisitorial judicial system that Taiwan's criminal justice reforms of the past decade were designed to eradicate. Especially appalling were the severe limitations upon the opportunities for the target and his counsel to identify and cross-examine the witnesses against him.

Given existing political constraints and other distorting influences upon Chinese courts, which significantly diminish prospects for independent judicial action, it would be most unfortunate if China should establish the equivalent of Taiwan's "security tribunals." That would impose further restrictions on fair court procedures while misleading the public into thinking that adequate court review was being granted. It would be far better for China's judicial resources to be expanded to ensure that

205

all decisions imposing or recommending RETL will receive in practice the same judicial review as currently available in principle under the Administrative Litigation Law. Taking reforms a step further, it would be even better if witnesses regularly appeared in court for many types of cases under both the Administrative Litigation Law and Criminal Procedure Law, as compared with current practice where witnesses are nearly always absent.

Of course, real change will also require that judges not only be adequate in numbers but also be willing to stand up to the police who bring cases before them. We recognize that empowering the Chinese judiciary to take a more assertive position vis-à-vis the police would be no easy task. Nonetheless, making sure that there are adequate numbers of judges to give each case serious scrutiny is a necessary first step. Our hope is that the prospect of a meaningful judicial review in every case where RETL is decided upon or recommended by the police will stimulate police to be more cautious in their appraisals and reduce the number of cases that come before the court.

III. THE BROADER LESSON OF TAIWAN'S EXPERIENCE

From a broader perspective, what might China learn from our examination of the life and death of the *Liumang* Act? Apart from the desirability of completely abolishing long-term administrative detention, we believe the attention of people in Mainland China should focus on the roles that democratic political-legal institutions played in its gradual reform and ultimate demise. Especially prominent was the role of Taiwan's Constitutional Court, an institution that, sadly, has no counterpart on the Mainland, where the Standing Committee of the National People's Congress (NPC) has the exclusive power to interpret the Constitution but, in practice, does not exercise it.

For a long period under the KMT dictatorship in Taiwan, the Constitutional Court served as mere window dressing for the system's rule of law charade. Yet, as the martial law regime began to unravel, the Court began to spread its wings and increasingly demonstrate a capacity for imaginatively and vigorously holding the other branches of government to the legal standards of government under law. In fact, many of the Constitutional Court's new interpretations stimulated, indeed insisted upon, further reforms in accordance with the Justices' impressive knowledge not only of the Republic of China's Constitution but also of the governments and legal systems of the principal Western democracies. The publishing of Justices' concurring and dissenting opinions along with the Constitutional Court's majority opinion has further spurred a robust debate over the meaning of the provisions enshrined in Taiwan's Constitution.

As we have shown in Chapter Four, the Constitutional Court's deft handling of the sensitive problems of long-term administrative detention, beginning in 1995 with the first of three interpretations that ultimately led to abolition, is a prime illustration of how constitutionalism can fruitfully take root in Chinese political-legal culture and benefit the development of democratic government and the rule of law. The Court's interpretations wisely selected from and responded to the broad range of requests presented to it by increasingly energetic legal and judicial experts. Those interpretations made clear that many of the features of the *Liumang* Act were inconsistent with the basic values of Taiwan's rapidly evolving democratic system. The Constitutional Court therefore required the legislature, with the assistance of the executive, to revise the offending provisions within a reasonable time.

The Constitutional Court's handling of these cases also illustrates the limits under which it exercises its powers. Despite the many constitutional failings of the *Liumang* Act, the Court did not believe itself free to invalidate the legislation in its entirety. Nor did it assert the power to address issues that were not raised by the applications for review that had been submitted. These constraints left the overall fate of this politically sensitive legislation to the democratically elected branches of government, and in 2009, as we have seen, the newly-elected KMT administration and the KMT-dominated legislature obliged by abolishing it. In this instance, the three main branches of the Republic of China's distinctive system of five branches of government performed in textbook fashion.

This example of the separation of powers among Taiwan's main branches of government and the ability of the Constitutional Court to act as a powerful final arbiter of constitutional issues is currently impossible to replicate in the PRC. There, at best, the branches exercise a separation of functions under the nominal control of the NPC and its Standing Committee, which, like the other branches, are under the actual control of the Communist Party.

Although this case history of the recent constitutional process in Taiwan should be of enormous interest to Mainland reformers, in the present political climate there is little prospect that the PRC is ready to consider establishment of a similar constitutional court. The most that many experts think feasible might be the authorization of a constitutional committee within the NPC that would scrutinize all proposed legislation in order to determine whether any provisions in the draft were inconsistent with the Constitution. Even that may well be more than China's current leaders are prepared to support. Interestingly, that is exactly what is provided in the new draft Constitution of the Socialist Republic of Vietnam, a Communist regime that bears many similarities to the PRC and has often been influenced by it. If the Vietnamese do adopt this provision, it will add to the arguments of Chinese experts and officials who have been advocating establishment of a constitutional committee.

We hope that our study offers further support for both the demise of RETL, in substance as well as name, and the establishment of at least a constitutional committee within the NPC, if not an independent constitutional court. As Xi Jinping and his cohort begin their terms, we also hope that the new leadership has the wisdom to see that RETL, like the *Liumang* Act, should become a relic of the past. Surely there are many Taiwan legal experts across the strait who are willing and able to provide valuable advice on charting a path to a RETL-free future.

APPENDIX

ABBREVIATIONS OF MAJOR LAWS
AND REGULATIONS

Abbreviation	Full English Name	Full Chinese Name
1955 Measures	Taiwan Province Measures on Repressing *Liumang* during the Martial Law Period	台灣省戒嚴時期取締流氓辦法
1985 Act	Act for Eliminating *Liumang* During the Period of Communist Rebellion	動員戡亂時期檢肅流氓條例
AAL	Administrative Appeal Law	訴願法
Additional Articles	Additional Articles of the Constitution of the ROC	中華民國憲法增修條文
ALL	Administrative Litigation Law	行政訴訟法
CIPL	Constitutional Interpretation Procedure Law	司法院大法官審理案件法
Court Matters or CM	Matters that Courts Should Pay Attention to in Handling Cases under the Act for Eliminating *Liumang*	法院辦理檢肅流氓條例案件應行注意事項

Abbreviation	Full English Name	Full Chinese Name
CPC	Criminal Procedure Code	刑事訴訟法
Cst.	Constitution of the Republic of China	中華民國憲法
Deliberation Committee Organizational Rules or DCOR	Organizational Rules of the Deliberation Committee for Administrative Appeals of the Executive Yuan and Administrative Agencies under the Executive Yuan	行政院及各級行政機關訴願審議委員會組織規程
Deliberation Committee Rules or DCR	Deliberation Rules of the Deliberation Committee for Administrative Appeals of the Executive Yuan and All Levels of Administrative Agencies	行政院及各級行政機關訴願審議委員會審議規則
DL	Detention Law	羈押法
Enforcement Measures or EM	Measures for Enforcing the Punishment of Reformatory Training	感訓處分執行辦法
Examination Provisions	Provisions on Examining the Results of Work to Eliminate *Liumang*	執行檢肅流氓工作績效考核規定
Firearms Act	Act for the Control of Firearms, Ammunition, and Weapons	槍砲彈藥刀械管制條例

Abbreviation	Full English Name	Full Chinese Name
Implementing Rules or IR	Implementing Rules for the Act for Eliminating *Liumang*	檢肅流氓條例施行細則
Liumang Act or LMA	Act for Eliminating *Liumang*	檢肅流氓條例
Organized Crime Act or OCA	Act for Preventing Organized Crime	組織犯罪防制條例
Police Provisions or PP	Provisions on Police Handling of Cases under the Act for Eliminating *Liumang*	警察機關辦理檢肅流氓條例案件作業規定
Review Committee Rules or RCR	Main Points for the Organization of the Police Committee for the Deliberation of and Objections to *Liumang* Cases	警察機關流氓案件審議及異議委員會編組要點
Reward and Punishment Provisions	Reward and Punishment Provisions for Police Handling of Cases under the Act for Eliminating *Liumang*	警察機關辦理檢肅流氓條例案件獎懲規定
Temporary Provisions	Temporary Provisions Effective During the Period of Communist Rebellion	動員戡亂時期臨時條款
WPL	Witness Protection Law	證人保護法

OTHER ABBREVIATIONS

Abbreviation	Full English Name	Full Chinese Name
appeals committee	deliberation committee for administrative appeals	訴願審議委員會
Constitutional Court	Grand Justices of the Judicial Yuan	司法院大法官
examination group	examination group for eliminating *liumang*	檢肅流氓審查小組
DPP	Democratic Progressive Party	民主進步黨 or 民進黨
KMT	Kuomintang	國民黨
NPA	National Police Agency	警政署
post-reformatory training *liumang*	concluded (reformatory) training, guidance *liumang*	結訓輔導流氓
PRC, China, or the Mainland	People's Republic of China	中華人民共和國
recidivist *liumang*	*liumang* who fails to reform after receiving a warning	經告誡不改過之流氓
review committee	deliberation committee for *liumang* cases	流氓案件審議委員會
ROC (Taiwan)	Republic of China	中華民國
serious *liumang*	*liumang* for whom the circumstances are serious	情節重大流氓
training institutes	vocational training institutes	技能訓練所
warned *liumang*	*liumang* warned and under guidance	告誡輔導流氓

GLOSSARY OF TERMS

English	Chinese Traditional Chinese Simplified Chinese	Pinyin
Administrative appeal	訴願 诉愿	Sùyuàn
Administrative divisions at district courts	地方法院行政訴訟庭 地方法院行政诉讼庭	Dìfāng fǎyuàn xíngzhèng sùsòng tíng
Administrative lawsuit	行政訴訟 行政诉讼	Xíngzhèng sùsòng
Administrative police	行政警察 行政警察	Xíngzhèng jǐngchá
Administrative re-appeal	再訴願 再诉愿	Zàisùyuàn
Arrest warrant	拘票 拘票	Jūpiào
Arrest with a warrant	拘提 拘提	Jūtí
Arrest without a warrant	逮捕 逮捕	Dǎibǔ or Dàibǔ (either pronunciation acceptable)
Bail	具保 具保	Jùbǎo
Bamboo Union [gang]	竹聯幫 竹联帮	Zhúliánbāng
Bodily freedom	身體自由 身体自由	Shēntǐ zìyóu

English	Chinese Traditional Chinese Simplified Chinese	Pinyin
Cancel confinement	撤銷留置 撤销留置	Chèxiāo liúzhì
Case reported *liumang*	案報流氓 案报流氓	Ànbào liúmáng
Celestial Alliance [gang]	天道盟 天道盟	Tiāndàoméng
Character of an offensive violation	積極侵害性 积极侵害性	Jījíqīnhàixìng
Character of being habitual	慣常性 惯常性	Guànchángxìng
Character of being unspecific	不特定性 不特定性	Bútèdìngxìng
Chief judge	庭長 庭长	Tíngzhǎng
Chosen lawyer	選任律師 选任律师	Xuǎnrèn lùshī
Coerce and cause trouble	要挾滋事 要挟滋事	Yāoxié zīshì
Coercion	脅迫 胁迫	Xiépò
Commendation	嘉獎 嘉奖	Jiājiǎng
Commissioner of the Criminal Investigation Bureau	刑事警察局局長 刑事警察局局长	Xíngshì Jǐngchájú Júzhǎng

English	Chinese **Traditional Chinese** **Simplified Chinese**	Pinyin
Commit to reformatory training	交付感訓 交付感训	Jiāofù gǎnxùn
Concrete facts and evidence	具體事證 具体事证	Jùtǐ shìzhèng
Confinement	留置 留置	Liúzhì
Confinement houses	留置所 留置所	Liúzhìsuǒ
Confinement warrant	留置票 留置票	Liúzhìpiào
Confront	對質 对质	Duìzhí
Consignment document	交付書 交付书	Jiāofùshū
Constitutional Court	司法院大法官 司法院大法官	Sīfǎyuàn Dàfǎguān
Consultation and investigation	諮詢調查 咨询调查	Zīxún diàochá
Control and training	管訓 管训	Guǎnxùn
Coordinate through writing	具函協調 具函协调	Jùhán xiétiáo
Crimes of coercion	強制罪 强制罪	Qiángzhìzuì
Criminal act	犯行 犯行	Fànxíng

English	Chinese Traditional Chinese Simplified Chinese	Pinyin
Criminal information system	刑事資訊系統 刑事资讯系统	Xíngshì zīxùn xìtǒng
Criminal Investigation Bureau	刑事警察局 刑事警察局	Xíngshì Jǐngchájú
Criminal Unit Brigade Commander	刑警大隊長 刑警大队长	Xíngjǐng Dàduìzhǎng
Custodial release	責付 责付	Zéfù
Database of criminal cases	刑案知識庫 刑案知识库	Xíng'àn zhīshìkù
Discipline group	管教小組 管教小组	Guǎnjiào xiǎozǔ
Decision	裁判 裁判	Cáipàn
Decision not to accept [the petition]	不受理決議 不受理决议	Búshòulǐ juéyì
Defendant	被告 被告	Bèigào
Defense lawyer	辯護律師 辩护律师	Biànhù lǜshī
Deferred prosecution	緩起訴 缓起诉	Huǎnqǐsù
Deliberation Committee for Administrative Appeals	訴願審議委員會 诉愿审议委员会	Sùyuàn Shěnyì Wěiyuánhuì

English	Chinese **Traditional Chinese** **Simplified Chinese**	Pinyin
Deliberation committee for *liumang* cases (review committee) or committee for the deliberation of and objections to *liumang* cases	流氓案件審議委員會 or 流氓案件審議及異議委員會 流氓案件审议委员会 or 流氓案件审议及异议委员会	Liúmáng Ànjiàn Shěnyì Wěiyuánhuì or Liúmáng Ànjiàn Shěnyì jí yìyì Wěiyuánhuì
Detention [judge-determined, short-term detention as an administrative punishment]	拘留 拘留	Jūliú
Detention [judge-determined as a criminal punishment]	拘役 拘役	Jūyì
Detention [pre-trial]	羈押 羈押	Jīyā
Detention houses	看守所 看守所	Kānshǒusuǒ
Detention request (written)	拘留聲請書 拘留申请书	Jūliú shēngqǐngshū
Determining police agency	認定之警察機關 认定之警察机关	Rèndìng zhī jǐngchá jīguān
Directly governed municipality	直轄市 直辖市	Zhíxiáshì

English	Chinese Traditional Chinese Simplified Chinese	Pinyin
Discretionary arrest	逕行拘提 径行拘提	Jìngxíng jūtí
District courts	地方法院 地方法院	Dìfāng fǎyuàn
Dongcheng Training Institute	東成技能訓練所 东成技能训练所	Dōngchéng Jìnéng Xùnliànsuǒ
Due process	正當法律程序原則 正当法律程序原则	Zhèngdāng fǎlǜ chéngxù yuánzé
Eat and drink without paying	白吃白喝 白吃白喝	Báichī báihē
Efficient weapon to crack down on crime	掃黑利器 扫黑利器	Sǎohēi lìqì
Emergency arrests	緊急拘捕 紧急拘捕	Jǐnjí jūbǔ
Enforce	執行 执行	Zhíxíng
Enforcement document	執行書 执行书	Zhíxíngshū
Ex officio	(依) 職權 (依) 职权	(Yī) zhíquán
Examination group for eliminating *liumang*	檢肅流氓審查小組 检肃流氓审查小组	Jiǎnsù liúmáng shěnchá xiǎozǔ
Executive Yuan	行政院 行政院	Xíngzhèngyuàn
Fixed-term imprisonment	有期徒刑 有期徒刑	Yǒuqí túxíng

218

English	Chinese **Traditional Chinese** **Simplified Chinese**	Pinyin
Forced work	強制工作 强制工作	Qiángzhì gōngzuò
Four Seas Gang	四海幫 四海帮	Sìhǎibāng
Grade for [*liumang*] appearing at the station and transferring *liumang*	到案移送的績效 到案移送的绩效	Dàoàn yísòng de jīxiào
Grade for [*liumang*] rulings by the courts	裁定的績效 裁定的绩效	Cáidìng de jīxiào
Grade for reporting [*liumang*]	提報的績效 提报的绩效	Tíbào de jīxiào
Green Island (prison for dissidents)	綠島 绿岛	Lǜdǎo
Guardianship	監護 监护	Jiānhù
Guidance	輔導 辅导	Fǔdǎo
Have not begun enforcement	未開始執行 未开始执行	Wèikāishǐ zhíxíng
High Administrative Court	高等行政法院 高等行政法院	Gāoděng Xíngzhèng Fǎyuàn
High Court	高等法院 高等法院	Gāoděng Fǎyuàn
Indictable only upon complaint	告訴乃論罪 告诉乃论罪	Gàosùnǎilùnzuì

English	Chinese **Traditional Chinese** **Simplified Chinese**	Pinyin
Institute Affairs Committee	所務委員會 所务委员会	Suǒwù Wěiyuánhuì
Interview in person	正面訪問 正面访问	Zhèngmiàn fǎngwèn
Intimidation	恐嚇 恐吓	Kǒnghè
Investigative teams	偵察隊 侦察队	Zhēncháduì
Investigators from the responsibility beat for crime monitoring	刑責區偵查員 刑责区侦查员	Xíngzéqū zhēncháyuán
Judgment	判決 判决	Pànjué
Judicial Reform Foundation	民間司法改革基金會 民间司法改革基金会	Mínjiān Sīfǎ Gǎigé Jījīnhuì
Judicial Yuan	司法院 司法院	Sīfǎyuàn
Key supervising guidance personnel	重點監管輔導人員 重点监管辅导人员	Zhòngdiǎn jiānguǎn fǔdǎo rényuán
Legal Aid Foundation	法律扶助基金會 法律扶助基金会	Fǎlǜ Fúzhù Jījīnhuì
Legislative Yuan	立法院 立法院	Lìfǎyuàn

English	Chinese **Traditional Chinese** **Simplified Chinese**	Pinyin
Listed-*liumang* guidance supervision card	列冊流氓監管輔導紀錄卡 列册流氓监管辅导记录卡	Lièce liúmáng jiānguǎn fǔdǎo jìlùkǎ
Liumang investigation materials form	流氓調查資料表 流氓调查资料表	Liúmáng diàochá zīliàobiǎo
Liumang listed in the register and under guidance	列冊輔導流氓 列册辅导流氓	Lièce fǔdǎo liúmáng
Local despots	惡霸 恶霸	Èbà
Local gang or local gang leader	角頭 角头	Jiǎotóu
Ministry of Justice's Investigation Bureau	法務部調查局 法务部调查局	Fǎwùbù Diàochájú
Ministry of National Defense's Military Police Command	國防部憲兵司令部 (now 國防部憲兵指揮部) 国防部宪兵司令部 (now 国防部宪兵指挥部)	Guófángbù Xiànbīng Sīlìngbù (now Guófángbù Xiànbīng Zhǐhuībù)
Morally corrupt	品行惡劣 品行恶劣	Pǐnxìng èliè
Must be proper in substance	內容更須實質正當 内容更须实质正当	Nèiróng gèngxū shízhí zhèngdāng

English	Chinese **Traditional Chinese** **Simplified Chinese**	Pinyin
Mutually set-off	相互折抵 相互折抵	Xiānghù zhédǐ
National Police Agency	警政署 警政署	Jǐngzhèngshǔ
Native, pre-1949 Taiwanese	本省人 本省人	Běnshěngrén
Noncommissioned officers	士官 士官	Shìguān
nulla poena sine lege (no punishment without a law authorizing it)	罪刑法定主義 罪刑法定主义	Zuìxíng fǎdìng zhǔyì
Occupy territory	霸佔地盤 霸占地盘	Bàzhàn dìpán
Oral arguments	言詞辯論 言词辩论	Yáncí biànlùn
Ordinary *liumang*	一般流氓 一般流氓	Yībān liúmáng
Organized Crime Affairs Section	檢肅科 检肃科	Jiǎnsùkē
Original determining agency	原認定機關 原认定机关	Yuán rèndìng jīguān
Other concerned public security units	其他有關治安單位 其他有关治安单位	Qítā yǒuguān zhì'ān dānwèi
Parole	假釋 假释	Jiǎshì

English	Chinese **Traditional Chinese** **Simplified Chinese**	Pinyin
Parole Examination Committee	假釋審查委員會 假释审查委员会	Jiǎshì Shěnchá Wěiyuánhuì
People of Mainland heritage	外省人 外省人	Wàishěngrén
Person caught in the act of committing a crime	現行犯 现行犯	Xiànxíngfàn
Person receiving the sanction of reformatory training	受感訓處分人 受感训处分人	Shòugǎnxùn chǔfènrén
Points deducted	扣分 扣分	Kòufēn
Police beats	警勤區 警勤区	Jǐngqínqū
Police department	警察局 警察局	Jǐngchájú
Positive citation	記功 记功	Jìgōng
Post-reformatory training *liumang*	結訓輔導流氓 结训辅导流氓	Jiéxùn fǔdǎo liúmáng
Precinct	分局 分局	Fēnjú
Predetermined standards for credits	預定積分標準 预定积分标准	Yùdìng jīfēn biāozhǔn

English	Chinese **Traditional Chinese** **Simplified Chinese**	Pinyin
Preliminary examination	初審 初审	Chūshěn
Preliminary examination meeting	初審會議 初审会议	Chūshěn huìyì
Principal supervising guidance personnel	主要監管輔導人員 主要监管辅导人员	Zhǔyào jiānguǎn fǔdǎo rényuán
Principle of clarity for criminal laws	刑法明確原則 刑法明确原则	Xíngfǎ míngquè yuánzé
Principle of clarity of crimes and punishments	罪刑明確性原則 罪刑明确性原则	Zuìxíng míngquèxìng yuánzé
Principle of equality	平等原則 平等原则	Píngděng yuánzé
Principle of legal clarity	法律明確性原則 法律明确性原则	Fǎlǜ míngquèxìng yuánzé
Principle of the division of powers and functions	權能區分原則 权能区分原则	Quánnéng qūfēn yuánzé
Principle of the prohibition against double jeopardy	雙重危險禁止原則 双重危险禁止原则	Shuāngchóng wéixiǎn jìnzhǐ yuánzé
Principle of the separation of prosecution and adjudication	審檢分離之控訴原則 审检分离之控诉原则	Shěnjiǎn fēnlí zhī kòngsù yuánzé

English	Chinese Traditional Chinese Simplified Chinese	Pinyin
[Principle that] the same act not be punished again	一事不再罰 一事不再罚	Yīshì búzàifá
[Principle that] the same act not be punished twice	一事不二罰 一事不二罚	Yīshì bú'èrfá
[Principle that] the same behavior not be punished twice	一行為不二罰 一行为不二罚	Yīxíngwéi bú'èrfá
[Principle that] the same matter not be tried twice	一事不再理 一事不再理	Yīshì bùzàilǐ
Private prosecution	自訴 自诉	Zìsù
Private prosecutor	自訴人 自诉人	Zìsùrén
Probation	保護管束 保护管束	Bǎohù guǎnshù
Progressive Treatment Examination Committee	累進處遇審查會 累进处遇审查会	Lěijìn Chǔyù Shěncháhuì
Prohibition against repeat punishments	禁止重複處罰 禁止重复处罚	Jìnzhǐ chóngfù chǔfá
Proper grounds, good reason	正當理由 正当理由	Zhèngdāng lǐyóu

English	Chinese **Traditional Chinese** **Simplified Chinese**	Pinyin
Proportionality principle	比例原則 比例原则	Bǐlì yuánzé
Provincial municipality	省轄市 省辖市	Shěngxiáshì
Public prosecution	公訴 公诉	Gōngsù
Public prosecutors	檢察官 检察官	Jiǎncháguān
Public security population	治安人口 治安人口	Zhì'ān rénkǒu
Public security tribunal	治安法庭 治安法庭	Zhì'ān fǎtíng
Question	詰問 诘问	Jiéwèn
Receive demerits	記過 记过	Jìguò
Receive reports	收報 收报	Shōubào
Recommendation	建議 建议	Jiànyì
Record indirect findings through observations	側面瞭解 侧面了解	Cèmiàn liǎojiě
Re-education through labor	勞動教養 or 勞教 劳动教养 or 劳教	Láodòng jiàoyǎng or láojiào

English	Chinese Traditional Chinese Simplified Chinese	Pinyin
Reexamination	複審 复审	Fùshěn
Reexamination and determination	複審認定 复审认定	Fùshěn rèndìng
Reexamination meeting	複審會議 复审会议	Fùshěn huìyì
Reform through labor	勞動改造 or 勞改 劳动改造 or 劳改	Láodòng gǎizào or láogǎi
Reformatory training	感訓 感训	Gǎnxùn
Reformed adversarial system	改良式當事人進行主義 改良式当事人进行主义	Gǎiliángshì dāngshìrén jìnxíng zhǔyì
Refuse a person for reformatory training	拒絕收訓 拒绝收训	Jùjué shōuxùn
Rehabilitation measures	保安處分 保安处分	Bǎoān chǔfèn
Reformatory education	感化教育 感化教育	Gǎnhuà jiàoyù
Rehearing	重新審理 重新审理	Chóngxīn shěnlǐ
Relief	救濟 救济	Jiùjì

English	Chinese Traditional Chinese Simplified Chinese	Pinyin
Repeat confinement	再予留置 再予留置	Zàiyǔ liúzhì
Reported person	被提報人 被提报人	Bèitíbàorén
Reprimand	申誡 申诫	Shēnjiè
Responsibility beat for crime monitoring	刑事責任區 刑事责任区	Xíngshì zérènqū
Restricted residence	限制住居 限制住居	Xiànzhì zhùjū
Right to institute legal proceedings	訴訟權 诉讼权	Sùsòng quán
Ruling	裁定 裁定	Cáidìng
Ruling-appeal form	抗告書狀 抗告书状	Kànggào shūzhuàng
Ruling re-appeal	再抗告 再抗告	Zàikànggào
Secret witness	秘密證人 秘密证人	Mìmì zhèngrén
Serious *liumang* (literally a "*liumang* for whom the circumstances are serious")	情節重大流氓 情节重大流氓	Qíngjié zhòngdà liúmáng

English	Chinese Traditional Chinese Simplified Chinese	Pinyin
Shelter and repatriation	收容遣送 收容遣送	Shōuróng qiǎnsòng
Soldiers	士兵 士兵	Shìbīng
Station	分駐所 分驻所	Fēnzhùsuǒ
Stop confinement	停止留置 停止留置	Tíngzhǐ liúzhì
Substation	派出所 派出所	Pàichūsuǒ
Sufficient to have undermined social order	足以破壞社會秩序 足以破坏社会秩序	Zúyǐ pòhuài shèhuì zhìxù
Summary procedures	簡易程序 简易程序	Jiǎnyì chéngxù
Summary procedures division	簡易庭 简易庭	Jiǎnyìtíng
Summon	傳喚 传唤	Chuánhuàn
Supreme Administrative Court	最高行政法院 最高行政法院	Zuìgāo Xíngzhèng Fǎyuàn
Supreme Court	最高法院 最高法院	Zuìgāo Fǎyuàn
Suspect	嫌疑人 嫌疑人	Xiányírén

English	Chinese Traditional Chinese Simplified Chinese	Pinyin
Taiyuan Training Institute	泰源技能訓練所 泰源技能训练所	Tàiyuán Jìnéng Xùnliànsuǒ
Target (e.g., of an investigation)	對象 对象	Duìxiàng
System where the decision of the second level court is final	二級二審制 二级二审制	Èrjíèrshěnzhì
To appeal [a judgment]	上訴 上诉	Shàngsù
To appeal [a ruling], interlocutory appeal	抗告 抗告	Kànggào
Transfer document	移送書 移送书	Yísòngshū
Transferred person (literally, "person transferred for a ruling" [by the police])	被移送裁定人 被移送裁定人	Bèiyísòngcáidìngrén
Tyrannize good and honest people	欺壓善良 欺压善良	Qīyā shànliáng
Unspecific people	不特定人 不特定人	Bútèdìngrén
Violent behavior	暴力行為 暴力行为	Bàolì xíngwéi
Vocational training institutes	技能訓練所 技能训练所	Jìnéng xùnliànsuǒ

English	Chinese Traditional Chinese Simplified Chinese	Pinyin
Wander and act like rascals	遊蕩無賴 游荡无赖	Yóudàng wúlài
Warned *liumang* (literally a "*liumang* warned and under guidance")	告誡輔導流氓 告诫辅导流氓	Gàojiè fǔdǎo liúmáng
Warning	告誡 告诫	Gàojiè
Warning police agency	告誡之警察機關 告诫之警察机关	Gàojiè zhī jǐngchá jīguān
Written decision	決定書 决定书	Juédìngshū
Written determination	認定書 认定书	Rèndìngshū
Written notice	通知書 通知书	Tōngzhīshū
Written objection	異議書 异议书	Yìyìshū
Written objection decision	聲明異議決定書 声明异议决定书	Shēngmíng yìyì juédìngshū
Written warning	告誡書 告诫书	Gàojièshū
Yanwan Training Institute	岩灣技能訓練所 岩湾技能训练所	Yánwān Jìnéng Xùnliànsuǒ

BIBLIOGRAPHY

CHAPTER 1

BOOKS

Biddulph, Sarah. (2007). *Legal reform and administrative detention power in China.* Cambridge, UK: Cambridge University Press.

JOURNAL ARTICLES

Lewis, Margaret K. (2009). Taiwan's new adversarial system and the overlooked challenge of efficiency-driven reforms. *Virginia Journal of International Law, 49,* 651.

Martin, Jeffrey. (2007). A reasonable balance of law and sentiment: Social order in democratic Taiwan from the policeman's point of view. *Law & Society Review, 41,* 665.

Tao, Lung-Sheng. (1971). Reform of the criminal process in Nationalist China. *American Journal of Comparative Law, 19,* 764.

Wang, Tay-Sheng. (2002). The legal development of Taiwan in the 20th century: Toward a liberal and democratic country. *Pacific Rim Law & Policy Journal, 11,* 554.

Winckler, Edwin A. (1984). Institutionalization and participation on Taiwan: From hard to soft authoritarianism? *China Quarterly, 99,* 491.

ELECTRONIC MATERIALS

Dui Hua Foundation. (2010, 8 December). Translation & commentary: More than a decade after "hooliganism" is abolished, one hooligan's re-incarceration sparks debate. Retrieved 7 August 2013, from http://www.duihuahrjournal.org/2010/12/decade-after-hooliganism-is-abolished.html

Judicial Yuan. (2009a). Judicial statistics yearbook (table 71). Retrieved 7 August 2013, from http://www.judicial.gov.tw/juds/year98/09/071.pdf (in Chinese)

Judicial Yuan. (2009b). Judicial statistics yearbook (table 72). Retrieved 7 August 2013, from http://www.judicial.gov.tw/juds/year98/09/072.pdf (in Chinese)

CHAPTER 2

BOOKS

Chen, Tsung-Fu. (2000). The rule of law in Taiwan. In J. A. Cohen (Ed.), *The rule of law: Perspectives from the Pacific Rim*. Washington, DC: Mansfield Center for Pacific Affairs.

Roy, Dennis. (2003). *Taiwan: A political history*. Ithaca, NY: Cornell University Press.

JOURNAL ARTICLES

Barmé, Geremie. (1992). Wang Shuo and Liumang (hooligan) culture. *Australian Journal of Chinese Affairs, 28,* 23.

Tao, Lung-Sheng. (1971). Reform of the criminal process in Nationalist China. *American Journal of Comparative Law, 19,* 761.

Wakeman, Frederic, Jr. (1988). Policing modern Shanghai. *China Quarterly, 115,* 408.

ELECTRONIC MATERIALS

Government Information Office. (2005). Taiwan yearbook. Retrieved 7 August 2013, from http://www.ey.gov.tw/ (in Chinese)

Judicial Yuan. (2012). Branches. Retrieved 7 August 2013, from http://www.judicial.gov.tw/branches/branches02.asp (in Chinese)

Judicial Yuan. (2012). Justices of the Constitutional Court. Retrieved 7 August 2013, from http://www.judicial.gov.tw/constitutionalcourt/ (in Chinese)

JUDICIAL OPINIONS

Jacobellis v. Ohio, 378 US 184, 197 (1964).

CHAPTER 3

BOOKS

Chin, Ko-Lin. (2003). *Heijin: Organized crime, business, and politics in Taiwan*. Armonk, NY: East Gate Book.

CHAPTER 4

JOURNAL ARTICLES

Decker, John F. (2002). Addressing vagueness, ambiguity, and other uncertainty in American criminal laws. *Denver University Law Review, 80*, 241.

Huang, Thomas W. (2005). Judicial activism in the transitional polity: The Council of Grand Justices in Taiwan. *Temple International and Comparative Law Journal, 19*, 1.

Jeffries, John C., Jr. (1985). Legality, vagueness, and the construction of penal statutes. *University of Virginia Law Review, 71*, 189.

Wang, Jaw-perng. (2008). The *Liumang* Act: One law, eight unconstitutional aspects 一個條例，八處違憲─論檢肅流氓條例. *Taiwan Law Review, 155*, 121.

CONFERENCE PAPERS

Wang, Jaw-perng. (2006, 14 December). Constitutionality of the *Liumag* Act. *National Taiwan University School of Law*. (Draft prepared for the Conference on Taiwan's System for Dealing with *Liumang*: Constitutionality, Criminal Justice, and Broader Implications.)

SPEECHES

Ma Ying-jeou. (2009, 22 April). The Taiwan Relations Act: Turning a new chapter. Speech at *Center of International and Strategic Studies*.

ELECTRONIC MATERIALS

Judicial Yuan. (2007). Judicial statistics yearbook (table 2). Retrieved 7 August 2013, from http://www.judicial.gov.tw/juds/year96/02/02_002.pdf (in Chinese)

Judicial Yuan. (2009). Judicial statistics yearbook (table 3). Retrieved 7 August 2013, from http://www.judicial.gov.tw/juds/year98/02/03-4.pdf (in Chinese)

JUDICIAL OPINIONS

Connally v. General Construction Co., 269 US 385, 391 (1926).